The Democratic Challenge

The Democratic Challenge

Rethinking Democracy and Democratization

Jorge Nef

and

Bernd Reiter

First published 2009 by
PALGRAVE MACMILLAN

Palgrave Macmillan in the UK is an imprint of Macmillan Publishers Limited,
registered in England, company number 785998, of Houndmills, Basingstoke,
Hampshire RG21 6XS.

Palgrave Macmillan in the US is a division of St Martin's Press LLC,
175 Fifth Avenue, New York, NY 10010.

Palgrave Macmillan is the global academic imprint of the above companies
and has companies and representatives throughout the world.

Palgrave® and Macmillan® are registered trademarks in the United States,
the United Kingdom, Europe and other countries.

ISBN-13: 978–0–230–51689–2 hardback
ISBN-10: 0–230–51689–0 hardback
ISBN-13: 978–0–230–51690–8 paperback
ISBN-10: 0–230–51690–4 paperback

This book is printed on paper suitable for recycling and made from fully
managed and sustained forest sources. Logging, pulping and manufacturing
processes are expected to conform to the environmental regulations of the
country of origin.

A catalogue record for this book is available from the British Library.

A catalog record for this book is available from the Library of Congress.

10 9 8 7 6 5 4 3 2 1
18 17 16 15 14 13 12 11 10 09

Printed and bound in China

Contents

Acknowledgements

Some of the material in Chapters 5, 7 and 8 is based on earlier work in Nef *Human Security and Mutual Violence* (Ottawa: 1999). It is used by permission of Canada's International Development Research Centre, www.idrc.ca.

Chapter 6 draws on the chapter "Poverty and Sustainable Livelihoods," in O. P. Dwivedi, Renu Khator and Jorge Nef *Managing Development in a Global Context* (Basingstoke: 2007). The material is used by permission of Palgrave Macmillan.

Some of the material in Chapter 7 was first presented in the article "Globalization and the Crisis of Sovereignty, Legitimacy and Democracy" in *Latin American Perspectives*, Issue 125, 29(5): 59–69. It is used by permission of Sage.

We would like to thank Dr. Rebecca Thornhill and Mrs. Paula Lezama-Romero for reading and commenting on the manuscript.

Introduction

Despite persistent claims since the late 1980s, the "End of History" has not arrived. Nor has democracy emerged as the world's political norm. Instead, we are becoming aware that democracy and the values associated with it – freedom, equality, and prosperity – continue to be challenged. Worse, not only have old threats to democracy not been successfully resolved, new ones seem to emerge as we enter a more inter-dependent and globalized reality. Insecurity caused by the ecological crisis, terrorism and counter-terrorism, and increased economic volatility resulting from deregulated financial markets, are posing new challenges to the well-being of humanity. If anything, we are increasingly conscious that we need more understanding of the potentially devastating roadblocks to democracy.

This is, however, not another account of democracy's "victory and crisis" throughout history. This history has already been written. Instead, we set out to tackle a more ambitious task: to discuss democracy from a multi-faceted perspective, broadening our focus to include factors habitually overlooked by mainstream social science. This book tells the story of democracy as a social practice, as an idea and a continuously developing ideal, of the social context into which democratic rule needs to be embedded, and of the different challenges democracy faces, some as old as the idea itself, other as new as the idea of the global war on terror.

We follow democracy's unfolding over time and the contestations and resistances it encountered and still encounters in the different geographical regions where it was able to set foot. Ever since the notion of democracy emerged in ancient Greece, its core idea was self-rule, thus threatening the claims of those seeking to rule over others. Many ideologies have been sought to justify domination over those deemed subordinate and when reasons did not suffice, violence and coercion were readily employed first to impose minority or single-person rule and then to secure the established order. But at the same time that those able to access power were resourceful enough to delay the spread of popular rule and the core values associated with it, commoners proved even more spirited in their consistent pursuit of freedom, equality and self-rule. Yet even though mass movements have at times been able to wring power from those that seek to concentrate it, their victories were never lasting, as the opponents of self-rule soon regrouped and found new ways to undermine the claims and the practices of the many. Democracy has remained an unfulfilled promise and whenever achieved is readily

1

contested by all those that have much to lose from its reign, namely the powerful and all those able to gain from manipulating and exploiting the masses. This book, then, is about the biggest struggle of humankind, initiated in some Greek city-states some 2,500 years ago, and fought in different arenas ever since. It thus describes a spectacular drama, with much heroism, sacrifice, phenomenal gains and tremendous losses, on both sides. The opponents are always the same, although taking on different forms and shapes in different times and places: in every battle the simple people fight against the few privileged, more educated and rich. The reason for the struggle has not changed since the old days: who shall rule over whom.

Instead of offering a complete and encyclopaedic discussion of democracy, we set out to offer a more critical and much more engaged approach. This is not an "objective" assessment of democracy and its challenges, if such a thing were possible. To the contrary, our starting point is explicitly normative. We are stern believers in and ardent defenders of democracy, both as a means and as an end, and as such, we offer our critical and engaged reflections and share our concerns and worries about certain developments we find potentially dangerous to the quality of democracy. As proud democrats, we find this to be not just morally important, but also scientifically sound, as we are sceptical of all those claiming to produce "neutral" and "objective" science in a field dominated by human interaction and the social construction of reality. More often than not, such "neutrality" is but a façade, unable to conceal ideological bias and hidden intent, clumsily covered by often unsound and tricky scientific methodology. As critical thinkers, we believe that reliability is achieved best through intellectual honesty and transparency, and we thus make no qualms about our aim of warning against the potential threats to democracy. To us, democracy is not just a way to rule among others; it is superior.

This book, then, represents a critical and engaged attempt to do what we perceive is part of the academic profession, namely to speak out against potential ills and to offer profound analyses of social problems so that they can be addressed and solved. Against all those demanding that scientific inquiry requires disengaged distance, we contend that to the contrary, reliable findings require that researchers and scholars lay bare their convictions. We also contend that the social location from where they observe, measure and explain reality has to be taken into consideration, thus producing a more reliable form of scientific enquiry and a harder objectivity (Harding, 1993). To all those who contend that there is no science able to capture human action, we say that we are not looking for explanatory laws guiding history. We are aware that there might be no such laws; rather, it is essential to gain understanding of the contingencies and conditionalities of democracy. Ours is a quest to establish an "if...then" logic, which allows us to point out both circumstances that put democracy at risk and others that favour its blossoming.

To the reader, we thus offer more than a textbook. Although we do provide the relevant background information that enables the reader to follow our reasoning, we want to raise questions that point beyond the concrete and the measurable and we hope to inspire our readers to discover and explore with us the many folds and often filigree and wide-spun capillaries of democratic processes and practices and the effects they produce on our lives.

Hence, this book is about democracy both as a phenomenon and as a normative ideal. It also deals with the dynamics of democratization and de-democratization; namely the processes of expansion and contraction of popular rule. For there is as much reason to think of democracy as a forward-moving process as there is also evidence of entropic tendencies. In this contradiction lies the dual nature of the democratic challenge. On the one hand government by the people under the rule of law poses a threat for authoritarian, abusive and corrupt regimes throughout the globe. On the other, the very notion of popular rule is contested not only by persistent worldwide autocratic and oligarchic tendencies; but by new, or seemingly new developments such as globalization, neo-conservatism, market fundamentalism, ultranationalism, the national security state and re-emerging religious messianism.

Democracy is a particular form of collective organizing for conflict management, as well as rule-making and implementation. Historically and semantically we can talk about numerous variations of the term, from "classical" to contemporary. We will examine these variations later on, in the search for persistent continuities and relevant discontinuities. Democracy as an ideal has a final goal: a desired form of political association of free and equal people living together under a form of legality based upon consensus. Yet, its concrete realization in the here-and-now remains elusive, as real politics is a changing, dynamic and often "messy" thing.

Democracy is an attribute, and unlike systems of management and organization in the field of administration it is not a tangible, material object whose existence can be easily verified and engineered. For Arblaster (1987: 1) it constitutes an abstract and essentially contestable idiom, without precise and agreed meaning. However, as a current practice it exhibits some common and conventional elements, or "common core of meaning lying beneath all the varied uses and interpretations which have been made of the term" (ibid.: 8). These traits include government by the people, equality, representation, inclusiveness, universal suffrage, frequent elections, majority rule, those who govern being accountable to the larger social constituency, consent, debate and freedom of speech. All this boils down to legitimacy based upon support by the people and the principle of "popular sovereignty," understood as the presence of "popular power." In a democracy, the people rule and popular rule happens when the gap between those who rule and those who are ruled remains minimal.

However, polities and their governments distance themselves from any ideal democratic benchmark over time and space. Real and concrete political systems exhibit to greater and lesser degree democratic and autocratic traits, the predominance of which depends upon internal and external factors. The latter define the context in which politics operates, being affected by such context, and in turn affecting it in multiple ways.

The Democratic Challenge is a critical study of the issues and debates around widely used concepts and trends in political science, economics, political economy and development studies. It aims at presenting a systemic, global and critical perspective to the analysis of the main views on democratization and de-democratization (Crenson et al., 2002). It combines empirical findings with theoretical reflection to examine the conjectures, assumptions and stereotypes existent in conventional theories and studies of democracy in the so-called new world order. It also proposes alternative perspectives for understanding democracy and democratization in the contemporary scene. Finally, it advances a number of hypothetical formulations to study the "real world of democracy" (Macpherson, 1969), by casting them in the perspective of human security and mutual vulnerability (Nef, 1995).

Far from postulating a universal and unidirectional democratizing trend, this study seeks to provide for history and context – ecological, economic, social and cultural – in a broadly comparative study focused on three interconnected processes: democratization, re-democratization and de-democratization. In fact, it questions the alleged convergence of globalization, liberalism and democracy as an adequate descriptor of the post-1989 democratic conjuncture, by contrasting discourse, ideology and rhetoric on the one hand, with concrete trends on the other. While focusing on the interplay among history, culture, ideology, economics and politics, our study approaches any overly deterministic explanations of democracy with scepticism and methical doubt. Instead, it presents a multi-varied, situational analysis instead of the self-congratulating discourses that, more often than not, dominate and obscure the discussion of democracy. As specific processes and circumstances are examined, unique tendencies and often contradictory patterns of democratization/de-democratization across the globe will be discussed, including emerging and as yet rather amorphous strains of democracy that could often be looked upon as anomalous.

In particular, this work concentrates upon probing into and also contesting three dominant themes in the discussion of democracy: (a) the so-called crisis of democracy; (b) the inevitability of democracy thesis extant in the End of History literature (Fukuyama, 1989); and (c) the globalization thesis and its contested corollaries – the erosion of sovereignty and the prospects for global democracy. In tackling these theses, we confront several intellectual challenges. One is to lay bare the major elements and assumptions in the study of democracy and democratization. Another is to define the terms and establish the interconnectedness among these elements and assumptions. This entails sketching some basic theory or conceptual framework to explain and understand the democratic phenomenon. A third and equally fundamental task is to articulate the set of conjectural propositions and implications of these conceptualizations.

Besides a systematic treatment of democracy following the paths laid by major theorists, this book will undertake a genealogical analysis of the idea and practice of democracy and their variations (Arblaster, 1987: 13–37). Our aim is to provide a general perspective of the theoretical and philosophical foundations and contributions to the explanation and understanding of democracy and democratization over time. One essential theoretical and practical aspect appearing and re-appearing in the diachronic (time bound) and synchronic/structural treatment of the subject is the uneasy relationship between liberalism and democracy. Another is the complex interplay between the notions of power, equality, liberty, freedom, justice, majority rule, inclusiveness and the like.

A main tenet of our approach to the subject is the need to examine differing democratic visions not as a lofty discourse but as a concrete and indeterminate process with multi-directional dynamics and possibilities. Far from seeing democracy as a stable and irreversible stage (in the sense of "development" envisioned by modernization theorists) our study emphasizes the essentially open and indeterminate nature of the democratic phenomenon as a complex historical, cultural and socioeconomic process. Nor do we look at democracy as a discrete purely institutional category, limited to formal, procedural and constitutional factors. To approach the subject from the proposed wide angle requires studying the relationships among various interconnected, though at times contradictory, levels of analysis. These constitute the structural foundations of democracy. They range from the broader social, economic and cultural regime, to the political community, the state, the government and the self (for instance, the interplay between culture and personality). This means focusing on democratic and antidemocratic attributes present in concrete social, economic and political institutions and practices. Such attributes present at various levels of analysis permit to ascertain the extent and nature of popular empowerment and disempowerment under several circumstances and historical moments. To accomplish its stated goal, the book is divided into nine inter-related chapters.

Chapter 1 presents an historical and structural overview of the concept of democracy. It outlines the key notions, ideas and evolving trends regarding democracy and the process of democratization, as well as its counter tendencies. The chapter briefly discusses democracy among a constellation of different models of conflict management. It also sketches the major theses and debates surrounding these and related concepts, as well as their contingent political use. Besides being a systematic treatment of democracy, this foundational chapter undertakes a genealogical analysis of the idea of democracy and its variations.

Chapter 2 examines, from an institutional viewpoint, the proposition that the varied definitions and conceptions of democracy often imply very different processes and organizational manifestations. This chapter takes a closer look at the dominant Western, liberal and representative paradigm of procedural democracy as characterized by Schumpeter (1942). From our perspective, formal procedures – though necessary – are insufficient to empower people in decision-making process and in the creation of a democratic ("civic") culture (Almond and Verba, 1965). The attributes of formal democracy are contrasted here with those of substantive democracy. From a substantive point of view, constitutions, elections, separation of powers, checks and balances, and responsible government can be seen as a necessary but by no means sufficient condition of democracy. Instead, such criteria as equal access to citizenship rights and self-governance are significantly more central to the meaning of democracy.

Chapter 3 concentrates on the uses, and abuses, of the democratic idiom in current discourse. After pointing out some of the inherent contradictions between democracy, understood as the rule of the people, and liberalism, with its emphasis on individual freedom, it examines how the perception of the word democracy has changed over the centuries; from one evoking mob rule to one where government by the people appeared as a political ideal. With the emergence and consolidation of the labour movement as a political actor in the later part of the nineteenth century, the struggle for democracy became equated with equity, justice, self-determination, majority rule, constitutionalism and the rule of law. For progressives, it came to signify modernity and also social change. In the post-World War I era democracy constituted a hegemonic concept. From left to right – including mainstream radicals, liberals, conservatives and even anarchists – the term evoked a positive connotation. Yet it was anathema to fascists and reactionaries, and to leftist groups who rejected its "bourgeois" trappings. This chapter seeks to elucidate the various meanings, extrinsic conditions and intrinsic traits of the democratic phenomenon. In so doing, it also attempts to provide criteria to compare and contrast the various manifestations of democracy, which allows us to challenge a number of propositions emerging, and derived from, the above-mentioned literature.

Chapter 4 begins by examining the relationship between democracy and sovereignty (who rules) and subsequently explores some of the implications of popular sovereignty, namely the question "who are the people." After developing some of the inherent complications that result from the pairing of democracy with economic liberalism, the chapter explores two important developments during the 1970s and 1980s that challenged the concept of democracy on a global scale. One was the shift from the idea of participation to the conservative notion of order, justified by postulating a crisis of democracy resulting from "over-participation." Another was the support by the West for ostensibly antidemocratic regimes elsewhere, justified by the need to fight communism.

This latter shift relates directly to the emergence of "transition theory." This theory provided a roadmap for controlled political openings, geared at maintaining both the socioeconomic order harboured by these regimes (and supported by the West) and the international alliances of the crumbling dictatorships. Transition theory became relevant to explain the fragmentation and reconfiguration of regimes in Eastern Europe at the heels of the collapse of communism and its replacement by liberal – though not yet democratic – systems of government. Besides addressing these historical developments, the chapter addresses a related but more contemporary issue. This is the movement away from democracy in the developed world and the multiple factors seemingly accounting for it.

Chapter 5 examines the relationship between human insecurity in its multiple global and subsystemic dimensions, and democracy. In particular, it studies how major international economic crises in recent decades, converged with globalization, state policies, and uneven distribution of income, to alter the socioeconomic conditions of liberal democracy. The recognition of this contradiction, as well as the inherent tension between legitimacy and effectiveness in democratic regimes, has led numerous analysts to speak of the profound and unprecedented crisis of democracy, referred to in previous chapters. Shrinking revenue and a new free-market paradigm has made untenable the notion of an expansive safety net once provided by a welfare state. In it, the contradiction between legitimation and accumulation has created conditions for both greater exclusion, and its enforcement via repression.

But the challenges to democracy also emerge from other international, regional, as well as national and more local threats. Issues like failed states, criminality and especially terrorism have a deleterious impact on democracy, not so much from the direct risks associated with these acts, but because of dysfunctional systemic responses. While the maintenance of security is a necessary condition for democracy, the "securitization" of politics carries with it a most destructive challenge for popular sovereignty under the rule of law.

Chapter 6 centres on the issue of structural inequality. The chapter explores the central proposition that liberal democratic consensus requires economic growth, employment, and equitable distribution. In the past this was facilitated in developed societies by the presence of a strong, efficient and effective administrative, and subsequently welfare, state. Under the management of a white collar middle class, its central function was to play brokerage between elites and non-elites, relying on the fiscal surplus generated by economic expansion to soften the often radical and socially undesirable consequences of unfettered capitalism. This "welfarist" model is there no longer and hence social frictions have intensified, whereas the room for compromise has shrunk. Without adequate distributive policies, it has become harder to manage conflict in a democracy, even with significant economic growth, as regressive distribution has a most negative effect on the aggregate level of human security.

Chapter 7 deals with the emergence, evolvement and entrenchment of "governable" and limited democracies in the context of neo-liberal reforms. Despite claims of a final stage of history characterized by global democracy, the outcome of this process of transformation is today uncertain. If democracy was ever thought to be a benchmark of political development in nation and state building, the contemporary situation appears to be one of de-development. Thus, this chapter also examines a paradoxical trend, taking place as many analysts proclaim the global triumph of democracy. It also addresses the factors underpinning globalization and the implications of these factors for democracy. In this sense we examine the retrenchment and erosion of democracy (or "un-doing democracy,") in the sense used by Close and Deonandan (2004), which is occurring not only in unstable polities, but also in reputedly developed and pluralistic regimes.

Chapter 8 concentrates on the antidemocratic effects of traits associated with the nature of the contemporary state. These include increased concentration of ownership of different media, an overdeveloped and increasingly autonomous defence and security apparatus, complex hierarchical and highly specialized bureaucratic structures of modern government, and a process of acute transnationalization of the economy and the state itself. The end of the Cold War affected the nature of global politics, rendering the "old" military industrial complex less instrumental to facilitate continuous growth. This transformation threatened the survival of this entrenched and relatively autonomous part of the administrative state and created conditions for its return under the mantle of a new perpetual state of war, exemplified by the "war on terror."

The combination of globalization with militarization, though intrinsically incompatible in the long run, has resulted in an erosion of democracy. This power deflation is rooted in the convergence of two opposite processes: *global* accumulation and *national* security. The nature of the contemporary state is being affected by these contradictory and essentially external gravitational pulls.

The chapter also explores the internal contemporary manifestation of Michels' "Iron Law of Oligarchy" applied to the crucial mechanisms of brokerage – interest groups and political parties – that define the open (inclusive) or closed (exclusive) nature of the state. Narrowing participation, the bureaucratization of representation, and the growing influence of electoral mega-machines create conditions for plutocracy, favouring a kind of restricted democracy without people. This is not without precedent or theorization in the historical journey of the democratic idea. The Greek polis and the predilections of some influential founders of the American republic, like Alexander Hamilton or James Madison, preferred a type of democracy distrustful of equality and popular rule. Only some of the people, but not all the people, were fit to rule.

We suggest in this chapter that democratic control seems to be constantly slipping from the hands of the common people, even in systems characterized as open and fair. Moreover, ever more entrenched global and internal inequality, combined with media concentration and a growing "securitization" of the state, create conditions adverse to popular rule. In the midst of these processes, the model of democracy proclaimed and prescribed by the West to the world becomes for many an empty shell: a cynical façade that masks authoritarian and predatory decision-making.

The concluding chapter synthesizes the various themes explored in the previous chapters, and looks for the common roots and circumstances of the alleged crisis of democracy. Is it a crisis of governability resulting from over-participation, or is it something else? In so doing, it re-examines the purposeful deconstruction of the popular component of democracy and its replacement with what Duverger called Pluto-democracies, and "democracies without people" (1966, 1967). It also calls into question the thesis that there is no alternative to the prevailing neo-liberal, free market model of limited democracy that is being peddled as the last and highest stage of political and economic development.

Some lingering questions

Any analysis of democracy confronts us with several recurring riddles. One of these is the problem of inevitability: is democracy an expression of an unfolding historically-determined trend, a slowly unfolding "*Zeitgeist*," as suggested by Fukuyama's take on Hegel? Or is democracy rather something that inevitably will decay as a result of its own contradictions, as Michels and more recently Huntington have implied? There seem to be strong arguments on both sides. Or is history bereft of any unfolding soul or spirit, as Nietzsche first suggested? A related question is the complex association between democracy and development. Is democracy a "luxury" that only prosperous and developed societies can afford? Alternatively, will prosperity, complacency and apathy ultimately smother democracy? (Stoker, 2006: 87–102).

Another very relevant question at present is the issue of portability and replicability: can democracy be "exported" and transplanted? Certainly, there is abundant evidence of imperial powers attempting to reproduce, or impose their version of a "benchmark" political system on others. But, has this worked? Some of these transplants seem to have survived; even been successful. More often than not, however, impositions and imitations have been dismal failures. Yet, this obvious lesson seems to be hard to accept by the foreign policy establishments of major powers; witness Soviet and American involvements in Afghanistan and beyond.

Democracy is ultimately self-government, in the sense of home-rule, and as such it cannot be imposed. Of course, societies learn from each other and therefore a great deal of borrowing, "hybridization" and imitation takes place. Yet, democracy appears to be a kind of social or "soft" technology that, after all the learning and borrowing is done, still needs to be home-grown. As an ambassador in Washington back in the 1920s put it, "we do not need so much a world safe for democracy, but a safe democracy for the world." Democracy is not just a piece of hardware that can be plugged in to produce instantaneous results. As a soft technology, it is not even in the same category as a managerial structure, accounting system or business plan; though little critical thinking often accompanies most incorporations of administrative know-how. Learning, context, culture and ethical considerations are extremely important, but these often tend to be ignored.

Our contention is that democracy is not an exclusive and perennial endowment of those chosen or fortunate enough to possess it. Nor is it something that once acquired is here to stay; let alone an object of passive contemplation. Instead, it is something that needs to be nurtured and contested in the practice in everyday life. Democracy, in this sense, always remains a challenge and a promise and as such, it is not restricted to the narrow field of politics. Not only have our expectations towards democracy increased steadily over time, we have also come to realize that democracy is a fragile and illusive practice. It is easily distorted by power, threatened by inequality, and promptly held hostage by what has been termed "the establishment," the "military-industrial complex," the "state apparatus," or simply, "the system." But democracy is not only threatened from above. To be meaningful, democratic principles must guide all levels of human interactions. To put it simply: there cannot be a democratic state ruling over an undemocratic society. Democratic practice needs to start at the individual and family levels for a democratic common sense to emerge and be able to slowly and gradually consolidate and become institutionalized. Ultimately, a democratic regime, which includes a democratic state and its diverse legal components, must grow out of a democratic society, where the process of gradual democratization is as important, maybe even more important, than the end result; meaningful democracy cannot be achieved by antidemocratic means. Hence the democratic quality of processes is of utmost importance for the establishment of democratic political regimes and anyone interested in democracy needs to include an analysis of the processes and paths leading up to the ideal of popular rule.

Chapter 1

Democracy as an Idea and as a Process

Democracy is illusive – both as an idea and as a practice. Before undertaking an analysis of the multi-sided challenges to democracy, we need to outline the different ideas associated with democracy, as well as the different practices derived from these democratic ideas. This chapter first provides an overview of the democratic idea in the form of a genealogy, followed by a brief discussion of the different concrete manifestations of democracy and the potential problems and pitfalls of each. The term democracy, with all its connotations and ambiguities, has been central to political analysis virtually since the birth of the systematic study of politics. This chapter sketches a brief history of democracy, since its invention in ancient Greece to its resurgence in the 1600s (Arblaster, 1987: 13–37), and its contemporary manifestations.

The word is derived from two Greek terms: *demos* (people) and *kratos* (government, power, or more precisely, steering). It means simply rule by the people. But this form of direct participation by the citizens of Athens 2,500 years ago did not extended to the majority of the population, constituted mostly by slaves and foreigners. Women were excluded too. True, all free Athenians could sit in the Assembly, debate, and vote in establishing and modifying their laws, could stand for official positions, could be selected by vote or by drawing lots, could partake in making collective decisions, or could collectively condemn and punish dissidents, and those violating their laws.

All in all, by many accounts non-citizens outnumbered citizens ten to one and inclusion, as well as exclusion were generally inherited. However, classical democracy, as it has been called, was an amazing experiment of direct, participatory government and has remained in the political imaginary ever since. For Aristotle (384–322 BC), the founder of Western political analysis, the concept was one of several forms of articulation between the ruler and the ruled. In his study of how Greek city states were governed, he used a tripartite classification: the government of one, a select few or many. Each one of these types could appear in either a virtuous or its opposite, illegitimate, form. Aristotle thus continued a line of thinking first presented to him by his teacher, Plato (424–348 BC), who firmly associated democracy with mob rule: a perversion of the government of the many and a polis gone astray. The implication is demagoguery, or to use a contemporary term, populism. In a similar way, Aristotle perceived the government of just the few (*oligos*), or oligarchy, as an impure mutation of aristocracy, rule by the best (*aristos*); while tyranny for him was a perversion of monarchy (*mono kratos*, or government by one).

Aristotle's concern was the issue of legitimacy and quality of government, not how representative or participatory it was. His normative preference was a form of mixed government in which elements of polis, aristocracy and monarchy combined in the pursuit of public virtues. It was Aristotle's most successful disciple, Alexander of Macedonia, "the Great" (356–323 BC), who finally put an end to Athenian institutions of self rule by around 330 BC, in his drive to establish the largest empire of the ancient world.

From polis to republic

The Roman equivalent of the Greek polis was the Republic (*res publica*, meaning the "public thing"). The Roman Republic persisted in various mutations since the overthrow of the monarchies in 510 BC until about 44 BC. Ever since, the basic idea of a republic has meant a "non-monarchy." Republican Rome was often ruled by a set of patrician land-holding families, articulated in a Senate and a plebeian Assembly of commoners. These collective bodies were often eclipsed by the power of a temporary Dictator, or a life-time Imperator. By the times of Julius Caesar (100–44 BC), the Republic had ceased to exist as a political arrangement. However, the notion of public affairs, as the order of those things of concern to all Romans (the *status quo rei romane*), or state, as well as the norms referring to those concerns (*publicum jus*, or public law) continued to evolve until the disintegration of the Western Roman Empire (476 AD). Even then, the body of practices, institutions and norms developed for over five hundred years continued in both the Roman Catholic Church and the Eastern Byzantine Empire (476–1453 AD).

Kings and barons

Throughout the early Middle Ages, the notion of Republic remained significantly absent. There were, however, persistent attempts by the landed nobility to wrestle power from kings. One example was the barons' rebellion in Norman England, leading to the *Magna Carta Libertatum* of 1215 and its subsequent developments. Another remarkable expression of limited monarchical rule was the assemblies of notables, such as the Scandinavian *Things*, especially in Iceland and Sweden, dating back to the tenth and eleventh centuries. But these were not expressions of popular power, or commoner's bodies by any stretch of imagination. Rather, they were manifestations of traditional autonomies by tribal chiefs and the landed nobility.

With the development of urbanization and trade, and with the ascendancy of a commercial class of burghers, some cities were given special status as free cities by papal edicts and royal charters (e.g. *frei burghs* in Germany). In Spain, these dispensations constituted traditional "rights" of commoners: *fueros* in which local assemblies or town meetings – *cabildos* and *xuntas* – exercised a limited degree of autonomy. The growing freedom of the bourgeoisie vis-à-vis the monarchy and the nobility was based upon their control of credit and finance. As feudal kings and barons became heavily indebted in warlike pursuits, including internecine wars and Crusades, the relevance of merchants and the contractual liens over their debtors increased. A new aristocracy of money emerged towards the end of the Middle Ages, especially in those regions with a dynamic commercial economy: Florence, Genoa, Venice, and throughout Northern Europe and the Baltic.

The term republic was resurrected with the maritime trade boom in fourteenth-century Venice. The "most serene" Venetian Republic (1223–1797 AD), was ruled by an aristocratic governing Council, increasingly setting limits to the power of the autocratic Doge. This arrangement configured a model in which guilds of rich merchants progressively took power away from princes and bishops. From the sixteenth century onwards, and in the context of the Reformation and the Thirty Years War (1618–1648), several merchant-controlled republics and free city states acquired notoriety throughout Europe. Earlier examples of these emerged in the Low Countries (the Unified Republics of the Netherlands, 1581–1795), the Baltic (the Hanseatic League, 1356–1669) and in Catalonia (the *Corts* of Barcelona dating back to 1283). Another republican example was the relatively short-lived Commonwealth of England, under the rule of Oliver Cromwell from 1649 to 1653, and his son Richard from 1659 to 1660.

Sovereignty and the nation-state

Europe, after the thirty-year war ended with a peace agreement, written and signed in Westphalia (1648), saw a slow consolidation of the principle of national sovereignty. The seeds for nationalism were thus planted, yet states continued to drive towards absolutism, and democracy was indeed a dissonant concept. Sovereignty was essentially something that in the emerging world system belonged to the monarchies that substituted for popes and emperors. The principle of *Rex est imperator in regno suo* ("the king is Emperor in his own Kingdom") became the banner of the new projects of dynastic states. Increasingly, however, rationalist theorists of politics, whose intellectual roots were in Aristotle and Machiavelli (1469–1527), began questioning the deistic foundations of authority laid down by mainstream scholastic Catholic thinking, dominated then by the works of Thomas Aquinas (*c*.1225–1275).

The key question was what defined the essence of sovereign power. The answer for Thomas Aquinas and the proponents of the thesis of divine power, like Bossuet (1627–1704) and other "Thomists," was simply "*omnia potestas a Deo*" ("all power comes from God"). For Hobbes (1588–1679), the answer began to take on a secular tone: the authority of the state – even that of an all-powerful, authoritarian Leviathan – came from a foundational social contract. In other words, the base of legitimacy was the consent of the governed and the body politic itself. Hobbes' formulation privileged the concentration of power to prevent chaos. Equally secular was Niccolò Machiavelli's (1469–1527) opportunistic view of the Prince's power and legitimacy as rooted on a mixture of skill (*virtu*) and circumstances (*fortuna*).

Yet other contractual theorists, chiefly John Locke (1632–1704) and Jean-Jacques Rousseau (1712–1778), traced the sources of sovereignty to the free will of the people who thus formed an association to be better off. That is, sovereignty ceased to be an autocratic attribute of the monarch, but one of citizenship. Reversing Louis XIV saying, *l'état c'est moi* (I am the state), the contractual idiom would affirm a collectivist: *l'état c'est nous* (the state is us). The idea of contract in the constitutional (public) realm here had its roots in the growing importance of contracts – secular covenants – as binding obligations in the civil-commercial sphere. It also set limits on the power of sovereigns, by making them responsible to the rule of law, the will of assemblies, constituencies, or by creating checks and balances and by dividing authority among the powers of the state (Montesquieu, 1748).

"People," bourgeoisies and revolutions

Though in the evolving literature on social contracts, responsible government and above all sovereignty, the idea of democracy as popular power had become a feature of political discourse, it continued to be stigmatized by the Platonic characterization of mob rule. Not until the times of the American and French Revolutions in the 1770s and 1780s, both inspired by the English Revolution of 1688, with its "levellers" and "diggers" would the word democracy acquire a more positive and acceptable connotation.

The "people" (*le peuple, das Volk*) as a concept was incorporated in the late eighteenth-century revolutionary political discourse as the representative of the nation and the ultimate depository of sovereignty. The "children of the Motherland" or "sons of Liberty" implied an emerging revolutionary legitimacy: a radically new vision of citizens as people in arms who took care of the business of governing by themselves for themselves, and did so by overthrowing an illegitimate government. Carnot's "*levée en masse*" (armed mass mobilization), and Washington's Continental Army, were telling examples of these citizen fighters. They were also examples of an effective form of participatory warfare, whose antecedents go back to Cromwell's Model Army, The Dutch Civic Guard, the Swiss Pikemen and the Athenian Hoplites.

Even then, and in the throes of a sort of global antidemocratic and conservative backlash, or second "Thermidor," to envelop Europe and the Americas with the defeat of the Napoleonic Empire, the constitutionalism to emerge after the Congress of Vienna (1823) set constraints to popular rule and gave rise to a phase of restoring monarchies (known simply as "the Restoration"). It took time in the Old and the New World for even republicans and liberals to use the "d" word without the radical implications of profound equalitarianism, expropriatory socioeconomic change, and the profound anti-clericalism, which the French Revolution represented (Arblaster, 1987: 47). Madisonian democracy in the United States was an attempt to engineer democracy without radicalism. For the American Founding Fathers, this was mainly to be achieved through forging equilibrium between majority and minority rule. In hindsight, their dedication to maintaining stability and avoiding what they perceived as the dangers of democratic excesses proved successful in establishing the union as a republic, yet it also helped anchor slavery and institutionalized inequality into the republican framework, thus providing it with an extremely consequential breaking point that not only weakened the legitimacy of the republic, but also its moral fibre and endurance. Leaving the democratic project unfinished eventually led to civil war.

However, with the French and American revolutions from the 1770s to the 1790s, the very notion of democratic and popular politics became associated with revolutionary politics (Arblaster, 1987: 38), even more so after slaves in the French colony of Haiti had started to take the writings of Rousseau seriously, proclaiming their freedom and killing their colonial overseers. Yet, while sharing zeal for preserving established social orders and fearing the kind of changes likely to be produced by "mob rule," the American and French versions of democracy also differed substantially. The more conservative and elitist Madisonian version to emerge in the nascent American republic in the earlier nineteenth century deliberately put restraints on popularly elected assemblies. "[E]lectors should choose to be governed by persons they recognized as better and wiser then the people themselves...A representative system of government, coupled with a division of powers, was seen as providing safeguards against the dangers of democracy" (Arblaster, 1987: 40–41). Meanwhile, "[in] France...a quite different tradition of thinking about democracy was developing...This saw the common interests as something other than the sum of, or compromise between, a diversity of group interests." Rousseau, the prime contractual theorist representing this tradition, was at the opposite side of individualistic writers, like Hobbes and Bentham (ibid.: 41–42), as well as Locke. For him, equality and the collective took pre-eminence over liberty and property.

In *Federalist Paper 10*, Madison argued that unrestrained by external checks, any individual or group would tyrannize others, depriving them significantly of their natural rights. Therefore, internal checks against the tyranny of the majorities are equally if not more important than protections against the tyranny of the powerful few. This becomes possible, according to Madison, whenever electors are numerous and diverse (Dahl, 1956: 18).

In Madison's days, with the experiences from the French "Reign of Terror" and the Haitian Revolution very present, democracy was still equated with radical equalitarianism and direct democracy. The term much preferred was "republic," meaning a representative and a non-tyrannical system of limited government with multiple checks and balances to prevent democratic excesses (ibid.: 10). The Madisonian "polyarchy" constituted a compromise between equal rights for all adults and the protection of rights of powerful and privileged minorities, namely Locke's basic right: property. Hence, majorities had to be constitutionally inhibited in order to protect powerful, yet potentially vulnerable elites (Dahl, 1956: 31), threatened by the envious action of the poor masses.

Aristotle, in *Politics,* saw democracy as equality, with liberty and majority rule as demagoguery, representing a threat to virtuous government. Madison, in turn, stood against Jefferson and Rousseau in asserting the need for checks on majorities: internalized, social, and constitutional. Populist democracy, based on the majority principle, constituted the antithesis of Madisonian democracy (ibid.: 34–35, 38).

As Arblaster noted, the idea of rule by the people, as the centrepiece of the democratic discourse, only gained popularity in the 1820s, precisely because working-class voting was still not perceived as a threat to aristocratic privilege and middle class rule (Arblaster, 1987: 47). Liberal politics in the eighteenth and nineteenth centuries, while championing elections, fundamentally excluded the non-property holders, which encompassed the bulk of the working classes and the majority of the population. The same was the case with women. "[M]ost of [the writers] were content to redefine democracy in such a way as to eliminate its traditional participatory aspirations. They were thus able to get the best of both worlds. They could claim to be defending democracy while simultaneously denouncing the very tendencies and aspirations which led their...predecessors to condemn and criticize democracy as such" (ibid.: 53).

Equally reactionary tendencies characterized the development of democracy in the "new world" of Latin America. Here, conservative-minded landowners and the planters also sought to avoid social re-structuring after independence while paying lip-service to democracy. For all the verbiage around the Rights of Man, liberty, representative and responsible government, and the rule of law, after the fever of *Cabildos,* calls for *Juntas,* and Benthamian constitutions, most Hispanic American Republics went from chaos to autocracy. Independence heroes like San Martin and Bolivar felt that they had "plowed in the sea." Only Haiti went through a profound social revolution that ended slavery and thus established the first and only true popular sovereignty in the Hemisphere, just to be outcast as an international pariah for several decades after its creation and Napoleon's failure to re-establish slavery.

Until 1888, Brazil remained as an independent Empire, though ruled by the same dynastic family that sat at the throne in Lisbon, and retaining the same slave-based economy. In sum, the old colonial social formations and their connections with the international division of labour, continued and even deepened under conservative guises. Mexico went from an independent Empire to an uneasy liberal (though not particularly democratic) republic, just to become a liberal dictatorship under the *Porfiriato* (1870–1910). In a few cases, national autocracies evolved into republican forms, like Chile's constitutional and legalistic "tory democracy" (Moreno, 1968) from the 1830s onwards. In a few other cases, like late nineteenth-century Uruguay, Argentina and Costa Rica, a central government and economic prosperity were also capable of preventing what were once perpetual civil wars and factionalism. These political formulas balanced a local variance of the French royalist and nobility pacts by proposing a civic coexistence of "king" and "barons" based on exclusion and financed by a booming export economy. But these constitutional aristocracies were "best-case scenarios" and certainly not popular democracies by any account.

In the Americas, for most of the nineteenth and part of the twentieth century the participatory and representative franchise was vested in a tiny minority of mostly white, educated, male property holders of European descent. Even when political democracy, based on principles of equality to elect and be elected, became entrenched as an acceptable practice – largely as a result of electoral reforms expanding the franchise into the working classes – the notions of social and economic democracy remained confined to the radical fringe. The US was not alien to this undemocratic experience. It took a Civil War (1861–1865) – for some "the Second American Civil War" – to eradicate slavery and proclaim "freedom for all," yet not desegregation, equality, or non-repressive labour practices. It would take another century to begin opening the gates for African-Americans and other minorities into even formal equality; and the struggle for substantive equality still continues.

Democracy, social imperialism and social contracts

All in all, by the onset of the Age of Imperialism (1878–1914), the democratic idiom had become both legitimate and widespread in the Western world, including Europe and the oligarchic confines of the Americas. In many respects, the expansion of the franchise, combined with nationalism and imperial expansionism, allowed otherwise conservative elites to co-opt the labour movement and a good portion of the underclass. The challenges posed by the socialist and anarchist factions (those identified respectively with Marx and Bakunin) of the International Workingmen's Associations (a.k.a. the First International, established in 1864) brought about gradual reformism to otherwise oligarchic regimes. Yet to the elites, domestication and symbolic reformism was in the long run more effective than direct confrontation, which after all bearded the risk of unleashing the ghosts of Robespierre and Dessalines.

The political establishments in the Americas and Europe accepted political democracy and reluctantly tolerated trade unions in exchange for keeping internal peace, and social and economic democracy off the agenda. In practice, this meant that the liberal but essentially non-democratic state would accept working-class parties as legitimate contenders. However the electoral franchise would be distorted by skewed forms of balloting, all the way from redesigning electoral districts in majority systems, to manipulating proportionality, as in the Belgian system of proportional representation. For the elites, parliamentary-representative democracy became a tool to deadlock and prevent fundamental social change.

In the richer countries vertical (inward), but more often horizontal or "outward" expansion of capabilities facilitated elite-mass accommodation and a form of social appeasement. The "social imperialism" of Rhodes, McKinley and Theodore Roosevelt (Worsley, 1975) are illustrative of this trend; so is the more socially progressive Swedish social pact of Prime Ministers Hansen and Erlander (1934–1969). Expansion and growth became an imbedded necessity to facilitate social peace and to sustain a seemingly solid social contract, as it avoided distributional disputes. As long as the pie was big enough and growing, the discussions about how to divide it could be avoided, or at least postponed. Without sustained growth, consensus would soon lead to protracted paralysis or stalemate. Protracted and entrenched deadlock could lead to breakdown and open the gates of social rebellion, or even revolution. More often than not, however, polarized paralysis could led to repressive (and at times counter-revolutionary) modes of conflict management.

Democracy as hegemonic concept

It took major social revolutions (Russia and Mexico in 1917, China in 1912 and 1949), two world wars and a cold war for the word democracy to become hegemonic. Many struggles for self-determination in Asia, Africa and the Middle East incorporated the democratic ideal to the call for political independence. President Roosevelt's and Prime Minister Churchill's Atlantic Charter (1941) promised a world of free and democratic nations, thus echoing President Wilson's call for a "world safe for democracy" a generation earlier. By the end of World War II, conservatives, liberals, radicals, anarchists and even some advocates of totalitarianism had incorporated democracy as both an ideal and as a benchmark of their respective political projects.

The World War II pitched the ideology of democracy (both liberal and "popular") vis-à-vis its natural nemesis – "totalitarian" fascism. At the war's end, and in the period of rapid decolonization that followed, democracy had become a nominal measuring rod for political development, together with "freedom," self-determination and independence. The constitutions of the numerous new states resulting from decolonization enshrined democracy and the Universal Declaration of Human Rights as intrinsic components of their institutional engineering. In the industrial societies, democracy came to be associated with big – and responsible – government, popular representation, and the welfare state. In mainstream political science discourse, democracy and political development ended up being seen as one and the same (Lipset, 1960). As Held noticed, "[d]emocracy seems to bestow an 'aura of legitimacy' on modern political life: rules, laws, policies and decisions appear justified and appropriate when they are 'democratic' " (Held, 1987: 1).

Hyphenated democracy

In the "old days" of the Soviet Union, the USSR-controlled Third International, with its movement of "democratic" trade unions sharply differentiated the "corrupted" and hyphenated term "bourgeois democracy," to refer to the alienated and alienating practices of the West. For them, this type of subjective democracy objectively prevented the realization of a true workers' democracy, defined as "really-existing socialism." Terms like "democratic" (as in the now-defunct GDR), "socialist," "popular," or "people's republic" were so freely used to the point that the term democratic became a codeword for Communist.

This exclusivist definition was not without its detractors on the left. For one thing, anarchists, social democrats and "scientific socialists" had been at loggerheads since the times of the Marx-Bakunin and Second International splits of the 1860s and 1914. These tensions would grow even more intense with the Russian Revolution (1917), the Spanish Civil War (1934–1939), and beyond. Equally bloody was the struggle between Stalinists and Trotskyites in the 1930s, as were the subsequent schisms in the once Communist bloc. The emergence of Marshall Tito's version of Yugoslavian communism (1947), as well as the aborted attempts in Hungary (1956) and Czechoslovakia (1968), not to mention dissidents like Djilas and Bahro, each in their own terms claimed to offer a democratic alternative to Soviet-style "proletarian dictatorship." Thus, each movement on the left, from moderate to radical, had its own very different version of socialist democracy.

Social democracy

Particularly interesting here is the situation of the Social Democratic parties affiliated to the Second International. While advocating a sort of mixed economy with a welfare state, parliamentary and representative democracy, and a significant presence of the now vanishing labour movement, they were clearly anti-communist and showed a marked disdain for anarchists. The British Labour Party, the German SPD, Canada's NDP, and their numerous European and Latin American counterparts, exemplify this much-tamed version of socialism. Even today, many on the left still see Social Democracy and its current "Third Way" (Giddens, 1989) vogue not too far from a manifestation of Western liberal democracy: more democratic that socialist; and in fact, more liberal than democratic.

In fact, for all its diversity and complexity, the so-called "democratic socialism" is part of an evolving continuum among political projects calling themselves democratic that are clearly more evolutionary, some even static, than revolutionary. This continuum begins on the right with neo-conservatives; continues with conservatives, libertarians, neo-liberals, and finally also includes liberals. From the centre to the centre-left the gamut runs from Christian Democrats, Liberal Democrats and what has been referred to as "New Labour." The key issue dividing these groups is not so much how "democratic" they are. They all support some formal, parliamentary and representative form of responsible government based upon competitive elections (the slogans "free and fair elections" and "effective suffrage" come to mind), checks and balances, and a commitment to human rights. Included in this category are those parties that partake in the running of what Duverger has called Pluto-democracies. What separates them is policy divergences on issues related to the economy, the environment, taxation, defence, immigration or regulation.

In the heydays of the Cold War, what brought an alignment of all the above-mentioned organizations was their semantic monopoly of a non-hyphenated version of democracy. The latter was used and abused as a codename for "free" associations. The same way as "democratic" was used by the USSR as a synonym for "Moscow-supported," the word free (as in the notion of Free Trade Movement) was often used to mean, Western, or more precisely US, or even CIA sponsored. This semantic abuse by both sides had the effect of making the democratic idiom devoid of substance, but at the same time, and paradoxically, something intrinsically "good." The alleged triumph of democracy from the 1990s and into the new century coincided with its growing meaninglessness. The main question today is to what extent this once radical concept has retained its substantive vitality, above and beyond the emotions it still evokes.

The above characterization of groups and movements under the "democratic" rubric does not include other more radical democratic movements on the left, like anarchists and the so-called "New Left." These groups' agendas and platforms go beyond purely political issues, centred on representation and procedures, and address basic democratization in the social and economic sphere.

Democratization and re-democratization

At present, "legal democracy" is the model of the New Right, while "participatory democracy," became the model of the New Left (Held, 1987: 225). The previous narrative has highlighted the fact that the term democracy has a long semantic and operational lineage. By contrast, the idioms democratization and re-democratization, implying a movement towards a democratic teleology, are relatively new. They acquired intellectual notoriety with the expanding literature on "transitions from authoritarian rule" of the late 1970s and early 1980s (O'Donnell et al., 1986). From its beginnings the vocabulary of transition theory and "Third Wave" democratization (Huntington, 1991) was inherently ideological and prescriptive. It constituted largely an attempt to justify Western support for antidemocratic regimes during the Cold War, by proposing the reversibility of friendly dictatorial rule. It conveyed the notion that at times popular democracy can be stymied in the here-and-now in order to support an elitist capitalist democracy in the long run. In this sense, the transition discourse re-configured the 1930s' dichotomy between "democracy" and "totalitarianism," by introducing the concept of "authoritarianism" as something intrinsically different from – and ethically better than – its totalitarian counterpart. The implication was that while totalitarian regimes (meaning Soviet-type Communism) involved persistent and entrenched dictatorships, authoritarian regimes could traverse the road towards democracy and thus presented a lesser of two evils. The analytical and practical validity of this assumption was indeed questionable, as otherwise seemingly monolithic Soviet-type regimes disintegrated virtually overnight in the 1980s, while right-wing authoritarian tendencies endured, under conditions of transition, or even seemingly perpetual free fall.

Participation, order and transition

The above-mentioned conceptualization emerged in the context of a dramatic change in the conventional paradigm of political development (O'Brien, 1972), the latter rooted among others in the works of Schumpeter (1942), Lipset (1960) and Dahl (1962). Three fundamental transformations in the prevailing understanding of the liberal-democratic state underpin this change.

(1) One was a major shift among mainstream thinkers in the late 1960s regarding the democratic ideal: from participation and majority rule to order, stability, governability and elitism. The Crisis of Democracy thesis was the articulation of this conservative and increasingly prevailing mode of thinking.

(2) Another related foundational transformation in thinking and policy was the distancing between Keynesian demand-side policies from the Western conception of democracy and its replacement by neo-liberal supply-side economics, involving a general retrenchment of the socioeconomic and welfare functions of the state. This trend highlighted a growing and re-emerging contradiction between democracy and liberalism, and between freedom and equality (as well as equity).

(3) A third fundamental change was that between the national character of politics in the post-Westphalian state and the pervasive nature of transnationalization and globalization (Held et al., 1999). This affected

the linkage between democracy and the role of internal and external constituencies in the state.

The transitions from authoritarian rule in Southern Europe, the induced and controlled re-democratization in Latin America in the 1980s (O'Donnell et al., 1986), and the subsequent collapse of Communism in Eastern Europe offered opportunities for testing propositions derived from this restricted view of democracy. The old fascist regimes of Generalissimo Franco in Spain (1939–1975) and Prime Minister Oliveira Salazar in Portugal (1934–1968), and the neo-fascist regime of the Greek Colonels (1967–1973), all rabidly pro-Western, went into a tailspin in the 1970s (Poulantzas, 1976). In turn, the national security regimes in Latin America and Asia began to collapse from within. Transition and democratization became household words, defining a kind of teleological, as well as inevitable imperative, under the rubric of the End of History (Fukuyama, 1989). Giddens observed: "The orthodox view of democratization makes a virtue of, or in Fukuyama's case a philosophical case for, the disappearance of historical alternatives" (Giddens, 1998: 106–107). Liberal capitalism and democracy – albeit of a limited variety – were made almost synonymous, not just as *a* possible way but as *the* only way.

A number of institutional intellectuals provided a rationale for this linking. They postulated that, with classical fascism gone at the end of World War II, the only real menace to Western democracy was Communist totalitarianism. Policy-making advisors like Jeanne Kirkpatrick, Henry Kissinger and Samuel Huntington also argued that these "Second World" – for then undesirable regimes – entrenched in the hearts and minds of their citizens, had created a sort of totalitarian legitimacy and could not be transformed into "true" democracies. Conversely, there were pro-Western, equally non-democratic "authoritarian" regimes that, according to these establishment intellectuals could – if properly guided – traverse the road to democracy largely because they had not been able to entrench a totalitarian ideology in their respective societies. Originally, this concept was developed by Juan Linz in his analysis of Franco's fascism in a post-World War II context. Despite the circularity of the argument, it provided some moral justification to double standards. It also became mainstay academic discourse.

Yet, the alleged inevitability of Western-style democracy as postulated by Fukuyama (2000) and others remains questionable. A more nuanced and empirically grounded treatment of the relationship between globalization and democratization is required (Held et al., 1999, 1987). Although the Spanish, Portuguese and Greek transitions from authoritarian rule in the 1970s provided the minimal political requirements to join the European Community years later, the Latin American experience was one of substantially incomplete and largely ineffectual transition. In this case, under the aegis of the Washington Consensus, economic liberalization was by far more valued by Western elites than political, let alone social, democratization. In many cases, beneath a democratic façade, the illusive transition meant hardly more than the consolidation of the socioeconomic order constructed by the dictatorial regimes in retreat. Here, order still provided the dominant doctrine applied to justify the curtailing of social and economic democracy. But, even beyond Latin America, an examination of transitions after the fall of Communism in Eastern Europe and Central Asia equally indicates a persisting contradiction between liberalization and democracy. East Asia, the Middle East and Africa offer even fewer and unconvincing examples of viable democratization.

De-democratization

Equally important in the analysis of democratization is to examine the flip side of the story: the noticeable process of de-democratization unfolding throughout the globe, including the older industrial democracies. This new wave of de-democratization goes beyond the "crisis of democracy" discussed in the Report to the Trilateral Commission (Huntington, Crozier and Watanuki, 1975). For all intents and purposes, numerous empirical (benchmark) indicators of democracy in the West highlight a common trend. Greater corporate and media concentration, de-industrialization, labour atomization and decline, the dissolution of the liberal-democratic social contract, expanding income inequalities, declining participation, corruption, electoral fraud, erosion of sovereignty, and the "thinning" of human rights point in the direction of inequality and increasingly oligarchic, plutocratic and authoritarian rule. The post-9/11 revival of aggressive national security policies and the militarization of domestic society and foreign policy have furthered this tendency.

In its milder and less dramatic forms, popular exclusion has taken the form of European and Latin American style consociationalism; that is, highly institutionalized pacts among political and social elites to ensure smooth and coordinated governance, "pluto-democracies" (Duverger, 1966), or plutocracies with popular support (India, the US), or outright kleptocracies (*kleptos*=thieves). The predominant trait of contemporary democracies is one of diminishing participation and declining opportunities for non-elite influence in the political process going hand in hand with a dramatic increase of income and corporate and media concentration. Michels' (1915) observation about the "iron law of oligarchy" at the turn of the twentieth century is applicable with a vengeance as a descriptor of a globalized and transnationalized world and so is Eisenhower's warning against the Military-Industrial Complex.

In a number of industrialized countries with high value-added production, and in those implementing Import Substitution Industrialization (ISI) strategies from the 1930s to the 1960s, the expanded administrative state indeed facilitated the creation of conditions for stable economic prosperity. This mode of national-capitalist "managerialism" (Jaguaribe, 1968) constituted the foundation of the implicit social contract between business and unionized labour, considered by many as the cornerstone of modern liberal democracy. This was possible only under national capitalist schemes, with high protectionism and where labour, through collective bargaining, had real influence as an artefact of the internal power balance. Tripartite workers-business pacts guaranteed by the government allowed for some regulated and limited form of surplus sharing in the Western economies. It also facilitated labour peace and the purging of communists and other leftists from union ranks.

Growing transnationalization of capital and a subsequent erosion of labour power (Rifkin's "end of work" thesis, 1995) broke the above-mentioned balance and accelerated a fiscal crisis of the state. A manifestation of this was the elitist "tax revolt" started in the 1970s in the developed English-speaking world (the US, the UK, Canada, Australia, New Zealand) towards the end of the Vietnam War. Fiscal crises and legitimation crises went hand in hand (Habermas, 1973; O'Connor, 1973). The new skewed social contract was largely facilitated by the end of the Cold War: business needed not pretend to adopt a conciliatory stand vis-à-vis labour any longer. Unions were weak, corruptible and in a defensive mode. Rather than a contractual formula as such, the new model of labour relations meant basically an imposition by internationalized business over blue-collar workers and the middle strata: a sort of "global terms of surrender." It is under these conditions that elite discourse (and that of their institutional intellectuals) increasingly trumpeted that the crisis of democracy was rooted in over-participation. Its prescription was to adjust democracy to come to terms with the new liberalism, re-invent government (Osborne and Gaebler, 1993) and implement sweeping structural adjustments to facilitate hyper-accumulation at a global and unprecedented stage.

Politics as the management of contradictions

To explain and understand the complex reality of the democratic phenomenon, it would be useful first to construct a typology of conflict management based upon the interplay of contradictions (Nef, 1978). Politics is about conflict and its management, and conflict is the expression of tensions and contradictions within and among social actors and organizations. To simplify, we can offer a tripartite classification of the sources of this conflict.

Capabilities versus expectations: One essential contradiction in any political system is that between the supply of various resources, or "valuables," to be allocated by acts of authority (Easton, 1957) and the aggregate level of expectations, or social "demand," for those resources. Valuables, as Lasswell suggested, are not limited to material wealth. They include other important intangibles and social assets like respect, rectitude, affection, well-being, skill, knowledge and above all power (Lasswell, 1951). *Ceteris paribus*, conflict can be managed to the extent that the combination of assets to be allocated meets or exceeds the level of aggregate demand at any given point in time. As in any form of human association, trust and credibility are at the core of political transactions. Valuables are more often than not expressed in symbolic representations (hopes and promises) of delivery of things people deem scarce and necessary and whose disposition is subject to constraints. For instance, the availability of a resource to satisfy needs is not simply a matter of how abundant, or scarce this resource is. There are issues of ownership, delivery, localization and opportunity, as well as efficiency.

Elites versus masses: A second fundamental contradiction, conditioned by the demand-supply tension outlined above, is that of "who gets what." In other words, this is the conflict between those who obtain most of what is to be distributed and the rest who get least: the tension between "have" and "have-nots" (have-more and have-less). Most social orders, old and new, are stratified along lines of privileges and inequalities; conflict occurs along these distributive and redistributive lines. All political systems possess governance mechanisms to protect and manage socio-economic and other related inequalities. These mechanisms range all the way from co-optation, to ideological persuasion, to naked enforcement. Of course, the greater the availability of resources as indicated above, the greater the probability of successful, non-violent management of the conflict between elites and masses.

Sovereignty versus dependence: The third contradiction is that between the autonomy of the polity vis-à-vis extra-systemic actors or polities that control the creation and distribution of valuables (Frank, 1966; Chalmers, 1974). Since ancient times it has been recognized that a fundamental attribute of a polity is its being able to operate with some degree of internal control, or sovereignty. While the two inter-related contradictions mentioned above – that between capabilities and expectations and between elites and masses – were essentially internal to the political system, the one between sovereignty and dependence occurs at the international and supra-systemic level.

This may need some clarification. Foreign rule, whether indirect or direct requires a form of incorporation of external constituencies in the internal decision-making process. Even under conditions of formal autonomy these constituencies tend to partake in the normal correlation of forces in the state. Dependency and independence are a matter of degree. Of all the constraints regarding distribution of valuables within society, including the tensions between capabilities vs. expectations and elites vs. masses, the one between subordination and autonomy is the most independent and central variable. Without autonomy no polity can effectively manage its environment, economy, decision-making processes or its cultural "software." The issues of decolonization, neo-colonialism, trade and imperialism are centred on this question. So is the issue of democracy.

Modes of conflict management

The pattern or modality in which these three basic contradictions are managed over time suggests a typology based upon four possible scenarios.

(1) Repression: One scenario is a zero-sum game (Rapaport, 1974) in which the elites are unwilling or unable to respond to demands from the non-elite sectors of society, and suspend or freeze these demands by force. This is the scenario most inimical to popular rule; in fact irrespective of rhetoric, repression is the antithesis to popular rule. Repression refers to a scenario in which elites clear the stage of "superfluous" political actors, imposing dictatorial rule. This modality of governance involves a significant presence of violence, as the act of closure either happens in response to attempts at reform, existing domestic turmoil or by itself generates a form of resistance, whether peaceful or armed. Force is the elites' trump card to attempt to maintain order in the absence of internal legitimacy, generally involving a substitution of external for internal sources of support. The latter may take the form of foreign aid, technical cooperation, troops, or a combination of all these.

Authoritarian regimes are sometimes a temporary device by elites to halt a deteriorating political situation. Yet, in practice they tend to linger on until they either prevail, disintegrate or collapse, are overthrown by insurgencies or a negotiated settlement emerges. In very rare cases such regimes are able to generate a counter-revolution and transform the socioeconomic order from the top, as in Wilhemian Germany,

Meiji Japan, or in Pinochet's Chile. More often than not, however, these regimes become puppet regimes, heavily reliant on external supports.

(2) Rebellion: A second scenario is also a zero-sum game, but in reverse: a popular response in which the masses – or counter-elite representing those excluded by the existing regime – are able to overthrow the ruling oligarchy by force. Unlike repression, in which elites retain or increase their share of valuables by means of force, rebellion entails a drastic redistribution of power and resources and at least a temporary unravelling of the structure of privileges and inequalities. If a rebellion goes beyond the overthrow of the existing government and the transformation of the superstructures of the state apparatus, and if it is able to institutionalize itself into a relatively irreversible new order of things in the socioeconomic and cultural realms, we can talk about a revolution. Revolutions are not only change of government but regime change. This means a turnaround of the foundations of society. In the same way that not all instances of repression become full-fledged counter revolutions, not all rebellions – in fact, very few of them – become social revolutions (Brinton, 1965). Historically, leaving aside the developments in seventeenth-century England (e.g. 1688), significant revolutions include the American (1776), the French (1789), the Haitian (1804), the Mexican (1910), the Russian (1917), the Chinese (1949), the Bolivian (1952) and the Cuban (1959). Many rebellions, and even institutionalized revolutions, have become frozen, reversed or gone astray; to the point that nowadays it would be difficult to find progressive traces beyond their rhetoric and mythologies. Many never pass the phase of rebellion. What "challenges from below" have in common is that at least in moments in their history, rebellions and revolutions possess strong popular and democratic characteristics. In numerous cases, some of these equalitarian, popular, libertarian and progressive traits have persisted with the inherent tendency towards fossilization.

(3) Consensus is a third modality of conflict management. Unlike the two categories discussed above, it is essentially a non-zero-sum game (or variable score game) in the language of game theory. In this scenario, resources are abundant and/or effectively managed and relatively free of external constraints; the relations between elites and masses are defined by a degree of trust and mutual acceptance of the rules of the game and the implicit "social contract." Political actors can express themselves with relative freedom and recognize themselves as more or less equal citizens with rights; this despite the existence of an underlying structure of privileges and inequalities. Unions, business interest groups, aggregative political parties, a free press, an independent judiciary and a professional civilian and military bureaucracy partake in a

form of institutionalized class conflict, based upon collective bargaining and public accountability. The political system is essentially autonomous and able to protect its sovereignty over rule-making, resources and enforcement. In many cases, colonial expansion into someone else's territories, as in the high noon of British, French, Dutch and American imperialism, permitted the imperial country to incorporate the masses into a "national" vision of manifest destiny. Even without aggressive imperialism, as in present day Scandinavia, most of Western Europe, Australia and New Zealand, the economy can expand through high value-added production. In this context, demands for more valuables tend to be matched by some elasticity of supply: the socioeconomic system can deliver by expanding capabilities without expropriating or redistributing resources away from the elites, or imposing mass austerity by means of dictatorship. Indeed, consensus is a statistically very rare occurrence. However, it is the model most discussed in textbooks as being "normal" and congruent and synonymous with democratic politics.

(4) Stalemate: This mode is a peculiar and not uncommon derivation of the consensual scenario (Crozier, 1964). It is also a form of institutionalized class struggle but in which the contextual conditions of production, sovereignty, trust and culture are either absent or only partially present. Thus, the "game" as in models 1 and 2 is essentially a zero-sum interaction in which actors can obtain only sham victories, obscured by a veil of structural inflation. This means that the deep schism between elites and masses is played through the wage-price spiral between salaried and capital sectors. In fact, it is a form of democratic conflict management in which the outward traits of consensus – a free press, political parties and the like – coexist with the reality of a deeply divided society with little "elbow room," and oscillating close to the abyss of potential repression and latent rebellion.

Examples of this precarious form of democracy have been abundant in the twentieth century, from the Weimar Republic, the French Third and Fourth Republics, Italy, Uruguay and Chile through the 1960s and 1970s, and also in Australia and the United Kingdom. Some of these stalemated forms of what Sartori (1976) called polarized pluralism have descended into thoroughly repressive varieties, while others have been able to pull back from the brink. The fact remains that as the tensions between and among capabilities/expectations, elites/masses and sovereignty/dependence grow, so does the fragility of democracy. For, contrary to popular belief, democracies are the result of delicate balances, the nature of which has to be nurtured and consciously preserved, not of homeostatic automaticity.

No concrete political system is entirely repressive, consensual, stalemated or in a state of rebellion in all its spatial, functional and historical dimensions. Actually-existing polities are, rather, a dynamic combination and coexistence of these different modalities, with predominant and persistent strains. Democratic and antidemocratic features are present in most political systems, or in some of their spatial and temporal domains. Therefore, when we use the terms "democracy" as an empirical generalization, we are talking about a form of government that is predominantly and predictably *mostly* democratic in a given point in time and space.

The survival and strength of democracy is not a preordained "legacy of history," a divine gift or a function of social atavism. Rather, as in Machiavelli's old formula, the existence of democracy is an artful interplay between circumstances (*fortuna*) and statesmanship (*virtu*) on the part of the leadership and the citizens, creating and protecting political space. Citizens have a dual capacity in their roles as rulers and those being ruled, and as agents of their own destiny. Democracy, like many other natural and human-engineered structures, is not a homeostatic arrangement, whose resilience is to be taken for granted. Rather, it is negotiated and re-negotiated every day.

The many faces and layers of democracy

The real gap between democracy and non-democracy is much thinner than most would like to think. The practice of the former goes beyond the institutions of government, the rule of law or the electoral franchise. These are merely the tips of the iceberg: necessary, but not sufficient conditions for its existence and reproduction. Democracy, if it means anything at all, requires social, economic and cultural foundations. It also requires a favourable international and regional environment. Political democracy without a significant degree of socioeconomic equality and opportunity is a sham. The opposite is also true: equality without the respect for liberty, diversity and the attributes of an open society is similarly empty. Worse, simple equality can lead to the monotony of party bureaucracy, autocracy or tyranny.

Consensus is a fundamental condition for democracy to exist and flourish, but uniformity – whether in the forms of conformism, apathy, consumerism, moral fundamentalism or chauvinism – constantly threatens to undermine its very essence. For democracy is nurtured by diversity, dissent and debate. If these attributes are taken away the term becomes mere rhetoric, hypocrisy, or an empty shell. Above all, it is not a copyrighted word to be sold and bought, conferred upon and removed as it appears fit. Nobody has a monopoly or franchise on it. Many antidemocratic regimes around the world exhibit democratic traces and practices that deserve special attention. The opposite also holds: numerous allegedly democratic regimes present nasty authoritarian and undemocratic tendencies. These too need to be studied and acted upon.

Chapter 2

Formal and Substantive Democracy

The discussion in the previous chapter leaves us keenly aware of the fragility of democracy. Not only has our understanding of democracy changed over time, we came to expect gradually more and more from it. However, in its practical application, at the same time that the democratic ideal expanded and was able to gain more influence, antidemocratic forces sought to block every step of this expansion and avoid any further attacks on their privileged positions in society and their exclusive access to power – be it state power, or simply the power over others in society. According to Fareed Zakaria (2003), democracy advanced whenever dominant power holders were weakened and, more often than not, this weakening resulted from a lack of unity among the powerful. In other words, the principles of liberty and equality – the core values of democracy – expanded whenever contenting forces were able to drive a wedge into the alliance of the powerful. Not surprisingly, every step towards more democracy triggered a reaction against it and democracy has remained an embattled practice ever since it first emerged.

However, before we can address the different challenges to democracy in more detail, we need to reach an understanding of what democracy is – and what it is not. More than a definition, this requires a brief discussion of the different elements that are the necessary ingredients to a democratic regime. This chapter thus sets the conceptual stage for the more empirical analyses to follow.

The meaning of democracy

Democratic theorists have long discussed the changing meanings and possible definitions of the concept "democracy." Larry Diamond (1999) distinguishes "minimalist," or procedural definitions, focusing narrowly on free elections as the main criterion to characterize a democracy from more substantive definitions that also take issues of social justice and participation into account. Substantive democratic theorists, such as Barber (1984) and Rueschemeyer (1998) stress that it is necessary to diminish the distance separating the ruled from their rulers through means of direct participation and the creation of institutions that enhance the government's accountability. A third school of democratic thought has gone beyond substantive definitions, although agreeing with its premises. Advocates of deliberative democracy focus their attention on the discursive *formation* of preferences and the importance of civil society and the public sphere as places to legitimize democratic rule.

"Minimalist models," go back to Joseph Schumpeter (1942). Robert Dahl (1971) and Samuel Huntington (1993) both follow Schumpeter in broad terms. For him, democracy was a system "for arriving at political decisions in which individuals acquire the power to decide by means of a competitive struggle for the people's vote" (Schumpeter, 1947: 269). Other authors in the same tradition understand democracy as a form of government where people periodically elect their representatives. If political and civil freedoms, such as the right to vote, secret ballots, the right to run for office, and the right to campaign openly are given, political elites compete for votes, on a market-type basis. If they perform well, they probably will get re-elected. If they don't, the people have the chance to replace them. The problem with this model is its difficulty in explaining why elected elites should produce policies that favour the citizens once they are elected, rather than designing policies that serve themselves. Its strong point is that such treatment permits a more objective treatment of democracy. Democracy, in this view, is present where representatives are elected in free, public elections. Any normative or substantive criteria are left out. According to Samuel Huntington (1968), direct citizen participation is not needed nor wanted in all countries as it might jeopardize political stability. Other advocates of minimalist definitions have argued that citizen participation in democratic governance is not desirable because it might distort outcomes in favour of more influential groups (Fiorina), and because citizens are not informed enough to make wise political decisions (Hinich and Munger, 1997).

Fiorina (1999) has argued that the rise of more participation in the US has led to more distrust as interest groups have used the new mechanisms that participatory democracy has provided to manipulate and influence political processes in their own interest. He calls this process one of favouring "extreme voices" that are able, through media manipulation, money donations, lobbying, corridoring, and the like, to influence politicians and the broader public. In his understanding, the broader American public has reacted by retreating from politics, disenchanted with the political manipulation that some strong and rich interest groups are asserting on the political process. To all those favouring minimalist treatments of democracy, the impact of citizen participation on democracy is not necessarily positive.

A second school of authors advocates for a more substantive understanding of democracy. Authors like Laclau and Mouffe (1985), Benjamin

Barber (1984), and Dietrich Rueschemeyer (1998) claim that democracy is more than just a way to govern; rather, it is a mode of collective decision-making. They seek to identify a form of collective organization that promises to diminish the gap between the rulers and the ruled. Such organization necessarily includes participation, and seeks rational, open argumentation in order to achieve desired preferences and legitimate collective decisions. Free elections are therefore not enough to define democracy; and participation, social justice, equity, governmental responsiveness, and transparency have necessarily to be taken into account. This tradition goes back to republican treatments of the "general will" (Rousseau) and the "common good" (Locke and John Stuart Mill). Following the substantive definition, democratization depends on effectively responding to the needs and wants of all the people, including the disenfranchised that have long waited for democracy, fought, suffered, and died for it.

Advocates of deliberative democracy, a third and less traditional school of thinking about democracy, have argued about how to integrate deliberative arenas into the institutional framework of contemporary complex democracies. This entails the idea of debates used in game theory, as opposed to "fights" and "games" proper (Rapoport, 1967: 1–14). While the latter two involve winning or losing something without a defined set of outcomes and rules, debates involve the redefinition of desired outcomes and means of interaction. Whereas one way to conceive deliberative democracies is to think about deliberative spaces within the state, the more widespread argument locates deliberative processes outside the state, although without disputing the importance of deliberations and debates within the state.

"Civil society" and the "public sphere" have been the two main concepts introduced to locate places outside the state where deliberation can occur, critical opinions can be created and interchanged, including those directed against the state, and where states can be held accountable and brought to perform better and more responsively. Robert Putnam has made an important and widely discussed contribution to this subfield with his study on democracy in Italy (1993). Writing about civic traditions in Italy and the United States, Putnam shows how traditions of mutual trust, associability, and participation are nurtured in such apolitical groups as bird-watchers and bowling leagues, and how such traditions can enhance democratic performance, turning governments more responsive and accountable, ultimately even leading to better economic performance. The concept of "social capital" became a slogan and key concept for the advocates of this train of thought. At the same time, other writers tried to define where, and how, associations can deliver the desired attributes to the democratic system, and what kinds of associations can do this best. We shall return to a more detailed discussion of the potentials of "deliberative" or "discursive" democracy in Chapter 3.

Democracy and elections

One of the most common contemporary fallacies is to equate democracy with elections. True, elections are a necessity in any representative or indirect form of democratic practice, but we should bear in mind that participation is much broader than elections. Nor does this mean that elections per se equal democracy. We should also bear in mind that direct democracy is participative, but it is neither indirect nor representative via elections of incumbents; though participation may take place in the form of voting or even drawing lots. Elections are neither synonymous nor relevant for democracy when the selection process for candidates is controlled by a few powerful moneyed or ethnic interests, a dictator or a dominant party. Ostensibly non-democratic regimes often use election for purposes of ritualization and international legitimation, as with Robert Mugabe's 2008 self-election in Zimbabwe. Many elections are effectively undemocratic when the accessibility to choices and resources to allow for inclusive representation is restricted, or where the policy choices are basically the same. Conversely, voting is relevant when its procedures are not tampered with, and the results are transparent and respected. They are also relevant where different parties present a multiplicity of platforms for consideration – not exclusively those favourable to one dominant group: the economic elites, the security apparatus, and the corporate media. What counts is not just the number of voices, but the inclusiveness and representational range of diversity. The issue of social equity and accessibility, as well as the probability of effecting change, are crucial too for a substantial definition of democracy.

Elections, whether majority or proportional, are mechanisms of representation of the civil society into the polity. Thus, their crafting and operation are indicators of the breadth and depth of democracy. Binomial and majority systems tend to eschew representation, as can the drafting and re-drafting of electoral procedures and districts. In turn, proportional representation, though more equitable in theory, tends to generate deadlock in polarized societies. Examining a wide array of data especially from Europe, Duverger concluded that the type of election mechanism had a significant impact on the party system. A single member district with majority representation tended to favour a two-party system, while discouraging smaller parties; proportional mechanisms favoured a multiparty arrangement. Another aspect of elections with potentially distorting or equalizing abilities is the expediency and/or difficulty for voter registration, and de-registration. So is vote-counting and tabulating as a manifestation of the degree of transparency (or lack of transparency) of the political process. More substantively is the educational and learning functions of electoral participation, or, using the words of Maturana and Varela, the autopoietic experience of building citizenship (1980).

Furthermore, if one agrees about the superiority of majority rule over other forms of collective decision-making in modern and complex societies, there inevitably remains the problem of what Tocqueville called "the tyranny of the majority." As Brian Barry (1979) argued in his article "Is Democracy Special?," structural minorities that have a different language, religion, or national identity than the majority in power and whose preferences are therefore consistently divergent from the majority, have a great risk of not being represented in majority rule systems. The liberal doctrine that guarantees individual freedom to all citizens, meaning first and foremost the absence of state coercion, necessarily comes into conflict with the basic principle of democracy: majority rule. In cases where minorities are neglected, not represented, or oppressed by ruling majorities, then we face the logical problem of two mutually exclusive principles: democracy and liberalism, understood as a form of governance that allows all individuals to be free and equal. We shall return to this tension later.

Constitutions, limited government, and the often illusive rule of law are equally problematic. Institutional procedures and rules matter where all the actors can have equal access to the government, public information, and resources, regardless of their ties to the ruling forces or the security apparatus. It has been estimated that "two in every three people in the planet – some 4 billion in total – are 'excluded from the rule of law' " (*The Economist*, 2008: 87). Moreover, constitutional procedures – including the oft repeated "due process" – make sense only where all the actors can partake in the "authoritative shaping and sharing of valuables" with a reasonable expectation of effecting change. They also matter where different brokers present a multiplicity of platforms for consideration – not exclusively those favourable to a single group.

Constitutions as political projects

Together with "free and fair elections," the notion of constitutional government is another term conventionally associated with democracy. It is important, however, to remember that not all constitutions are democratic, nor that the rule of law per se guarantees fairness, freedom or equality. Nevertheless, all democratic forms require a constitutional foundation setting the institutional blueprint and the basic rules of politics. Thus, while all democracies are constitutional regimes, not all constitutional regimes are democratic.

The word constitution in continental Europe and Latin America generally evokes the notion of an inscribed discourse, or text, from where both the legitimacy and the exercise of the public power emanate (Duverger, 1956: 4). Nevertheless, at close examination, it is not a precise and widely accepted concept. It is crisscrossed by different legal and philosophical interpretations that lead in many different directions. For instance, in the British mould the constitution refers to a set of practices and conventions, some of them non-written, that govern the body politic. Conversely, the continental European conception of constitution, which has had significant worldwide resonance, is that of an, often detailed, legal document. Although the British Empire left a deep imprint in India's practices and institutions, this country's 1947 constitution is an extremely detailed and explicit document.

A very ample and operational characterization of the concept would include written, consuetudinary, and mixed forms. The term "national constitution" is used by political leaders and by academics to refer in general to the official collection of the principles and fundamental norms that define the sources, uses, purposes and limitations of state power. This collection of principles and rules is contained in most cases in a single written document – though no meaningful study of a constitutional system can be limited to such central document alone (Duchacek, 1973b: 23).

For the purposes of our analysis, constitutions can be studied from the prism of three main conceptual models, or "visions;" namely (a) *organic*, (b) *literal*, as a written text or, (c) as a *substantive* manifestation of political goals, rights and obligations.

The organic paradigm

This perspective sees the constitution as a living, slowly evolving and essentially conservative construct: an established order of things and practices transcending any written text and literal interpretation. This understanding of the constitution as an *ordum seclorum*, or *status quo rei publicum,* has a historical lineage going back to ancient Greece and Rome. Aristotle's comparison of the constitutions of the Aegean city-states in his *Politics* was not a just an exegesis of written laws and texts, but a study of how power was actually generated and exercised in each political community. This way or pattern of practices and core values related to running civic affairs was *the* constitution. Traditional, non-secular systems, like the Pashtun *Jirga* are consuetudinary mechanisms for conflict resolution where norms are defined by imbedded practices, not written rules.

The United Kingdom, the United States, and to a lesser extent Canada are examples of this model. English constitutionalism includes numerous documents, beginning with the *Magna Carta Libertatum* (Great Charter of Freedom of 1215), the Bill of Rights (1689), consuetudinary practices and common-law traditions, as well as various institutions and Statuses under the Westminster system that guarantee the rule of law. In turn, the US tradition, though branching out of British constitutional developments, essentially centres on a succinct, formal and highly emblematic written document: the Philadelphia Constitution of 1787, complemented by numerous constitutional legislation and amendments to the constitutional text. For Corwin, the Constitution of the United States is much more than the written text. It includes it, or a good deal of it, but it also includes some important statutes, and government practices which have evolved since the enactment of the formal constitution. It also encompasses in a material sense a wide array of judicial decisions that inductively define the spirit of the formal constitution (Corwin, 1925: 291). Besides Great Britain, there are only two countries that do not have a written constitution codified under a single text: Israel and Saudi Arabia. One is a Western-style democracy; the other an absolute and traditional monarchy.

Constitutions as inscribed discourses

In contrast with the aforementioned organic tradition, the literal or nominalist model emphasizes the deductive legal interpretation (exegesis) of written norms. Continental European constitutionalism and its Thomistic varieties in Ibero-America emerged from this formal and logical foundation. However, this strain has been strongly influenced by secular and liberal social contract theories born out the Enlightenment and ultimately the French Revolution (1789–1795). For rationalist eighteenth-century philosophers, constitutionalism was understood as an expression of a social contract, or covenant, between the constituent power of the citizenry and the constituted power of the state, reflecting and representing this citizenship. In this mode of analysis it is essential to understand the meaning, form and intent of the contractual text and its intrinsic relationship with the various declarations on the Rights of Man and the Citizen (inspired by the French and American revolutions), structured by this text.

Despite its deductive, as opposed to inductive foundation, the contractual tradition is more than superficially related to the Anglo-American pattern of constitution-building – for instance, Montesquieu's reference to "the Constitution in England" in the development of his often misunderstood thesis of the separation and balance of powers contained in his *Spirit of the Laws* (1777). The European constitutional experience is fundamentally rooted in a deductive tradition, or frame of mind, whose original source is Roman and subsequent Cannon law. In this scholastic mould, upon which Continental positive law has been carved, the written law, rather than tradition or convention, play the central role. Text, not practice or context, are the primary sources of the juridical and legal order.

This is not to say that contractualisms, especially those of Thomas Hobbes (1588–1679) and John Locke (1632–1704), did not have an important role in the development of Anglo-Saxon constitutionalism. On the contrary: these philosophical sources were fundamental in such development. In fact, the social contract or pact became the political correlate of the expanding contractual-commercial practices of the emerging English or American bourgeoisie. True, for Hobbes a social contract as covenant and the idea of authority were conditions of survival for the constituents of the social order. To make this order possible, the contracting parties delegated the entirety of their sovereign and individual power to an authoritarian state: the Leviathan. For Locke, on the other hand, the social contract was connatural to any social order centred on property – and thus on social inequality, and liberty. Individuals delegated part of their power to the state, and the latter returned these delegated powers in the form of civic rights. Citizens always retained a reservoir of constituent power. The concept of freedom is here a categorical imperative for a system of market and market-like transactions (von Hayek's "catalaxia"). To fully appreciate these constitutional ideologies in a broader context is necessary to relate Locke's theses with the formulations about possessive individualism (MacPherson, 1964: 1–8) of classical liberal economists, like Adam Smith, or David Ricardo.

In turn, early constitutionalism in France and Spain (respectively 1790–1793 and 1812–1814), and that of their former New World colonies, were deeply influenced by contractual theories, such a Jean-Jacques Rousseau's *Social Contract* in which equality, more than liberty (for Locke the very foundation of society), was the cornerstone. According to Rousseau, the transfer of sovereignty from the citizens to the rulers was a rational act to enhance collective well-being. In this sense, the nominalist and normative philosophical strain of Rousseau's argument emphasizes the formal and explicit nature of the collective will, as well as the equalitarian basis of a constitutional regime.

The French revolutionary constitution, its Spanish counterpart, and those to emerge in the colonial insurgencies of New Spain, New Granada, La Plata, and throughout South America (1809–1824) formally abolished slavery – something the US Constitution did not do. Emancipation and abolition were the logical corollaries of the principle of equality. They also erased by decree the privileges of the colonial nobility. Needless to say, this declaratory idealism soon entered into conflict with the entrenched practices of servitude and vassalage present in latifundia, plantations, and other extractive operations, which provided wealth and power to the New World oligarchies. The early "liberal" constitutions in Latin America were soon displaced by force of arms by more conservative documents, whose central preoccupation was the establishment and maintenance of public order over equalitarian notions, or citizen's rights.

The substantive paradigm

We can identify a third and more contemporary view of constitutions. For lack of a better term we could call this the substantive or teleological perspective. The constitutional order here is structured around the ends and purposes of the state, more so than in reference to the means, forms and procedures which are instrumental to attain those purposes. The above-mentioned ends refer to two types of human rights. The first group of rights includes those called individual, or "subjective," already recognized in organic and nominalist constitutional doctrines in the late eighteenth and early nineteenth centuries. The second group is constituted by the so-called "objective" human rights: employment, education, health, housing, access to land, social security and the like. This constitutional doctrine not only proclaims those material rights. It also sets limits to private property (the social function of property) to satisfy social well-being, in clear opposition to nineteenth-century liberal principles and Locke's foundational prime directive. By and large, the substantive paradigm does not displace liberal civil and individual rights. It rather expands collective rights to all citizens and puts human rights, not tradition or the letter of the law, at the centre of the constitution.

Two examples of this type of constitutionalism were articulated in the 1912 Chinese provisional constitution of Nanking and in the Mexican constitution of 1917. China's experiment emerged from the ouster of the Qing (Manchu) dynasty by the forces of modernizing republican leader Dr. Sun Yat-Sen and the subsequent proclamation of the Chinese Republic. The constitution was based on Sun's Three Principles of the People (nationalism, democracy and people's livelihood), proclaimed in 1905. Mexico's constitution, in turn, also emerged from another popular uprising: the social revolution started in 1910. In both cases, the "social question" (in China the issue of people's livelihood) found itself at the centre of the debate on the role of the state. In Mexico, this paradigmatic shift took place in an historical moment in which socialists, anarchists, populists, and even a conservative Catholic Church, were questioning the alienating character of liberal modernism and industrial capitalism. In these two examples, some of the underlying constitutional principles were influenced by British, French and American legal traditions.

In spite of their open antidemocratic proclivities, the fascist regimes of the First post-war introduced substantive and interventionist clauses in their corporatist constitutional charters. In turn, the self-proclaimed "real socialisms" imbedded these principles, as in the case of the Soviet constitution of 1936 and the derivative texts that proliferated in Eastern Europe since the end of the Second World War. Yet, in the totalitarian, fascist and communist versions of substantive constitutionalism, the "objective" rights were often a justification to violate "subjective" individual rights.

The substantive constitutional paradigm, however, remained limited to new political Marxist–Leninist, fascist and populist projects (as in China, Mexico, or Kemalist Turkey) until the 1930s. Even regimes with entrenched liberal constitutions were dramatically affected by the Great Depression of 1929. The crisis created the conditions for the emergence and consolidation of an interventionist Administrative State with a developmental and welfare agenda. This was certainly the case with Keynesian policies of economic reactivation and full employment in North America, the United Kingdom, Scandinavia, and throughout Europe, as well as the Import Substitution Industrialization (ISI) model in Latin America – the foundation of national development policies in Mexico, Brazil, Uruguay, Argentina and Chile in the 1930s and 1940s. But this encompassing Administrative and Welfare State did not always manifest itself in ostensible constitutional changes – as was the case with Getulio Vargas *Estado Novo* (1937–1945) in Brazil, or the Cuban constitution of 1940. More often than not the new paradigm involved adding programs and agencies, not fundamental transformation of the "power map." At any rate, the substantive paradigm became the template for many emerging states; it inspired some of the ideas of the Atlantic Charter, European integration and reconstruction, the United Nations, and the Universal Declaration of Human Rights of 1948.

The above Declaration in its evolution recognizes two types of rights for all people. One group, called "first generation" rights are those individual civil rights, many of which derived from liberal constitutions, whether organic or nominalist, during the eighteenth and nineteenth centuries. The other group of rights is the "second generation" social and economic rights that put an emphasis not only what the state *cannot* do, but on what the state *must* do. This third perspective on constitutionalism found expression in the constitutional development of what Carl Friedrich referred to as "neo democratic constitutions" (both, social-democratic and social Christian) in post-World War II Europe, especially in the then Federal Republic of Germany and Italy. Though these tendencies are partly rooted in the "subjective" attributes of individual freedom – of cult, thought, expression, association – and the *habeas corpus*, their cornerstone is the explicit recognition of concrete social and economic rights the state has an obligation to protect and attain.

Constitutions: text, subtext and context

Building upon the work by Duchacek (1973), it is possible to examine constitutions in relation to the main functions they perform in the larger political system, especially as they affect the nature of the democratic phenomenon. (1) A primary function is foundational: being the basic document or charter establishing the principles of government and organization. (2) Another is that of providing a blueprint, or "power map," defining both the political actors, the organizational structure of the state – what is called "the form of government" – and the rules of the game. (3) Last, but not least, is the most important and substantive function related to the ends of the state: the declaration of rights guarantees and obligations.

Therefore, the relationship between constitutionalism and democracy is in practice rather indirect. All three models discussed here could support democratic as well as non-democratic regimes. It is not possible to conceive a democratic regime without a working constitutional formula, including texts, traditions and a robust set of substantive rights. But the constitution, whatever its definition, is not the only element that makes a regime. As with elections, democracy, to be real, involves above all a persistent political practice by and for its citizens. But this practice, in turn, requires to be rooted in an open, inclusive, and democratic social, economic and cultural foundation. Without this base, and without the democratizing effects of such foundation and political practices upon its political superstructure, the political process is mere ritual, or empty rhetoric.

Indeed, as Jürgen Habermas has argued, "the *de facto validity* of legal norms is determined by the degree to which such norms are acted on or implanted, and thus by the extent to which one can actually expect the addressees to accept them" (Habermas, 1998: 30). Both continental Europe and Latin America and to some extent Asia, however, inherited a tradition of code law rooted in the legal practices of the Roman Empire and spread across the globe by Spanish and Portuguese colonizers, which is deeply marked by legal idealism. Legal idealism characterizes a system where laws are created and codified by elites, who take little interest and are indeed often unfamiliar with the reality of the majority. Under such circumstances, legal codes do not necessarily articulate the consolidated practices and norms of "the people." Rather, they represent the definition how a society ought to organize according to societal elites; and they thus contain an inherent paternalistic and antidemocratic trait of elite-tutelage. The most immediate result of this tension between legal codes and social realities is that in many societies a tremendous gap separates realty (or "facts," in the terminology of Habermas) from legal norms, thus casting severe doubt about the relevance of more or less aloof institutional frameworks for the organization of societal reality according to democratic guidelines.

Certainly there is much more to politics and democracy than constitutions that define the rules of engagement as well as the power maps, and electoral processes and taxation systems that generate incumbents and resources. All of these have an impact on the democratic, or non-democratic, nature of politics, being, in turn affected by the political process. Contrary to a widespread belief among political scientists of the 1960s, though culture, attitudes and behaviour are important attributes of democracy, institutions cannot be ignored. This is especially the case if we go beyond purely legal and formalistic categories and focus on institutions as purposive organizations, possessing a culture, a social fabric and a significant permeability to larger societal and extra-societal environments.

Generation and exercise of authority

Generally speaking, and as suggested above, political institutions perform two interrelated functions that connect the state and more specifically the government, with the civil society. First of these processes is the generation of authority, in the form of incumbents and resources, transforming "private" into "public" power. When the latter is recognized by society as appropriately acquired and legitimate, we are talking about authority. The very idea of democracy presupposes legitimacy and majority rule by consensus. Incumbents, whether appointed or elected (or hypothetically chosen by lot, drafted, or volunteered) bring into the government projects, perspectives, mindsets and ideologies. In other words, they import objectives (teleologies) in the form of utopias to be attained and conversely dystopias (undesirable states of affairs) to be avoided, ways of doing things and practices (deontologies), and value systems and beliefs (axiologies). The manner in which incumbents, resources and perspectives are generated – that is, how they perform the "script" – have a direct impact upon democracy, or its absence. The dialectics between taxation (resource extraction), broadly defined, and representation is one of the basic lines along which democratic struggles have been fought throughout history. There are also other less frequent but not necessarily exotic mechanisms to affect power generation. These include petitioning, initiatives, commissions, access to information (and its opposite, secrecy), and recall; all having an effect upon the openness of government.

The generation of incumbents is a process particularly relevant to a democracy. So is, nowadays, the notion of universal suffrage (Arblaster, 1987: 99). There are two general ways to generate incumbents. The most traditional and authoritarian form is bureaucratic: by appointment. It should be kept in mind that most incumbents in any state, even the reputedly most democratic of them all, are appointed. The other, more democratic and less frequent mode of generation of incumbents implies one of three political artefacts: direct participation (as in the classical Greek polis or in some Swiss cantons); selection by chance (drawing lots); or representation by election.

Since direct participation is increasingly rare throughout the world, elections have become, since the eighteenth century, the mechanism of democratic incumbency generation par excellence. As mentioned earlier in this chapter, there are two basic electoral devices. One is the majority system, with either single or binomial-member districts, in which the one who obtains the majority of the ballots is elected. This electoral practice tends to favour in most cases a two-party government-opposition mould, discouraging third party participation. The other, generally claimed to be more democratic, is the plurality or proportional representation system. In it, those with the largest plurality of the balloting get elected in districts with multiple memberships. This mechanism, which is nowadays the most common worldwide, tends to favour, by and large, multi-party arrangements.

Of course, the degree of democracy of a government cannot be directly inferred by its having a higher ratio of elected positions. Nor is democracy a direct consequence of a more proportionally representative modality of voting. These traits may facilitate or impede democracy, but what counts at the end is a multiplicity of cultural, structural, procedural and conjunctural factors. Things like who is allowed to register as a voter, and how; who votes, how are the votes counted, and the existence of institutional devices to mediate electoral disputes are equally important. Above all, while instruments are not inconsequential, democracy depends on the attitudes and behaviours of the citizens and the government.

The second process is the one we could call exercise of power, or, in more conventional terms, what is often referred to as the form of government. It involves three inter-related structural patterns of relationships:

(1) Interplay and balancing among the major decision-making organs that compose the superstructure of government. This arrangement refers to the conventional tripartite division and interaction of the "powers of the state" outlined by Montesquieu: rule-making, rule-executing and

rule-adjudicating. Historically, the idea of popular rule has been linked to the notion of checks and balances among these organs and functions. To some extent this involves some sort of parliamentary-legislative control over executive decisions and the ability of the judiciary to intervene in jurisdictional disputes as well as in interpreting the law. Executive supremacy has been, in theory, associated with the notion of authoritarianism, and arbitrary rule, while legislative (collective) dominance, with greater pluralism and diversity. In practice these distinctions that highlight the parliamentarism vs. presidentialism debate are more complex than the prima facie democratic credentials of these systems based on purely formal criteria. Parliamentary systems can be as undemocratic as their presidential counterparts, depending upon how the real political game is played and upon the degree of competition, openness, transparency and accountability. Apartheid South Africa was a parliamentary republic, as has been the case with contemporary Iran – both with opposition parties. The American presidential model in its application has generated anything from pluralistic democracies like post-1948 Costa Rica to authoritarian-corporatist forms like Brazil's national security regime from the mid-1960s through the mid-1980s.

(2) Besides the relations between the individual Executive and the collective assembly, there is another pattern defining the form of government. This is the interplay between the central government and territorial units, along the continuum between decentralized federalism and a centralized unitary state. Equally important is the role of local, municipal governments, vis-à-vis the central administration. In general, greater territorial autonomy, as opposed to high centralization, has been associated with democracy. However, this relation is more equivocal than that related to legislative supremacy; think about state rights in the Southern United States under Jim Crow norms of racial segregation (1876–1965).

(3) The third structural pattern associated with the exercise of power that is relevant to the institutionalization of democracy is the relationship between the above-mentioned higher decision-making organs (the executive, the legislature and the judiciary) and the techno-bureaucracy that theoretically implements laws and executive decisions (orders, decrees, ordinances). In most modern states there is a separate identity between the executive (or the office of head of government – whether a President or a Prime Minister) and the complex bureaucratic and security apparatuses that implement the day to day operations of the state. Public management especially in developed societies has become highly professionalized and technical, to the point that its operations often escape the grasp of the public it serves, or that of the elected officials that are to keep bureaus responsible to the public interest. Moreover, complexity tends to generate inwardness and secrecy.

Bureaucracy, security and democracy

There is an inherent tension between bureaucracy and democracy, related to the fact that most bureaucracies, by their very nature, are reluctant to operate in any other way but through a highly hierarchical and oligarchic mode. Bureaus function in a very compartmentalized fashion and often strive for autonomy. This is the case for even those agencies that are formally decentralized. Power in bureaucratic organizations is closely connected with control over the sources of uncertainty (Crozier, 1964); therefore, secrecy and lack of transparency are valued assets, as power tends to decrease in direct proportion of one actor's predictability. At times, agencies develop strong clientelistic ties with their specific constituencies, circumventing the jurisdictional control of elected officials. The professionalization of the civil service – a necessity for achieving efficiency in a world of complexity – in no small manner strengthens a separation between "politics" and "administration," and allows for the entrenchment of corporate interests.

This lack of political control is even more acute when it comes to the security establishment: the military, police and intelligence agencies. Most professional security agencies learn to have a very low opinion of democracy and other civic (and civilian) attributes, especially when the security apparatus ends up defining itself as the only true upholder of virtue, patriotism, the "national interest," and the like; even democracy itself. In fact, they often perceive democracy, transparency and accountability as a nuisance impeding the effective pursuit of their professional mission. Military or military-dominated regimes are illustrations of this praetorian (Huntington, 1968) antidemocratic pathology. However, other seemingly civilian-controlled governments end up adopting the same militaristic values in a sort of civic religious patriotism (e.g. "my country, right or wrong"). Worse, many such entities blend this civic, state-centred devotion with professional (deontological) zeal and conventional religious fundamentalism, creating a most dangerous antidemocratic cultural mixture: what journalist Christiane Amampour has called "God's warriors" (Young, 2007; Suskind, 2004).

We should remember that the security apparatus constitutes an insurance policy of last resort to protect the socioeconomic order. Many a politician has been tempted to bang at the doors of the barracks to ask for military intervention to bring back "order," or morality, or to combat the "enemies of the nation," both within and without. In turn, the officer class is often all too compliant to heed the call. Having been socialized and trained in a heroic vision of their role, members in the security establishment may see themselves as messianic saviours. Militarism, "securitization" and praetorianism, that is the rule of second-rank bureaucrats, are not things of the past, but according to some a real and present danger, even in some of the more developed societies, including Western Europe and the US (Ganser, 2005). This challenge to democracy is all the more serious since security agencies tend to operate as international conglomerates, or cartels, radiating from the centres of wealth and power down to branch plant managers of violence in client states. In this case, security ceases to be an attribute of sovereignty, as is often portrayed, to become, especially in less developed countries, a prime vehicle for dependency.

Chapter 3

Myths and Misconceptions about Democracy

The term liberal democracy is very often used in current discourse to characterize the type of political regime prevalent in most western nations. Giddens provides a basic definition of this construct:

> Liberal democracy, I shall accept with Weber and Bobbio, is essentially a system of representation. It is a form of government characterized by regular elections, universal suffrage, freedom of conscience, and the universal right to stand for office or to form political associations. Defined in such a way, democracy is normally understood in relation to pluralism and the expression of diverse interests. (Giddens, 1994: 112)

Having introduced the potential challenges to democracy and laid out what democracy is, as well as what it is not, we can begin to formulate a concept of democracy that reflects all its normative and operational dimensions. We are now also in a better position to evaluate the different challenges to democracy. One of the oldest, most discussed, and yet still unresolved, challenges to democracy results from an inherent tension among the basic principles of democracy and liberalism – both economic and political. This tension has attracted so much reflection and produced such a vast amount of scholarly discussion that we need to dedicate some space to its discussion and provide some relevant background information in order to allow for an adequate grasping of this old problem.

Liberalism and democracy

The uneasy relationship between liberalism and democracy is both a theoretical and a practical problem. This means delving into the complex historical and structural interplay between the notions of power, equality, liberty, freedom, justice, majority rule, inclusiveness and the like. In its most elementary sense, democracy is majority, popular rule. Liberalism, on the other hand, means safeguarding individual liberty, first and foremost, against a potentially coercive state. In practice, however, liberalism is often simply equated to market politics: a model of decision-making and social order based upon private property, and free competition. Yet even at this very basic level, contradictions readily emerge. Majority rule, the most central tenant of democracy, bears some inherent tensions with liberalism. That is, if one agrees about the superiority of majority rule over other forms of collective decision-making in modern, complex societies, there inevitably remains the problem of what Tocqueville called "the tyranny of the majority." Structural minorities that have a different language, religion, or national identity from the majority in power and whose preferences are therefore consistently divergent from the majority, have a great risk of not being represented in majority rule systems (Barry, 1979). The liberal doctrine that guarantees individual freedom to all citizens, meaning first and foremost the absence of state coercion, thus necessarily comes into conflict with the basic principle of democracy: majority rule. In cases where minorities are neglected, not represented, or oppressed by ruling majorities, we face the logical problem of two mutually exclusive principles: democracy and liberalism, coexisting as a form of governance that allows all individuals to be free and equal.

This is an old problem. Several solutions to it have been advanced. John Stuart Mill proposed a reduction of majorities from 51 percent to 26 percent, and elections requiring more than one step. Not too long ago, William Riker (1982) saw as the only possible solution the limitation of what democracy possibly can mean, to a model where the main function of democracy is to enable citizens to remove elected officials in periodic elections. Another group of solutions comes out of the opposite corner: republicanism. For Rousseau, political dissent is an error, a misunderstanding of the *general will*. Therefore one can ignore political dissent. The utilitarian solution, on the other hand, declares the superiority of the collective will over the individual wills, relying on the ideal of the "greatest happiness of the greatest number."

With John Rawls *Theory of Justice* (1971), there was a revival of political theorizing about the dichotomy of liberalism vis-à-vis democracy, which has received an even stronger attention since the "third wave" of democratic transitions of the 1980s. But Rawls' *ex-ante* commitments to justify the possibility of political liberalism and welfare state policies have restricted the scope of his critique, letting him use restrictive definitions of public reason, civil society and deliberation. In addition, as Chantal Mouffe (1996) has pointed out, Rawls' project to justify liberal democratic regimes has led him to associate opponents of political liberalism with unreasonableness. Although his theory allows for a modern, non-religious foundation of principles of justice, Rawls stops short of providing theoretical solutions for problems of diversity and difference. Defining reasonable persons as being morally independent and willing to cooperate with other members of their society, Rawls ultimately restricts democratic legitimacy to the negotiation of *reasonable doctrines,* thereby declaring moral or political disagreement unreasonable (Rawls, 1993: 55).

Jürgen Habermas presented his *Theory of Communicative Action* in 1981, and Bernard Manin wrote an important article on the subject in 1987, offering a third group of solutions to the problem of democratic legitimacy. According to authors like Hannah Arendt (1970) and Michael J. Sandel (1996), who are associated with republican conceptions of the common good, democratic legitimacy refers to the degree that the authority exercised over citizens results from the consent of those same citizens. These authors shifted their attention from problems of aggregation of preferences, to a more basic one: the *formation* of these preferences. For Habermas and Manin, and the many authors they have inspired, individual preferences cannot be understood as given and stable, but as influenced by economic, social and cultural conditions. Seyla Benhabib argues that "legitimacy in complex democratic societies must be thought to result from the free and unconstrained public deliberation of all about matters of common concern" (Benhabib, 1996: 68).

A whole set of assumptions – particularly influential in economics, where individual preferences are not only treated as a given, but are also held as being rationally ordered, "transitive," in the economic jargon – is thereby put into question. This shift marks an orientation towards a more sociological view of basic assumptions about individuals, and their relation to society, ideology and culture. The main question therefore shifts from how to aggregate individual preferences so as to prevent coercion of minorities, to the question of how processes of deliberation on both the individual and the collective level can be established and lead to decisions based on those deliberations. In political theory, this shift meant looking at how persons arrive at their preferences. Manin writes:

It is, therefore, necessary to alter radically the perspective common to both liberal theories and democratic thought: the source of legitimacy is not the predetermined will of individuals, but rather the process of its formation, that is, deliberation itself. An individual's liberty consists first of all in being able to arrive at decision by a process of research and comparison among various solutions. As political decisions are characteristically imposed on all, it seems reasonable to seek, as an essential condition for legitimacy, the deliberation of all or, more precisely, the right of all to participate in deliberation. We must, therefore, challenge the fundamental conclusion of Rousseau, Sieyès, and Rawls: a legitimate decision does not represent the will of all, but is one that results from the deliberation of all. (Manin, 1987: 351f)

At once, other problems appear. How can one think of enhancing open and deliberative processes at the individual and at the collective level? Jürgen Habermas' writings address exactly this point. Again, the proposals are not new, but go back to classical thinking and nineteenth-century writings. John Stuart Mill questioned the legitimacy of secret ballots and pointed to the necessity for government and institutions to "promote the virtue and intelligence of the people themselves." The first question in respect to any political institution is how much it fosters in the members of the community the various desirable qualities, moral and intellectual (Mills, 1958 [1861]: 25). Alexis de Tocqueville saw that the loci where this deliberative competence can be cultivated are in political and civil associations.

Habermas adopted this reasoning and defined the *conditions* for collective deliberative processes to take place, laying out the philosophical ground on which "communicative action" can grow. For Habermas, the main condition for democratic learning and legitimate collective decision-making consists of maintaining institutional frames that allow for a communicative interchange of reasonable arguments, where all those potentially affected by a decision have a right to voice their point of view. He alerts us to the fact that power, tradition and privilege easily distort this "ideal speech situation," potentially leading away from rational and democratic decisions. Undemocratic collective decision-making for Habermas is based on such principles as self-interest, accumulation of wealth, power seeking, prestige enhancement, or the advance of individual benefits at the cost of others. The discussion on democratic agenda-setting demonstrated just one aspect of this weakness, as it alerts us to the fact that some decisions are made by the people who define what will be discussed by a broader public *before* the actual democratic decision-making process starts (Lukes, 1977).

The promises and problems of deliberation

Four reasons to favour the deliberative conception of democracy (as superior to both the "minimalist" procedural, and the substantive conceptions of democracy) are commonly given. First, deliberation assures legitimacy, following the reasoning outlined by Manin. Second, deliberation leads to more reasoned decisions, as information is shared in dialogue and different perspectives are taken into account and interchanged. Third, through deliberation, individual preferences become more reasonable and ordered, as preferences cannot be thought of as given, but rather as the result of dialogue. Preferences that are the result of reasonable discourse are "more enlightened" and rational. Fourth, the publicity and reflexivity of public discourse allows for a constant redefining and questioning of what is perceived as "good" and "right," which is particularly important under conditions of modernity, characterized by a plurality of worldviews. Exposing one's opinion in public also offers the possibility of sorting out antidemocratic arguments, as these arguments are likely to be challenged. Furthermore, deliberation promises more individual enlightenment. In the absence of restrictions, participants in a dialogue are permitted and encouraged to be self-critical. Echoing Manin's earlier words, Benhabib (1996) writes that "legitimacy in complex democratic societies must be thought to result from the free and unconstrained public deliberation of all about matters of common concern. Thus a public sphere of deliberation about matters of mutual concern is essential to the legitimacy of democratic institutions" (p. 68).

The problems of deliberative forms of democracy are of two types. First there are those concerning the conditions for deliberation to occur and prevail, as manipulation can easily destroy the framework that allows for deliberation. If people have no real power to influence decisions they will not continue participating. The eloquence of some can easily influence others. Power rooted in prestige, money, tradition or violence can easily distort democratic dialogue. Special knowledge, or even the successful claim of possessing such knowledge, opens the door for manipulation. Claims for superior esoteric or religious knowledge have the same effect. If the conditions described earlier are not met deliberation ends.

Secondly, another group of problems derives from the potential that deliberative associations can work too well. Interest groups can advance their particular preferences against the will of a less organized majority. Under such conditions, political decisions do not represent the general will, but the special interests of some groups that are more organized, vocal and better able to influence political decisions. In other words, interest groups that defend their claims *against* others might distort democratic decisions to their own favour, as Barber and Fiorina have pointed out. As liberal authors have argued since John Locke, the basic principle of one person one vote would be in danger of distortion if people gather in interest groups, being able to make stronger claims than single individuals. Fiorina (1999) has termed this problem one of "extreme voices." The history of ancient Athens is rich with narratives of eloquent orators, like Demosthenes or Themistocles, and less famous demagogues who could influence the Assembly by their oral skills.

Feminist theorists like Iris Young (1996, 2000), Jane Mansbridge (1990) and Nancy Fraser (1997) have raised another set of problems concerning deliberative democracy. They have argued that most deliberative theorists insist on a common culture (Rawls) or a universalist conception of reasonable procedures and outcomes (Habermas) as the basis allowing for mutual understanding. They point to the fact that in many societies men talk more than women, hence effectively excluding them. They also highlight that sitting down at a table to discuss problems using reasonable arguments is in fact a culturally biased, Western way to resolve collective problems. It excludes other, more emotional utterances and potentially favours those with more eloquence and formal education.

Young argues that other cultures resolve their collective problems differently, in less verbal and differently structured ways. In addition, she points to the fact that historically Western public spaces have been highly exclusionary, not allowing for women and non-whites. She proposes a wider definition of communicative practices, allowing for the recognition of difference and of different styles of argumentation and verbal and non-verbal participation. Young argues that, "emotional and figurative expressions are important tools of reasonable persuasion and judgment [and that] the privilege of allegedly dispassionate speech styles, moreover often correlates with other differences of social privilege" (Young, 2000: 39).

Young's scepticism about the possibility of reaching one single, reasonable outcome through continued deliberation leads her to propose a model of "communicative democracy," which makes weaker claims about universalist reasonable agreements. Her definition also allows treating difference as a resource and not as a problem to be "solved," as communicative processes still have the effects described above, even if no single agreement is reached. According to Young, group differences are not absolute, but relationally situated to a given issue-area in question, and group affiliations are multiple and shifting within individuals. Under such a perspective, deliberation facilitates the understanding of the reasons why one group holds a certain position. In general, deliberative or communicative forms of democracy specify the necessary but not the sufficient conditions for democratic legitimacy and reasonable decisions, as deliberative processes can be easily distorted.

Several conditions need to be met in order deliberative processes to take place without distortion and to be maintained. First equality and symmetry of the participants must be assured. All must have the same chance to speak and be heard. All must have the same right to question the agenda setting. All participants must have the right to challenge the procedural rules that organize the discussion, as there can be no fixed rules that limit the agenda and exclude certain topics. All individuals that are potentially affected by a decision must be able to participate in the process of decision-making. This is what Habermas has called the "ideal speech situation." Additional problems of feasibility also arise from the understanding that in large complex democracies not all those potentially affected by a decision can effectively participate in the making of this decision. The most convincing solution lies in the definition of civil society and the role of the state itself.

Benhabib (1996) explains that deliberative models of democracy share a *"plurality of modes of association* in which all affected can have the right to articulate their point of view. These can range from political parties, to citizens' initiatives, to social movements, to voluntary associations, to consciousness-raising groups, and the like" (Benhabib, 1996: 73). For Benhabib, deliberative processes should happen in all these different forms of associations, allowing for an "interlocking" and the creation of "networks" of spaces for deliberative reasoning. This definition comes closest to the model Cohen and Rogers (1995) have called "egalitarian pluralism," understood as a set of institutional designs allowing for associations to influence legislative and administrative arenas. In short, if deliberation is a desirable goal, democratic institutions should provide as many deliberative spaces as possible – inside and outside of government.

But several authors have pointed to the inherent conflictual nature of governmental decision-making that works against more consensus-aimed deliberation. The solution to this problem goes back to Alexis de Tocqueville's argument that the conflictual nature of democratic government should be counterbalanced by associations acting outside established governments, in the realm of civil society. "Neo-Tocquevillian" political theorists argue that civil society is the realm where individuals can meet to associate freely around the interest areas of their choice. Authors like Cohen and Arato (1995) argue that the state and the economy do not allow for systematic democratic discourse aimed at reaching consensus, because the actors of political and economic society are directly involved with state power and economic production, which they seek to control and manage. They cannot afford to subordinate strategic and instrumental criteria to the patterns of *normative and open-ended communication* characteristic of civil society. Civil society, to the contrary, can be the realm of free communication and consensus finding, because civil society is the realm where people meet freely and outside their potential coercive work environments.

According to Cohen and Arato, the term "civil society" was first introduced by Aristotle, who spoke of *politike koinonia*, referring to political society and political community. Later it was translated into the Latin *societas civilis*. These authors argue that the shift towards modern usage of the term occurred under European absolutism. The monopolistic holder of the legitimate means of violence was understood as standing on one side and estates and corporate bodies on the other, forming the civil society. Hegel's treatment of the concept was far reaching and still influences the debate of civil society. In his *Philosophy of Rights,* he presented civil society as a realm outside the economy and the state.

Nevertheless, most theorists argue that deliberation can happen in varied places, both inside and outside the state. Within the state, it is in parliaments and debates where elected representatives should pursue rational discourse in order to reach the most enlightened decisions. But, as Arendt has argued, democratic legitimacy ultimately rests on public consent. Therefore, the public sphere is one major societal place where deliberation must happen. The public sphere is characterized by a plurality of associations, including political parties, unions, voluntary associations, neighbourhood groups, recreational groups, or just spontaneous gatherings and meetings. For some authors (Walzer) the state itself is but one association among others, embedded in the broader society, although it has a more powerful and enduring position compared to other associations.

The discussions about deliberative democracy suggest that democracy rests on more than just the free election of representatives. In this view, democratic legitimacy ultimately rests on the deliberative participation of the people. Although deliberative theorists have found solutions to the problem of feasibility, they also point to the social prerequisites on which deliberation, and therefore democratic legitimacy, rests. Power, threat, authority, unequal access to information, racialized and gendered patterns of formal or of subtle dominance, and unreflected traditions easily distort deliberative processes. Models of deliberative democracy offer solutions to the problems of democratic legitimacy, the representation of structural minorities, and the renewal of a society's moral grounds through communication, but they also point to the weakness of these processes and their susceptibility to internal and external threats that have the potential to distort those communicative processes. The promise of deliberative democracy remains just that: a promise.

In the meantime, the most common definition of democracy that is engendered by the dominant Western paradigm of representative and liberal democracy is largely procedural (Schumpeter, 1942). As explained above, Schumpeter's definition centres on a "method," not on substance, as an "institutional arrangement for arriving at political decisions in which individuals acquire the power to decide by means of a competitive struggle for the people's vote" (p. 269). In this interpretation, people actually do not rule, but regularly and intermittently participate in elections. However, the democratic phenomenon is not a purely formal ritual. Constitutions, suffrage, elections, separation of powers, checks and balances, and responsible government can be seen as a necessary but by no means sufficient condition of democracy. Nevertheless, in the last analysis, institutions are relevant, particularly when formal procedures represent real structures and processes in civil society.

As this discussion highlights, the practice of democracy goes beyond the institutions of government, the rule of law or the electoral franchise.

The latter are just the tip of the iceberg; and paradoxically this tip may rest on socioeconomic conditions adverse to its emergence and sustainability. A real democracy requires social, economic and cultural foundations for democratic practices and institutions to be resilient and sustainable. No matter how minimalist one wants to define democracy, its legitimacy must ultimately reside in a democratic society, where the core value of democracy, namely having access to basic citizenship rights, is guaranteed. A democratic political system working smoothly in an undemocratic society is an absurdity. After all, democratic legitimacy must ultimately rest on public consent and it must be embedded in a democratic society for this consent to form without excluding significant parts of the citizenry.

Ultimately, collective-will formation must be achieved discursively and behavioural and moral standards must be formed, consolidated, and become institutionalized in the form of legal standards, as Emile Durkheim has already stated in the late nineteenth century. Democratic legitimacy, therefore, must rest on a democratic public sphere that is open to all citizens, where the public sphere is understood as an open (public) domain of political-will formation and discussion. In short, political democracy without a significant degree of socioeconomic equality and opportunity is a mere façade without content (Reiter, 2009). The opposite is also true: equality, without respect for liberty, diversity and the attributes of an open society, including responsible government and the rule of law, leads to the monotony of party, or bureaucratic autocracy, or tyranny.

The gap between democracy and non-democracy is much thinner than most would like to think. Consensus is a fundamental condition for democracy to exist and flourish, but uniformity – whether in the forms of conformism, consumerism, moral virtue or patriotism – undermines its very essence. For democracy is nurtured by diversity, dissent and debate at the same time that it requires the taking of binding collective decisions.

Democracy: beyond institutions

In the twentieth century, with the rise of the labour movement, democracy increasingly became associated with the notions of equity, justice, self-determination, majority rule, the rule of law, responsible government and modernity. President Wilson's plea during World War I to make "the world safe for democracy" seemingly stood against an old imperial and Eurocentric world order based upon dynastic privilege and exclusion. The early part of the twentieth century was rich in democratizing experiments. Revolutionary modernizers in Mexico, Russia, China and Turkey demolished old autocracies and oligarchies, replacing them with radical and unprecedented forms of embryonic popular rule. As liberating and progressive as they may have been, these transformations – like their predecessors in seventeenth-century England, and eighteenth-century North America and France – were attained through much violence and bloodshed. Many mutated into extremely authoritarian regimes, even if for brief periods of time. However, these revolutions succeeded in undoing an old order of things and ushering in new practices and institutions. Most important, irrespective of how profound and irreversible their attainments, the sociopolitical order they created was more open, secular and inclusive than the one they replaced.

From the World War I onward, the word democracy was used more and more as a positive, if not outright hegemonic symbol for mainstream liberals, conservatives and even radicals. Yet, class based movements and parties claimed ownership of the democratic idiom. For the working classes and the union movement, democracy meant essentially rule by the majority of working people and their transformative agenda. For the professional and bureaucratic middle classes, democracy meant compromise and centrism around a moderately progressive program, representing the public interest. For conservatives, democracy meant a system of balances and entrenched legal rules that allowed the protection of their interest by means of institutional safeguards to maintain the status quo. As Lipset noted (1960), democracy rested on a compromise of various classes around a formula that provided different actors with regular opportunities to attain official positions by contending for political office. This notion was quite similar to Schumpeter's characterization of formal and procedural democracy.

Nevertheless, despite the acceptance of this narrow definition, and perhaps because of it, democracy was not an acceptable notion in many quarters, especially in the turbulent years leading to World War II. Extreme nationalists and reactionaries, represented in the tide of fascist parties to sweep Europe in the 1920s and 1930s, as well as those on the militant left – hyphenating bourgeois to the term democracy – denounced anything merely resembling, or done solely in the name of, popular rule as a fraud. This bitter clash of ideologies and social forces reached its climax during the Spanish Civil War (1936–1939). In it, the unified Nationalist forces of the Spanish right defeated a fractious Republican alliance of democrats and antidemocrats on the centre and left. External actors supported both sides of this Civil War. The latter included Hitler's Germany, Mussolini's Italy on the Nationalist and Stalin's Russia on the Republican side. With the qualified exception of France, most Western liberal democracies stayed out of this "rehearsal" of a coming global conflagration, thus facilitating a fascist victory.

World War II pitched the ideological banner of democracy (both liberal and "popular") vis-à-vis the biological determinism of totalitarian fascism represented by the Axis powers: Germany, Italy and Japan. The war was construed by President Roosevelt and Prime Minister Churchill as a struggle not only against fascist totalitarianism but as one for democracy, human dignity and self-determination. These principles were central tenets of the Atlantic Charter, signed by Britain and the US in 1941. At the war's end, and in the period of rapid decolonization that followed, democracy had become a nominal measuring rod for political development, together with "freedom," self-determination and independence. The constitutions of the numerous new states, resulting from decolonization, enshrined democracy and the Universal Declaration of Human Rights as intrinsic principles of their institutional engineering.

In the capitalist industrial societies during the post-war period, democracy came to be associated with big – yet responsible – government, popular representation and the welfare state. This combination of political democracy with induced development and the promotion of social welfare had been originally paired together during the New Deal in the 1930s, and had become a standard feature in the UK and Scandinavian countries. It also constituted the backbone of European reconstruction under the Marshall Plan. Formulas along these lines of government-induced development had also emerged in the more developed Latin American countries under the rubric of Import Substitution Industrialization (ISI) policies. In mainstream political science discourse, democracy and sociopolitical and economic development ended up being seen as one and the same (Lipset, 1960; Rostow, 1959).

With the advent of the Cold War, however, the term (in its liberal and socialist variances) became almost a trademarked instrument in the hegemonic domain of both superpowers. In the East it meant "people's democracy" in contrast to "bourgeois" rule. In the West it stood in direct opposition to the uniformity of Communist totalitarianism. Thus, this use of the word conferred an almost mystical and beneficent quality to all "free-world" regimes, irrespective of their actual repressive nature or their human rights record, as in the cases of Franco's Spain and China's Chiang Kai Chek. Like development, democracy throughout the 1950s, 1960s and 1970s was made another ideological construct to legitimate and justify contingent policy options, such as foreign aid, military alliances or military and covert intervention. This distortion persisted despite the end of the Cold War, with ideologues in the West claiming by then virtual "ownership" over the term, as a historically determined and universal type where neo-liberalism and limited popular rule converged in a postulated global age. Under the discourse of a pretended "clash of civilizations" democracy continues to be another civilized weapon in an ideological and semantic arsenal, providing instant justification to all manner of interests and contingent policies.

The liberal-democratic hybrid of today is indeed the result of a rather uneasy amalgam between economic liberty (whose cornerstone is private property) and social equality (Macpherson, 1977). As many historical cases demonstrate, as long as the political system provided with sufficient surplus to accommodate increasing expectations with expanding capabilities, the contradiction between economic liberty and equality could be kept at bay. Historically, and contrary to widespread ideological mythology, liberal capitalism has however been quite compatible with aristocratic and oligarchic rule. In fact, as the examples of nineteenth-century Europe and the Americas indicate, economic liberalism flourished under constitutional monarchies or republican regimes, where the very word democracy was anathema. Moreover, philosophically progressive, modernizing autocrats like Czar Alexander II of Russia (1855–1881), Mexico's Porfirio Díaz (1876–1911) and Brazilian Emperor Dom Pedro II (1841–1889), all of them influenced by Positivism, favoured the development of a strong national capitalist class. In turn, domestic and foreign investors profited from the pro-business climate and enthusiastically supported these regimes.

In all these cases, the state, the government and the "rule of law," acted as protectors of an unequal socioeconomic status quo in a clear Madisonian logic "to protect the minority of the opulent against the majority" (Madison, 1787, in Dahl, 1956). Likewise, the advent of "modern" capitalism did not bring about pluralism or democracy on its own, as we shall explore later. Authoritarian capitalism in the later part of the nineteenth century (Meiji, Bonapartist or Bismarckean), and its post-World War II varieties (Korea, Chile, Argentina, Brazil, or Apartheid South Africa) has not been an uncommon blend. In its milder and more consensual forms, popular exclusion has taken the form of what in the European context Arendt Lijphart has called consociationalism (pacts of elites to maintain the status quo). Transition theorists and practitioners favoured and engineered such pacts in the 1980s in the orderly movement from national security regimes to limited democracy in Latin America. Pro-Western and pro-capitalist Asian autocrats, in the context of the Cold War argued that they were presiding over guided or tutelary democracies, a simple euphemism for heavy-handed personal dictatorship. Other exclusive though less extreme forms of façade democracies encompass the notions of "democracy without people," "Pluto-democracies" (Duverger, 1966) or what we can call plutocracies with popular support.

At any rate, the notion of democracy is not just a teleology, or desired end-state. It is an open-ended *process* with multi-directional dynamics and possibilities. Far from being at a stable and irreversible stage (in the sense of "development stages" envisioned by modernization theorists) democracy is essentially a multi-linear and indeterminate, complex, changing, historical, cultural and socioeconomic phenomenon.

It is perfectly possible, and in fact it is not uncommon, for a socio-economic order based upon liberal principles to be undemocratic and even antidemocratic. Nineteenth-century England had a liberal, parliamentary and responsible government, but it could be only nominally democratic. In fact the British elite's contempt for democracy could be aptly summarized in Prime Minister Disraeli's statement: "The world is wearied of statesmen whom democracy has degraded into politicians" (quoted in *American Opinion*, April 1971, p. 75). The more open form of revolutionary liberalism to emerge in the former British colonies in North America was more attuned to represent, in theory at least, the will of the majorities. However, it excluded from the onset large segments of the population and was to all intents and purposes a social order based upon slavery. Incipient democracy emerged in the republican polyarchy (Dahl, 1956, 1973) as social groups and movements struggled for citizenship; a struggle that is far from over.

The repressive military and civilian dictatorships that proliferated in Latin America, Asia and to a lesser extent Africa in the 1960s through the 1980s, also known as National Security regimes, were largely staunch supporters of the West and devotees of free-market policies. A number of them, under the auspices of Western economic and political interests, were at the vanguard of the set of structural reforms that became the foundation of neo-liberalism, and precursors of structural adjustment. These policy packages were subsequently adopted en masse in Eastern Europe, Central Asia and even communist China. The democratizing impacts of market-friendly policies on either the political or social order have been minimal and have largely failed in setting up the basis of a still elusive open society.

The current form of global neo-liberalism, persistently hailed in business circles, is, in the last analysis, incompatible with democracy, other than its most strictly limited and nominal manifestations. These include ritualized elections, a privately-owned and concentrated "free" press and the formalities of legal-institutional procedures. Short of dictatorship, that raises the problem of enforcement cost and illegitimacy, the most congenial hegemonic form of government to protect such neo-liberal order is a low intensity strain of elitist and formal democracy. This model is essentially a sanitized variety of the above-mentioned polyarchy, adapted to non-Western conditions.

Not only is the intentional confusion between liberalization and democratization a major fallacy, but other manufactured misconceptions need to be addressed as well. One of these is the attempt to equate a transition from an authoritarian state to more open politics and democratization: not all such transitions are democratization. Another is the reductionist and formalistic view equating democracy with formal procedures and elections. Yet another misconception about transition is the confusion between democratization and economic changes towards market economies (liberalization). An example of it is the term "transitional" applied by mainstream academics to the former communist states in Eastern Europe and Central Asia. While these countries have significantly privatized, de-nationalized and liberalized their economies, democratic reforms have fallen far behind. The fact is that a regime could be in transition towards greater liberalization, or even become fully liberalized in its economic base, without ever becoming more democratic.

Equally important here is the artificial demarcation of the economic and social spheres on the one hand, with the specifically political on the other. This mode of thinking privileges descriptive over substantive criteria: formal democracy centred on electoral and procedural mechanisms, not its socioeconomic underpinnings and effects. The nominalist view posits that the exercise of such political rights as freedom of speech, press and assembly combined with competitive elections, are in fact democracy. This type of analysis privileges a linear, a-historical and fairly a-critical stand. It simply assumes actually existing Western (US-type) democracy being both the irreversible end of ideology and that of history itself. While from this conventional point of view democratization and re-democratization are conceived as possible paths, de-democratization is excluded as a possible scenario.

As MacPherson (1977) noted, present day liberal democracies were liberal long before they were democratic. The democratic character of many modern governments was the result of pressure from below: unions, the poor and the disenfranchised. As said, liberalism above everything else refers to a socioeconomic order built upon private and individual property and the notion of markets as distributive, but not redistributive, transaction mechanisms (*catalaxia*). Its political manifestation is "market politics" based on contracts and bargaining (Hayek, 1978). Freedom, more than equity, is its ontological pillar. Despite its bourgeois revolutionary origins (for instance in the American and French revolutions), liberalism does not necessarily express itself in democratic terms. Rather, throughout the nineteenth century, limited franchise to those with property, belonging to the dominant ethnic group, and with significant exclusion of all others (women, the poor, the young or those deemed "racially inferior") predominated. In the twentieth century, the examples of Apartheid South Africa and the American institutionalized racism, commonly known as "Jim Crow" (Myrdal, 1995: 198), constituted glaring examples of police states, while outwardly exhibiting many of the traits of economic liberalism and polyarchy.

On the other hand, democracy, in its nineteenth and twentieth-century versions has emphasized equality and popular rule. The opening of the political system and the electoral franchise was the result of pressures and struggles by those excluded, especially by labour, social-democratic, independentist and revolutionary movements. By emphasizing "democratic elitism" and polyarchy, mainstream theorists have underestimated – if not completely deconstructed, or worse, demonized – the role of social movements in advancing democratic rights. This way, democracy is not presented as contested territory, in which non-elites fight for and open up new political spaces, but as a generous gift of the elites to the masses.

This contradiction has been a persistent feature of contemporary politics, as common people pushed the envelope of inclusion and participation. It has re-emerged as contested territory with the demise of the Welfare state and the end of what has been referred to as *political* liberalism. "Liberal" in current neo-conservative verbiage in the US is used in the sense of "leftist," not middle-of-the road or a supporter of market ideology. The main contention by the proponents of the crisis of democracy thesis (Huntington et al., 1975) was that democracies had become ungovernable because of uncontrolled participation; a subject that we will return to in the following chapters. Thus, too much democracy is, in the eyes of the proponents of the crisis thesis, at the core of the problem of un-governability and institutional decay.

The recipe for those advancing the crisis thesis was and remains making it limited or restricted (Chomsky and Herman, 1979). This thesis was once again advanced as a prescription by those who advocated for a peaceful return to democracy, or re-democratization, in Latin America at the end of the Cold War. While reactionary economic policies inspired by the Chicago School, favouring the affluent, were entrenched by anti-democratic regimes, the advocates of limited democracy proposed a return to normalcy where "the rights of the bourgeoisies are untouchable" (O'Donnell et al., 1986: 69). This unbridled economic liberalism, later articulated in the so-called Washington Consensus, required a highly demobilized polity, in which the electorate faced extremely narrow, undifferentiated and largely irrelevant choices.

In most of those countries that were once referred to as the Third World, the conditionalities of Structural Adjustment Policies (SAPs) attached to debt relief schemes brought an end to import substitution, developmental and welfare policies, and transformed the states into transnationalized and weak receiver states (Nef, 1985). In the more developed societies, supply-side economics transformed the implicit social contract, while tearing down the welfare state and redistributive policies. Political neo-conservatism went hand in hand with neo-liberal economic policies, based upon deregulation, privatization and exclusion. The impact of these measures on democratic processes was to dismantle bargaining and mobilization in favour of demobilization, de-unionization, de-industrialization, and de-nationalization. Concentration of capital, information and power soon shifted the nature of politics into an increasingly elitist, ritualistic and meaning-less process.

In the relatively more developed industrial and post-industrial societies disillusionment with politics has, as usual, begun eroding the consensual foundations of the political system and the structures of representation (e.g. political parties and interest groups) supporting that system. This has happened at a time in which tax revolts by the very wealthy, and their ability to transfer assets globally has fuelled a severe fiscal cri-sis. In turn, in less affluent and institutionalized societies, administra-tive decay, corruption and state failure have become ever more present prospects. Therefore, whether in the developed or the lesser developed world, democratic processes have been compromised; even the very maintenance of "politics as usual" is much at stake.

Thus, the narrowing of participation in the input side and the shrink-age of real policy alternatives in the output side of the political process is not only a feature of post-dictatorial and transitional Latin America. The same type of arrangement, under different labels and covers, has existed since post-Thatcher Great Britain and in the US since the 1970s, even before the Reagan administration. If we look around the world, the coexistence of neo-liberalism and what Duverger once called "democracy without people" (Duverger, 1967) has become a frequent trait. Beneath the rhetoric of the triumph of democracy, formal electoral regimes have been quantitatively expanding, but participatory and substantive dem-ocracy is qualitatively at a standstill, if not in frank retreat. Electoral participation and public confidence are at an all time low across the globe, and this is strongly associated with the limited possibility for common people to affect policy outcomes.

In the "old" and "new" global peripheries (often referred to as the "global South"), the conditionalities of the aforementioned Structural Adjustment policies (SAPs) attached to debt relief schemes succeeded in dismantling industrial and social policies, the welfare state and national development policies. In the less affluent and poorly institutionalized periphery, the breakdown of the governmental machinery has become an ever more present prospect. In either case, democratic processes have been compromised. Mismanagement, criminality and urban decay go hand-in-hand with fiscal and legitimation crises, creating conditions adverse to democracy.

Democracy challenged

While global participatory democracy is now widely publicized as part of the newly arrived age of "democratization for the world and dem-ocracy for all," the real practice of democracy is far different from the discourse. Fewer and fewer of the non-elite strata partake in the decision-making process, which as a result is becoming increasingly less competitive. If US liberal democracy is the paradigm for democratization, a careful analysis of its actual functioning suggests that it presents severe problems (Crenson and Ginsberg, 2002). As participation shrinks in the seemingly open but vacuous process, voter turnout plummets; and an ever larger proportion of registered voters do not even bother to go to the polls. Many others choose not to register. Manipulation, exclusion and fraud are not rare occurrences, as was the case in the 2000 US presidential election.

Meanwhile, more top-down decision-making, incipient autocratic rule and denial of basic human rights have emerged, as national security is becoming paramount in the context of an almost Orwellian "War on Terror." All this has a most direct effect upon a culture of cynicism and illegitimacy; a far cry from the once-hailed civic culture (Almond and Verba, 1964) of mature political systems.

"Low intensity" democracy (Gills et al., 1993) is not working too well either in those countries where transition from authoritarian rule was induced decades ago. There is widespread anger and popular despair at the economic deprivation and political marginalization that the "new" democracy has brought in much of Latin America. In Mexico the corrupt and authoritarian PRI, ruling the country since 1917 (and increasingly unable to respond to popular demands), has been replaced by a much more conservative party, the National Action Party (PAN), which is even more oblivious of non-elite sectors. Elected leaders have rapidly lost their support and legitimacy in Bolivia, Argentina, Ecuador and Peru as the masses find that their desires and needs are not represented by these individuals. The current wave of left-wing populism to sweep the region since 2000 is an indication of the failure and outright rejection of the model of restricted and un-participatory democracy extant in the Washington Consensus, with its neo-liberal economic recipes. The election of former Tupamaro Tabaré Vásquez in Uruguay, Nestor and Cristina Kirchner in Argentina, Daniel Ortega in Nicaragua, Rafael Correa in Ecuador and Evo Morales in Bolivia, not to mention the entrenchment of populist nationalist Hugo Chavez in Venezuela and Luiz "Lula" da Silva in Brazil, point in the direction away from US hegemony. They also point towards an as-of-now amorphous and evolving alternative model of democracy, away from Madisonian traditions and neo-liberal prescriptions.

Authoritarian rule by refurbished *"nomenklatura"* elites is still present in Eastern Europe and Central Asia; while East Asian nations like Indonesia, Thailand, Taiwan, South Korea and Singapore exhibit only the most minimal and regressive democratic attributes. Old dictatorial methods have made a comeback, as in Pakistan and Thailand, while in

China democracy is defined in purely liberalizing market trends, such as mass production and the expansion of consumerism. Meanwhile decision-making continues to be extremely authoritarian: the "People's Republic" mixture of economic capitalism with political communism is ostensibly repressive. In Africa the most vibrant democratic institutions were those that existed at the village level before Europeanization began. They were once the banners of decolonization, just to become the casualties of corruption, the cold war, state crises and the neo-liberal onslaught associated with structural adjustment and globalization. The continent is still characterized by authoritarian and often ineffectual rule. In the best of cases, severe conflict coexists with the facile imitation of formal aspects of Western liberal institutions. Failed statehood is becoming a common trait.

Authoritarian preserves in the socioeconomic order

Across the globe there are other persistent de-democratizing factors at work in the larger social and economic order. A country can have a reputedly democratic government but rest upon a non-democratic civil society and traditions. In moments of crisis, these persistent authoritarian features become more pronounced and often replace those traits associated with the open society. Most educational systems, primary social structures and the workplace remain utterly undemocratic everywhere. Deference, patriarchy, class and caste, race, age, community values, religion and traditional authority often define the degree of democratic tolerance – or more properly lack of democracy and intolerance. The persistence and at times the backlash and resurgence of nationalism and fundamentalist religion, despite their undeniable populist (and popular) appeals, are often factors working against democratization. Most nations put a premium on assimilation into a modal pattern, or are established on ethnic or religious supremacy, equated with loyalty and patriotism. Neither of these are harbingers of democracy.

But undemocratic social and cultural preserves are not only in the realm of pre-modern legacies. Neo-liberal thinkers extol the democratizing features of markets and the equalizing role of consumerism; but consumers are not citizens and markets are not intrinsically democratic, but plutocratic. Nor are most business practices manifestations of an open society or democratic considerations. If anything, a business culture privileges wealth and those who control it. In such culture, compassion, solidarity and equality are mere Paretian "residues." State structures – including bureaucracies, the judiciary and the security apparatus – of themselves are at best partially democratic and many of them are quite the opposite: authoritarian and non-representative. This means that even the apparently most popular of governments rest upon layers on non-democratic institutions, from the state itself to the family.

In this sense, rather than focusing exclusively on the forms of government and the facile labelling of democratic, partially democratic and non-democratic, as found in the terminology of Freedom House (2007), we need to look at democratic and antidemocratic attributes present in civil society and the larger regime. This perspective centred on interconnected levels of analysis addresses the problem of empowerment and de-powerment, rather than the crisis-of-democracy as un-governability rooted in over-participation (Huntington et al., 1975). Intertwined with the above-mentioned analysis is the need to understand democracy and democratization, as well as de-democratization as they relate to other processes and conceptual frameworks such as modernity, human security and globalization (Held, 1996, 2004).

This way of questioning the "world out there" contrasts substantively with the crisis-of-democracy thesis centred on the misconstrued idea of over-participation. The root of the crisis is far from being too much democracy on the "demand side" of the political process. Instead, the problem is basically on the supply side: a democratic deficit. What is in crisis is a particular and dysfunctional form of limited democracy based on the culture of possessive individualism and inequality. The simultaneous crisis of accumulation and legitimation, intertwined with a fiscal crisis, results from the increasing transnationalization of capital, information and power, combined with a decline of labour on a global scale. Seen from a systemic and long-run perspective, the once heralded optimism related to democratization and re-democratization of the 1980s and 1990s has been replaced with the reality of eroding democracy, outright de-democratization and new forms of social exclusion.

Alternative sources and practices

It is important to distinguish between the formalities of a nominal democracy from the substance and content of participatory democracy. Merely representative, even parliamentary, electoral democracy can emerge, and in fact prosper, under conditions of extreme exclusion, inequality and abuse. As mentioned, parliamentary democracy evolved in nineteenth-century England and throughout Europe within societies with deeply repressive and oligarchic features (Chomsky, 1995). Democratic inclusivity was a relatively long evolutionary process punctuated by popular challenges and confrontations. In turn, the American polyarchical tradition "was founded on the principle, stressed by James

Madison in the Constitutional Convention in 1787, that the primary function of government is *to protect the minority of the opulent from the majority*" (ibid.). In these circumstances, the liberties of the minority are to be protected at any cost.

There is indeed much more to democracy than a label, its foretold demise or the facile characterization of its inevitability. Often, underneath the mainstream official and academic discourse, there are numerous vital and rich manifestations of democratic practices that need to be analysed. To do so, it is essential to re-examine first the legacy of traditional strains of effective participatory democracy (*real* democracy as Crenson and Ginsberg call it) as they relate to the concept of "popular power" (Arblaster, 1994). These include historical practices of some Swiss Cantons, the New England Town Meetings, the French Commune of 1871, worker-run factories in post-World War I Italy, during the Spanish Republic, and the embryonic democracy of the soviets in the early, pre-Stalin years of the USSR.

Secondly, it is necessary to focus on viable forms of substantive microdemocracy that have actually empowered common people in more recent times. These "experiments" include worker self-management in Western Europe and the US, the Mondragon movement in Spain, community organization and grass roots democracy in North America and Western Europe, the mass organizations that developed in Latin American countries in the seventies and eighties such as the ubiquitous Christian Base Communities, and the peasant movements inspired by Liberation Theology. It also includes the participation of the students, workers and common citizens in Paris, Prague and Mexico City in 1968 and more generally the multiple experiments on participatory democracy of the 1960s.

Then there are specific and very current varieties of democracy that must be carefully examined: Green party democracy as practiced in Western Europe, and mass movements and local decision-making in India, Africa and Latin American. The latter includes examples like the National Confederation of Indigenous Nationalities of Ecuador, the Landless Movement in Brazil (MST), the Zapatista *caracoles* in Southern Mexico, the decision-making processes in Brazil's Workers Party (PT) – in particular the participatory budgeting making process practiced in municipalities under Workers Party control in southern Brazil – and the spontaneous forms of grassroots democracy emerging in the recent institutional breakdowns and popular mobilizations in Argentina (2001), Ecuador (2000) and Bolivia (2003).

Also, neo-populism of the kind emerging in Bolivia, Peru and Venezuela cannot be simply dismissed as heresy, or just another dysfunctional rarity. On the contrary, this re-emergence of "the popular" should not be easily dismissed. It needs to be re-assessed objectively by concentrating on both its democratizing and de-democratizing characteristics. In this perspective, special attention needs to be devoted to social movements, past and present, in opening participatory gates and in removing structures of inequity. These movements are challenging not only the status quo but the theory and practice of democracy as well.

Chapter 4

Popular Sovereignty, Citizenship and the Limits of Liberal Democracy

We have now reached a point where we are able to analyse the different dimensions of democracy as an ideal type and to appraise how close – or far – various political practices are in reference to this ideal. As stated earlier, democracy is challenged from different sides, and new challenges have arisen, whereas old ones remain. The tension between liberalism and democracy is certainly one of the oldest and most analysed, and yet most controversial, of the "old" challenges. The "new" world order and globalization have added a new twist to economic liberalism and led to a renewed interest in discussing the conflictive nature of this relationship.

However, one question might be even more fundamental than the tension between democracy and liberalism, and that is the question of citizenship. This chapter will thus turn to yet another of the traditional and "old" challenges to democracy, namely the question of citizenship. Once a group of people establish that they, "the people," shall be the sole source of all power exercised over them, they need to answer the first question that automatically grows out of such an assertion, namely: who are the people? In other words, the principle of popular sovereignty produces the necessary corollary of citizenship and its limits. To adequately capture this challenge we need to start with an analysis of the principle of popular sovereignty, which will provide us with the basis to discuss citizenship.

Popular sovereignty

The most widely known definition of democracy is that of Daniel Webster, later found in Abraham Lincoln's First Inaugural Address of 1861: "the government of the people, by the people and for the people" (Bartlett, 1919). This implies a political system in which the people – a collective expression referring largely to commoners – are the main cause and prime effect of institutional organization. They are also the agent of political life. People as constituency are the source of power and

70

sovereignty; only they can create and change institutions and the rules of the game. It is also "the people" and/or its delegated representatives who retain, use and ultimately control that power. Finally, it is the people who are simultaneously those who exercise power and for whom the exercise of power takes place. For Lincoln, it was people who retained in their hands full constituent power: "This country, with its institutions belongs to the people who inhabit it. Whenever they shall grow weary of the existing government they can exercise their constitutional right to amend it, or their revolutionary right to dismember or overthrow it" (*First Inaugural Address*, 1861: 25).

This particular popular tradition assumes a number of substantive as well as formal characteristics. The substantive attributes refer to traits that are intrinsic to the very idea of democracy. They include the following:

1. Popular rule.
2. Majority rule.
3. All participants are considered effectively equal.
4. Participation by an active citizenry.
5. The institutions, offices and officials are subject to scrutiny, and checks and balances.
6. Responsible and accountable government.
7. A significant degree of consent among the actors: an explicit or implicit "social contract."
8. Participants' autonomy and limited coerciveness in their action.
9. If coercion is applied, its use is duly authorized, and all instruments of coercion are subordinated to legitimate authority.
10. Representation of diversity and inclusivity.
11. Accessibility and transparency.

In addition, there are more formal attributes, relating to the instrumentalities contributing to the operation and continuity of democratic practices. These include: (a) constitutionalism and the rule of law; (b) fair and accessible mechanisms of electoral representation; and (c) the existence of structures and procedures to secure ways of solving conflicts and for acquiring, distributing and managing resources. Arblaster offers a synthesis of these descriptive and normative elements:

The substance [of democracy] is the power of peoples to make government, and make their representatives, to accede to the popular will and popular demands. Democracy involves debate and discussion, but these are not enough if they remain inconclusive, and ineffective in determining actual policies. The outcome of such discussions should be popular decisions and popular demands; and since in a democracy it is the people, and not the government or parliament, which is sovereign, it is the business of government to accept and to implement the popular will. (Arblaster, 1987: 98)

In addition to the above traits, democracy also rests upon an uneasy but necessary balance between legitimacy and effectiveness (Lipset, 1960). Effectiveness means actual performance; not only efficiency in a technical sense, but ability to deliver. In turn, legitimacy refers to the subjective perception by the constituency that the system, its structures, incumbents and modus operandi are proper and respectable, and therefore are widely supported by social consensus. Central in a legitimate political order is the determination of who is "the sovereign" and therefore has the right to rule and determine what the common good is.

For traditional monarchists in seventeenth and eighteenth-century Europe, like Bossuet or Le Maistre, and in general for those arguing for the *"Thèse Royaliste"* (Royalist Thesis) of Divine Right, the source of sovereignty was the ruler. The Thomistic principle, *omnia potestas a Deo*, stated that all power comes from God; only God (or more to the point the Church) could anoint the monarch as the depository of divine will. The ruler, as an agent of Divine Providence, defined the common good. On the basis of such principle, as discussed in Chapter 1, an absolute king, like Louis the XIV could say *"l'etat c'est moi."*

For those advocating the contractual and secular thesis of sovereignty (Hobbes, Locke or Rousseau), political power comes out of the will of contracting parties. Therefore, sovereign power emanates from the political community, defined either as a nation (national sovereignty) or the people (popular sovereignty). The power of the state could be overwhelming, as in Hobbes' Leviathan, or be limited as in Locke's or Rousseau's view of the social contract. The common good in all three cases is seen in secular terms as a common interest. Inverting the above-mentioned dynastic formula by means of a republican twist, the expression would be "the state is us."

The riddle here remains the meaning of the collective noun "us," which is connatural to the idea of nation (literally birthplace). We could outline three possible approaches we have already touched upon. (a) The so-called *"Thèse nobiliaire"* (Nobility Thesis), a feudal and pre-absolutist tradition which challenged royal prerogatives by stressing the inherent rights of noble peers. The collective representing the common good is the assembly of aristocratic barons. This formula was characteristic of the Roman Republic as well as other ancient republics and aristocratic councils in Europe. We should be reminded that the term *"patria"* or *"patrie"* (Fatherland) is derived from the *pater familiaes*, the heads of notable Roman families. (b) In the French and American revolutionary versions, the collective is the commoners (the "Third

Estate"): the bourgeoisie, or, in general, major property holders. (c) From a radical point of view, the basis of legitimate power is, and can only be, the people – specifically the popular classes: the proletariat, or the workers; in one word, the majority. From this perspective, these large grassroots constituencies are the ones that represent the common, national, or public interest.

But even if popular sovereignty became the main, maybe even the sole, basis for providing democratic legitimacy to the rule of the few over the many, the drawing of the borders of belonging always was, and has remained, problematic. If all power rests with the people, the next question automatically is: who are concretely and specifically the people? Once states were formed and democracy had initiated its slow, but steady, march forward, state elites could no longer rely on coercion alone in order to get people to pay taxes and enlist as soldiers. As Hobsbawm (1992) explains, once subjects became citizens, their adherence to the state and their new, elected, rulers had to be secured with a strong ideology, able to replace the idea of divine rule. Nationalism thus became the almost necessary side-product of democracy, because even democratic states needed to levy taxes and motivate its citizens to fight. The ideology that proved strong enough to mobilize people and ready them to die, if necessary, was the idea of nationalism. The love of God and King of yore was converted into the love of country, as the mover of primeval and "tribal" emotion. The rise of nationalism and the "nation-state" in the Europe of the eighteenth century brought about one of democracy's most troubling sidespins, namely the need to exclude certain groups from the benefits associated with living in a democratic state.

Historically, nationalism replaced older modes of organizing people around a leader, namely the religious community and what Benedict Anderson has termed the "dynastic realm." This realm was characterized by a strong centre without clear borders, as borders, or even "belonging" mattered little, both to the ruler and the ruled alike. Popular realities remained strictly separated from the sacred realms of the Roman Catholic Church and those of Kings by Divine Grace. It is thus not surprising that most European princes did not speak, or understand, the vernacular languages of their many and diverse subjects.

According to Anderson,

as late as 1914, dynastic states made up the majority of the membership of the world political system, but...many dynasties had for some time been reaching for a "national" cachet as the old principle of legitimacy withered silently away. While the armies of Frederick the Great (1740–1786) were heavily staffed by "foreigners," those of his great-nephew Friedrich Wilhelm III (1797–1840) were, as a result of Scharnhorst's, Gneisenau's and Clausewitz's spectacular reforms, exclusively "national-Prussian." (Anderson, 2006: 22)

According to Hans Kohn (2005 [1944]),

> At the end of the eighteenth century, nationalism began to supply that emotional warmth, that intimacy of union which religion had provided and the separation of the emotional and the political forms of men's lives ceased: both sprang again from the same soil and reached out for the same heaven. Nationalism made the new State legitimate and implanted it deeply in the hearts and wills of its citizens. The expulsion of the Turks from Central Europe and the extinction of the Spanish Habsburgs, the last dreamers of a Christian world empire, at the end of the seventeenth century marked the definite end of medieval universalism. (Kohn, 2005: 188)

When it came to drawing the borders of belonging, revolutionary France and the newly independent America offered political opportunities, and space, for new ways to draw these borders. Both countries made belonging a civic-legal matter. After the French Revolution, everybody willing to join and underwrite the Spirit of the Revolution could become French, and being French was dealt as a gift to all those willing to embrace it. Similarly in the United States of America, citizenship rights were offered not to a group clearly demarcated by ethnic lines, but to all those willing to subscribe to its core ideological foundation – liberty, equality, and democracy. Both countries, however, also excluded blacks, indigenous groups and women from full citizenship rights, which points to the limited reach of democracy even in those places where democracy was at the forefront of history. In the rest of the world, where states came into being only reluctantly and did not provide for the means to effectively regulate belonging, culture and language served as the main criteria to forge community, thus making exclusion a central element of state- and nation building.

Although the stark differentiation between purely "*jus-solis*" states, regulating belonging with reference to being born in a place, and "*jus-sanguinis*" cases, where belonging depends on descent, is no longer valid, the dichotomy proposed by Brubaker (1992) is still very telling. Most contemporary states have created some form of mixture between *jus solis* and *jus sanguinis* principles, yet the post-9/11 United States and the post-Maastricht European Union have both shifted away from a civic-legal treatment of defining their respective national communities towards a more ethnic one. The discussions about the ability of "Hispanics" to blend into the Anglo mainstream (Huntington, 2004), as well as the questions about tolerance of religious symbols in French and German public institutions, all point to the resurgent importance of ethnicity and culture as criteria to decide who should be entitled to the benefits of democracy and who should not.

From a legal standpoint, what matters is of course not if one wears a headscarf or not, but if one supports democracy. Yet even the use of civic criteria to draw the borders of belonging requires exclusion, simply in order to be able to draw a border. The almost automatic association of certain cultures and religions with antidemocratic and anti-liberal attitudes is a particularly vicious one, and has produced much resentment among those affected by it. It has also pitched them against those engaged in such flimsy arbitrations and must thus be seen as one of the main factors of new, post-9/11, constellation of the world. Huntington's "Clash of Civilizations," instead of providing an explanation of contemporary conflict, rather explains how conflict is created and reproduced, namely by labelling some cultures categorically undemocratic and inferior to the West.

Historically, nationalism seems inevitably linked to democracy, at least up to the current state of affairs, and Hans Kohn might have been right when asserting: "Nationalism is inconceivable without the ideas of popular sovereignty preceding – without a complete revision of the position of ruler and ruled, of classes and castes" (Kohn, 2005: 3). Nationalism, then, is a discursively constructed seriality (Anderson) that comes to bear real consequences in people's lives. The categorizations of "us" versus "them" are maintained and disseminated through the media, the main means of opinion-formation available to political elites. Habermas (in Beiner, 1995: 257), taking account of these insights, has therefore defined nationalism as "a form of collective consciousness which ... presupposes a reflexive appropriation of cultural traditions that have been filtered through historiography and which spreads only via the channels of modern mass communication."

Furthermore, according to Tajfel (1986), a sense of group identity is fostered through the drawing of borders that separate those inside from those outside. This drawing of borders not only permits the effective separation of one group into two or more, it also constitutes each group with reference to the other. Tajfel's main dialectic insight is that one group can only exist by defining itself as different from another. In other words, difference and identity are constituted together, by defining oneself as different from others. National identity, analysed from this social-psychological framework, results from the contrasting of those that belong from those who don't. It is in this sense that Anderson (1991) talks about "imagined communities," thereby linking the political to the social-psychological. We are indeed still far from Habermas' utopia of global citizenry and it remains unclear if the benefits of democracy can ever be extended across the globe to include everyone.

Given the strong association between economic liberalism and political economy that has come to dominate our understanding of democratic possibilities, it rather seems likely that by opening the door of democracy to economic liberalism we have introduced the most corrosive force of capitalism into the heart of the system, namely perpetual and ever increasing competition. The modern welfare state might need to be embedded into a broader system of inequality in order to deliver the goods and services its citizens crave, or rather: in order to satisfy the subjective needs of those benefiting from living in "advanced democracies."

Citizenship

In his seminal work on *Citizenship and Social Class*, T. H. Marshall (1950) argued that, in Europe, civil rights preceded political rights and once both these rights were achieved, social rights would follow. Marshall predicted that the twentieth century would see an expansion of social rights, which he defines as

> the whole range from the right to a modicum of economic welfare and security to the right to share to the full in the social heritage and to live the life of a civilized being according to the standards prevailing in society. The institutions most closely connected with it are the educational system and the social services. (Marshall, 1992: 8)

When the twentieth century came to an end, it became clear that Marshall's prediction was too optimistic. In 2008, many European citizens were effectively still excluded from social rights, to the point were some analysts argue that Europe is developing an apartheid system (e.g. Balibar, 2004). Racism is at the core of this exclusion and it is Marshall's underestimation of racism that led him to formulate overly optimistic predictions about Europe's democratic future.

In Europe, as elsewhere, racism continues to be functional for the maintenance of inherited privilege. Under conditions of increased market competition, characteristic of advanced capitalist systems, the importance of racism grows, because whiteness functions as an additional capital, bestowing competitive advantages on those able to claim it (Hasenbalg et al., 1988; Harris, 1993). The economist Fred Hirsch (1976) further points out that advanced capitalist markets' competition for "positional goods" increases as capitalist development advances. According to Hirsch, positional goods derive their value not from their absolute utility, but rather from their relative position to others. Education is a central case in Hirsch's model. If everyone has access to higher education, the effect of leading to better jobs is thereby neutralized. Job requirements simply rise, making higher investment necessary, giving the better off an advantage over the less well off. At the same time, the costs in terms of investment required for the same outcome rise, in a process he calls "screening." When overall educational levels rise, a job formerly open to high school graduates now demands a college degree. The maintenance of the privilege of access resides on a better starting position. The traditionally included are able to hold the distance to the historically excluded by simply raising the value of the positional good. Historically excluded groups will therefore never be able to catch up. Under such circumstances, education becomes a means to create and protect social prestige, potentially losing all of its emancipating potential and its functionality of producing knowledge. Racism serves as a symbolic tool to defend privileged access to positional goods.

Almost 60 years after Marshall's lecture we are in the position to realize that social rights have not followed equally for all people once civil and political rights have been achieved. Especially non-traditional, non-white European citizens see their civil rights curbed by the forces of prejudice and racism. In many countries they are treated as foreigners and intruders despite their legal citizenship. Instead of social rights following civil and political rights, it rather appears that the exercise of civil rights depends on the previous achievement of social rights, as racism is undermining the effectiveness of civil and political rights of all those stigmatized as the "Others Within."

According to Jürgen Habermas, "only in an egalitarian public of citizens that has emerged from the confines of class and thrown off the millennia-old shackles of social stratification and exploitation can the potential of an unleashed cultural pluralism fully develop" (Habermas, 1998: 308). For many minorities, systematic misrepresentation translates into second-class citizenship, as it undermines their trust in public institutions. If citizens are stigmatized and feel underrepresented and unprotected by the state, the exercise of their civil and political rights is endangered. Instead of feeling protected by the state, they perceive state power as disciplinary power.

Europe's and the United States' difficulties to integrate non-Europeans and the trumping of nationalism over citizenship, as well as the related trumping of particularism over universalism, put them in company with other regions and countries of the world that face similar challenges of redefining belonging under conditions of ethnic and cultural diversity, increased trans-border migration, and heightened market competition.

Hannah Arendt has long since explained, that "of all forms of government and organizations of people, the nation-state is least suited for unlimited growth because the genuine consent at its base cannot be stretched indefinitely, and is only rarely, and with great difficulty, won from conquered peoples" (Arendt, 1966: 126). In her analysis of *The Origins of Totalitarianism*, Arendt further argued that,

Conquest, as well as empire building had fallen into disrepute for very good reasons. They had been carried out successfully only by governments which, like the Roman Republic, were based primarily on law, so that conquest could be followed by integration of the most heterogeneous peoples by imposing on them a common law. The nation-state, however, based upon a homogeneous population's active consent to its government (*"le plebiscite de tous les jours"*), lacked such a unifying principle and would, in the case of conquest, have to assimilate rather than to integrate, to enforce consent rather than justice, that is, to degenerate into tyranny. Robespierre was already well aware of this when he exclaimed: *Périssent les colonies si elles nous en coutent l'honneur, la liberté.* (Arendt, 1966: 125)

Lefebvre (2003), in turn, argues that, "Homogeneity is the precondition for the unity of the *pouvoir constituant,* and the goal of the constitution is not the organization of the life of the nation, but the establishment of government rules" (p. 18). This argument is proven right by Gary Wilder (2005), who demonstrates that the French Imperial Nation-State was never able, or willing, to expand full and equal citizenship rights to its conquered peoples in the Caribbean. According to Wilder, "republicanism, bureaucratic authoritarianism, and colonialism were internal elements of an expanded French state that were articulated within an encompassing imperial system" (Wilder, 2005: 26). On a similar note, Laurent Dubois (2004) depicts the difficulties that the first Republic encountered in accepting and integrating its former slaves in Guadeloupe. His detailed historical analysis of the years immediately following the French revolution allows us to witness the racist bias of colonial masters, who had much to lose with granting slaves citizenship rights, but also some mainland revolutionaries that sought to uphold culturally biased definitions of the "universal rights of men." Dubois' account of Guadeloupe's history also allows us to grasp the Caribbean roots of European citizenship as it points to the important, but often neglected, contribution of former slaves to the creation and active expansion of a discourse and practice of rights.

Accordingly, the whole set of assumptions on which liberal democracies rest is biased. The modern republic, from its very beginning, was unable to embrace its internal diversity. The case of Caribbean French citizens clearly points to the limits of the French citizenship from the very start. Although many countries have sought to overcome the racist undertones of their early democratic histories, many contemporary democracies have yet to live up to the abstract principles upon which they were founded. Second-class citizenship based on racism and aimed against non-traditional citizens is not a thing of the past. The case of contemporary France, Germany, Denmark and many others provides yet more evidence for the inherent restrictions of citizenship. It also provides the last episode of a continued history yet untold – the history of second-class citizenship, as old and as influential as the history of citizenship itself.

Transition to what?

Historically, the model of democracy based upon popular sovereignty manifested itself not only a nineteenth-century ideal, but also a standard benchmark of political analysis and assessment since the beginning of the twentieth century, and more so after World War II. During the 1970s and 1980s two important and related developments challenged the concept of liberal, representative and participatory democracy in the Western core. One was the shift in the normative political ideal among official intellectuals, from the notions of participation and people's rule, to the conservative obsession with governability and order (O'Brien, 1972). This right-wing critique, today referred to as neo-conservatism, emerged in the late 1960s as a hard-line reaction to the challenge posed by the New Left and other forms of extra-parliamentary opposition. The argument centred on government ineffectiveness (un-governability) eventually leading to a breakdown and ultimately a crisis of legitimacy.

Before delving into the argument of the crisis of democracy thesis as such, some historical grounding is necessary. In the context of the quagmire of the Vietnam War, with a mounting economic recession and disillusionment with mainstream liberal policies in Western societies, dissident voices had grown louder in tone. In the case of the US, there was unrest in university campuses and in urban ghettos. There were militant social movements, and the most vociferous critics within the left of the Democratic Party became rejected outsiders, giving birth to the radical SDS (Students for a Democratic Society). Black liberation movements emerged from the frustration with the Civil Rights Movement, especially after the assassinations of Malcolm X and Martin Luther King. There were Farm Workers movements, like César Chávez's NFWA, struggling for inclusion and the right to a fair wage. So was the case with First Nations' movements, attempting to redress historical injustices. Middle-class student mobilizations emerged out of the irritation and frustration with the Vietnam War, the draft and the spiralling confrontations with the police and security agencies.

Co-optation having failed, establishment responses either attempted to ignore or silence these dissonant voices, while disqualifying and side-lining opponents. Often dissidence was confronted with massive and invasive surveillance, and disproportionate force. The effect was further alienation and isolation of an opposition that had been already virtually cut off from the media and conventional channels of interest articulation and aggregation. Militancy, including armed grandstanding, as with the Weathermen and the Black Panthers, conveyed an image of impending crisis. Urban riots, marches and counter marches, punctuated with bloodshed, as in the Chicago Democratic Convention of 1968, or 1970 Kent and Jackson State universities, contributed to a conservative backlash. It culminated with the election of Republican hard-liner Richard Nixon to the presidency in 1969. However, the government's heavy-handed tactics, including bizarre episodes like the Watergate incident (1972–1974), exacerbated polarization, culminating with the toppling of the administration, a severe crisis of legitimacy, and almost systemic breakdown.

Europe and other countries in the Americas were not exempt from this, by then incipient, global turmoil. From Mexico's Tlatelolco student mobilization and massacre in 1968, to the Prague Spring of the same year, to Paris, to Berlin, to Turin, frustration with politics as usual led to increasingly militant extra parliamentary movements, which ultimately escalated into violent opposition. This included urban terrorist groups like the Red Brigades (*Brigatte Rosse*) in Italy, the Baader Meinhoff "gang" in Germany (*Rote Armee Fraktion*) and the various manifestations of violent irredentist urban guerrillas, like the IRA in Northern Ireland or the Basque separatist ETA in Spain.

The ever-harder line that until then seemingly tolerant governments across the globe took against protestors had the effect of enhancing the conditions of leftist militancy, while simultaneously failing to eradicate it. What began as an ideological right-wing response to radical left-wing challenges to the existing order soon mutated into a critique not only of radicalism but also of mainstream political liberalism. It also became a critique of democracy and a prescription of how to make it governable. Its central argument was articulated in the so-called crisis of democracy thesis (Huntington, Crozier and Watanuki, 1975). According to this, the ostensible erosion of authority and governability in contemporary societies was a consequence of "over-participation." In other words, and simplifying: the root cause of the crisis of democracy was the over-permissiveness of democracy itself, and authority its solution (Chomsky, 1979).

From a slightly cynical point of view, it could be argued that the liberal-democratic hybrid which had served the wealthy classes well for over a century had suddenly become obsolescent, too expensive or unable to serve accumulation on a global scale. Thus, a new model of conflict management, legitimation and enforcement, and above all elite accumulation, appeared necessary. As Keynesianism was replaced by von Hayek's and Friedman's economics, and the very wealthy initiated a "tax revolt," a more limited democracy was called upon. Its role was to legitimate and enforce a new social contract that excluded most blue-collar labour and the clerical and professional middle classes. It also heavily relied upon a transnational integration of the super rich as the basic condition for regime stability.

Justifying antidemocratic regimes

The other related ideological shift that challenged the previous model of representative and participatory democracy was the need on the part of Western governments, particularly Cold War liberals and authoritarian conservatives in the US, to justify their support for ostensibly antidemocratic regimes. These included anticommunist allies and bulwarks of market capitalism, like the Shah of Iran (1953–1979); Generals Ayub Khan (1950–1968), Yahya Khan (1971–1978) and Zia (1978–1988) in Pakistan; Mobutu in Zaire (1965–1997); Suharto in Indonesia (1967–1988); the Greek Colonels (1967–1974); and Chile's Pinochet (1973–1990). All of these regimes were encouraged, brought to power or courted by Washington. Before the end of the decade of the 1970s, the old pre-World War II fascist regimes of Spain (Franco) and Portugal (Oliveira Salazar) and the aforementioned neo-fascist regime of the Greek Colonels went into a tailspin. The same was the case with apartheid South Africa (1948–1993). Meanwhile the US-sponsored national security regimes in Latin America and Asia began collapsing from within during the decade of the 1980s. Paradoxically, the very excesses of the Nixon administration were perceived by right-wing intellectuals who once applauded his antidemocratic deeds as the administration's lack of authority and decisiveness. The blame was not put on the transgressions, but on his being caught red-handed in the murky Watergate affair. At any rate, the Republican defeat in 1977 and the ascent of the Carter administration was a critical interlude to "old" Cold War policies. However, it opened the door to the very Trilateralist (Sklar, 1980) ideas and modes of thinking that reflected the crisis of democracy and transition theories.

Seen from a long-range perspective, the praise for authoritarianism was a direct solution of continuity with the subsequent vogue: transition theory, a seemingly more benign flip side of the same coin. As we discussed in Chapter 1, a number of conservative policy advisors (e.g. Kissinger, Kirkpatrick) rationalized this policy, arguing that with classical fascism gone at the end of World War II, the only real menace to Western democracy was Communist totalitarianism. They also argued, quite erroneously in light of post-1989 developments, that existing socialist regimes, entrenched in the hearts and minds of their citizens, had created a sort of totalitarian legitimacy (Huntington, 1968) and could not be transformed into democracies. Conversely, these policy advisors suggested that equally non-democratic but pro-Western "friendly authoritarian regimes" if properly guided, could traverse the road to democracy. In their eyes, this was possible largely because the proto-fascist governments in those countries had not been able or willing to embed a totalitarian ideology in their populations. Despite the circularity of the argument, it was used to provide some moral justification to otherwise unjustifiable practices, and expectedly this ideology became mainstay academic discourse.

Transition in theory and practice

"Transitology" provided a teleological rationale and a roadmap for an orderly change of the guard in many pro-Western client states. This type of democratization was aimed at preserving both the socioeconomic order and the security apparatus entrenched by repressive regimes. It also maintained intact the international alliances with Cold War allied elites that had permitted their assent and continuity. A similar conceptual framework (albeit more refined) was at hand a decade later in cheerleading the transition from communism to liberalism – not necessarily democracy – in Eastern Europe.

From a broad perspective, the prevailing linear and unidirectional model offered by transition theory has not provided analytical tracks to explain a parallel, and in our view more significant, phenomenon. This is the retrenchment and erosion of democracy (or "un-doing democracy," in the sense used by Close and Deonandan), even in the context of shrinking participation. What is analytically and practically relevant to this trend away from democracy is that it is occurring not only in new, weak and fledgling polities, but also in older and reputedly more stable regimes with seemingly deeply-rooted democratic practices and values.

Democracy is often used as a seal of approval centred on "technical" factors, like electoral mechanisms and market friendliness, not on a regime's socioeconomic underpinnings and social effects. A great deal of the "metrics" of democracy generated by Western think tanks is quite biased in this regard. Furthermore, the analysis has concentrated on a linear and fairly a-critical (and largely non-historical) stand that simply assumes existing Western (US) democracy is both the end of ideology and that of history itself (Fukuyama, 1992). From this perspective, democratization and re-democratization are conceived as possible global trends; a peculiar reification of the "invisible hand." However, neither the crisis of democracy nor transition theories are able to generate hypothetical interpretations regarding de-democratization, let alone the retrenchment, or slippage," of democracy currently happening in reputedly developed regimes.

Democratic consolidation and stability

A closer examination of the alleged democratizing trend suggested by Fukuyama (1989, 1992) reveals a much more complex pattern than a predictable and unidirectional path to democracy the world over. In the 1980s and 1990s numerous regimes traversed the road from a certain state of authoritarianism and repression to a less certain one of liberalization and limited opening. But liberalization has advanced at a higher and more resolute pace than democracy. In the last 20-year period, very few formerly non-democratic nations have become full-fledged and inclusive democracies. For an overwhelming majority of people in Asia, Latin America, Central Asia and Africa, not to mention the Middle East, transition has been at best a slow movement into a limited, restricted, conditional or low-intensity democracy, not popular rule. On the flip side, many governments have reverted to authoritarianism.

Three Southern European countries (Spain, Portugal and Greece) in the 1970s, and a bunch of East European states (Poland, Hungary, the Czech Republic and the Baltic republics) in the 1980s and 1990s present the most successful cases, evolving into full-fledged liberal democratic status. In the Southern and Eastern European cases the EEC, and its successor the EU, undoubtedly played a major role in the transition. They provided both positive and negative economic incentives and political pressures to move into political practices and standards compatible with those of their West European would-be associates. The successful cases are those in which democratic practices and institutions were consolidated into an apparently less reversible system, with strong support by the regional and international community.

The next layer is provided by the less successful cases of Latin America. They point to a consolidation of a socioeconomic order designed by the previous dictatorships of the 1970s and their military and economic constituencies in the US, while developing a mostly formal and fairly inconsequential political façade. In fact, despite a decline in reported cases of extreme violence (e.g. dirty wars, torture and disappearances), Latin America, with few exceptions, is not only not fully democratic yet, but also some countries (like Colombia, Guatemala and El Salvador) show severe deterioration. Moreover, unlike the functional relationship between the EU and fledgling democracies in Eastern and Southern Europe, most American attempts at consolidating democracy in Latin America have been less than successful. This reflects a global trend: US efforts at democratization anywhere appear to be increasingly ineffectual. This trend needs to be studied in depth and in the context of long-term tendencies, as we will attempt in a subsequent chapter. Many countries in the Latin American region are today less democratic than they were before the military and US interventions, from the 1950s to the

1970s. The more hopeful signs in the region are not those predicted and favoured by transition theorists but the consequence of new grassroots social movements that emerged precisely *against* the prescriptions of neo-liberal transitions and the Washington Consensus.

A similar yet much more acute dysfunctional pattern evolved in the least successful cases encompassing most of Africa, the Middle East and Central Asia. Not only did democracy make little or no progress, measured even by the most minimal standards, but political, as well as socioeconomic conditions significantly deteriorated vis-à-vis the post-independence period for Africa and post-Soviet rule in Central Asia. Worse, the crises in many cases went beyond chronic political instability, persistent turmoil, authoritarianism and un-governability, and human misery. They became outright governmental unravelling, civil war and state failure.

Russia and China remain very special but significant cases of liberalization with very limited democratization. These examples are relevant not only with reference to the statistical fact that both countries encompass a very large proportion of the world population and economy. Qualitatively they represent cases of rapid conversion to capitalism, accompanied by distinct oligarchic tendencies. In Russia, the collapse of communism brought to power a new *nomenklatura*, made of former Party officials, bureaucrats and members of the security apparatus, interacting with the new "oligarchy" of robber barons; all fighting for the spoils of a now privatized economy. Though the country shows noticeable and even dramatic economic gains in terms of growth and investment, income distribution and basic living standards for most of the population, including life expectancy, have dramatically deteriorated. So has personal security. In China, the Communist Party reigns dictatorially and supreme over a society and a polity resting basically on a capitalist foundation. Its economy is sustained by a virtually inexhaustible supply of very cheap labour, which the Communist Party is eager to maintain. Thus, although China's economy has been growing at a historically unprecedented and sustained rate of 10 percent per year, so has the inequality between the rural and the urban population. In both cases, systemic corruption and repression, not popular rule, are central parts of the regime's mode of conflict management (TI, 2006).

De-democratization in the developed world

The democratic trend in the already established political systems is also less than stellar when closely examined. One common denominator is a significant historical decline of electoral participation, combined with an important downturn in the registration of new (i.e. young and foreign-born) voters. Attitudinal studies confirm a trend of growing cynicism and alienation from the political process: a general decline of citizenship and civic orientations. Apathy rather than interest and participation have become the predominant orientation in the political culture throughout the West.

A related factor negatively affecting democracy in industrial and post-industrial societies is unbridled transnationalization and globalization. These two traits should not be confused with regionalization and internationalization, based upon the construction of trust and cooperation, as in the European examples mentioned above. In a highly penetrated and exposed state the citizenry at large lose their grip on the economy. The potential tax and investment base, as well as sources of employment, escape to friendlier havens, all this encouraged by supranational regulation and de-regulation upon which they have little control. Therefore, the fiscal capabilities for problem-solving and elbow room to reach social compromise decline. In light of the analysis presented in Chapter 1 regarding the parameters of conflict management, sovereignty – the ability of the polity to be master in its own territory – is lost to increased globalization, supranational economic integration and external constituencies. This means that available capabilities at the national level are shrinking, while expectations and demands keep on growing.

Simultaneously, with such processes as outsourcing and capital and tax flights in continuous motion, the ability to reach some degree of consensus between elites and non-elites is severely reduced. Loss of purchasing power, of employment, of social benefits and safety nets affects an ever larger section of the population. The implicit social contract breaks down and so does public trust. Unless larger and encompassing supranational safeguards and networks are in place, as in contemporary Europe, social and political cohesion are likely to fall by the wayside.

In this context the political system ceases to be an inclusive and integrative arrangement for conflict management and the shaping and sharing of valuables under popular rule, but a plutocracy, a kleptocracy, or both. The policy alternatives also close dramatically, leading to an exacerbation of elite rule: a government of the few, by the few, for the few, with cosmetic rhetoric substituting for equity. Oligarchy displaces democracy, and, if the former fails, repression under the mantle of states of exception and surveillance become the way to maintain privilege and the status quo.

If we examine the Americas, a collective noun for the Western Hemisphere, a similar malaise can be detected. It is extremely acute in most of Latin America and the Caribbean, though these antidemocratic features, as noted earlier, are confronting vigorous social mobilizations challenging the existing order. Following the Argentinean, Mexican, Brazilian, Ecuadorian and Bolivian economic debacles of the 1990s and

2000s, all bearing the sign of neo-liberal stabilization schemes, social movements and reformist political alternatives have proliferated. Some of these have been able to generate new governments with open sensitivities to the demands of the previously excluded majorities. Bolivia, Ecuador, Uruguay, Nicaragua and, to a lesser extent, Brazil, Argentina and the populist Bonapartist experiment in Chavez's Venezuela, point to a region groping for political alternatives to the formula of neo-liberalism with restricted and exclusionary democracy.

In the United States the crisis is profound, multi-faceted and dramatic; perhaps in the same magnitude as it was towards the end of the Nixon presidency. It is also unprecedented in the sense that it is a juxtaposition of numerous structural malfunctions compressed in time and space. Moreover, it is highlighted by an obsessive proclivity of an increasingly authoritarian administration to use international conflict and national security as a strategy to rally around the flag and quell opposition. The conscious strategic restructuring of the judiciary along neo-conservative lines has compromised the old checks and balances among the "powers of the state." It has become a government of Executive supremacy, whose antecedents go back to the 1969–1974 era; though the Thirty-Seventh President did not then enjoy the support of a subservient judiciary. The War on Terror, in fact a perpetual state of emergency, has given security agencies and the military the ability to "manufacture consent" outside the usual opinion-making mechanisms, and circumvent democratic controls. Civil rights have been severely compromised, while praetorianism and government by deceit has become a common practice.

The current political landscape is characterized by a process that favours the very rich. Elections and other mechanisms for brokerage and citizen's representation are multi-million-dollar operations that effectively give a dominant role to big business. Thus, the super-rich became the major power contenders, with the ability to put elected officials in the highest offices. This oligarchic tendency is compounded by a managerial, cultural and economic implosion. Examples of these are the inability to address the devastation caused by hurricane Katrina; the insecurity posed by what Huntington called the "Hispanic Threat"; and, in 2007 and 2008, the meltdown of the housing and financial markets. All these appear beyond the capacity of official Washington and the country's power elites to handle. Meanwhile, social movements have lost the strength and appeal of the past, as with the Civil Rights, anti-war, environmental, feminist and other progressive movements of the 1960s and 1970s. Rather, a well financed, organized and aggressive extreme right has filled the vacuum and taken the initiative in the midst of public apathy.

In Canada, a highly dependent and penetrated polity, the collapse of the long-reigning Liberals in 2006, in the midst of a corruption scandal, brought to power a neo-conservative coalition with a regressive agenda not too dissimilar to that of their Republican neighbours to the south. Without effective political alternatives to the neo-conservative and neo-liberal onslaught, and without real safeguards for authoritarian rule, or a republican tradition, the prospects for real democracy in the Dominion look dim. This weakness is compounded by the continentalist policies favoured by most of the business elite and the transnationalized security apparatus. With the Canadian state being dismantled by continental economic and security policies, the "spine" of the once inclusive multicultural nation has been severely weakened. In its place centrifugal regional and ethnic tendencies could combine with oligarchic colonial traditions threatening pluralism as well as the vertebration and unity of the nation itself.

Chapter 5

Democracy and Insecurity[1]

There can be no political order if some basic human needs are not satisfied first. Put very simply, people need to be able to eat, have shelter and feel safe so that they can enjoy the benefits of democracy. Without human security democracy will be at risk and lack of human security provides a formidable challenge to democracy. This chapter thus delves into the complex relationship between the realms of politics and insecurity. Human security, understood as the reduction of people's vulnerability and uncertainty, is a multidimensional phenomenon (Nef, 1999: 23–26). It encompasses environmental, economic, social, political and cultural traits central to the realization of human dignity. However, the political dimension holds the key to the safeguarding of physical-environmental, economic, social and cultural "rights." Politics, understood here in its most conventional sense – the "allocation of valuables" through "authoritative choices" (Easton, 1957) – constitutes the organizing principle of a community's life. Without it, the realization of other forms of security could be impossible. The term authoritative is of crucial importance, as it means legitimate power, resting upon consensus. The alternative to authority is the display of force and violence to attain compliance.

Substantive, as well as procedural, democracy lies at the core of political security. As mentioned, politics involves the ongoing conflict management (and resolution) of contradictions between economic capabilities and social expectations, elites and masses, and sovereignty (autonomy) and subordination (Nef, 1983). The ability of a polity to overcome crises and provide security for its members depends less on its resource base and autonomy than on its learned capacity for conflict management – in a word, governance (Nef, 1992). Conversely, increased levels of insecurity relate to greater scarcity, to severe reductions in autonomy, and especially to ineffectual and authoritarian conflict management. A primary function of the polity is to provide security or, conversely, reduce insecurity and vulnerability for the population. The kind of security we are discussing here goes beyond the narrow and macro-aggressive notion of national security, centred on a military foundation. Human security does not necessarily exclude the latter. Rather, it enriches the analysis of complex systems by bringing in essentially the realization of human dignity as an ethical principle.

Threats to human security

Security threats emerge as a direct consequence of dysfunctional environmental, economic, social and cultural regimes in their multiple, though overlapping, subsystemic dimensions. The reproduction and expansion of mutual vulnerabilities (and insecurity), at both the micro and macro levels, expresses itself through closely related and interconnected thrusts. The same is the case with its opposite, security. Security threats are systemically related, so that dysfunctions in one sphere tend to express themselves in other subsystems. That is, mutual vulnerability is constituted by numerous reciprocating dysfunctions sequentially and structurally linked in vicious circuits of multiple causality. Security so defined implies the intersecting between global and domestic spheres.

Between 1945 and 1989, the functioning of the global and international conflict management regime was based on the intersection of two patterns of confrontation. The primary contradiction was a bipolar and seemingly symmetrical stalemate between the United States and the Soviet Union and their First and Second World allies. The principal source of global insecurity in the East–West confrontation was the nuclear arms race, underpinned by contending ideologies, economies and political systems. The bipolar global order defined the main spheres of interests and influence. Collective defence agreements, such as NATO or the Warsaw Pact, gave an institutional basis, as well as military muscle, to the global divide.

The secondary worldwide contradiction was that between a developed North and an underdeveloped South. The latter constituted the Third World of "developing," "new" and "non-aligned" nations or, more specifically, their ruling elites attempting to maintain an uneasy balance between the two blocs. More often than not this allegedly independent stand was an illusion. Despite the rhetoric, nonalignment for Africa, most of Latin America, the Middle East and the bulk of South and East Asia was conditioned by neo-colonial patterns of trade and military ties with the West. Some of the new radical regimes, such as Angola, Cuba, Mozambique and Vietnam existed in a client relation with the Soviet Union. In fact, only a few large states (including China, India, post-revolutionary Iran, and Iraq) played an intermittent non-aligned role, but with no common bonds among themselves. In other words, the Third World, despite claims to a "spirit of Bandung" (1955) was more a systemic feedback of the confrontation between the First and Second Worlds than a consequence of their leaders' ostensible attempts to ascertain the sovereignty of their respective nations.

Until the 1990s, the global system involved a wide array of linkage groups connecting both centres and their respective cores with their peripheries and semi-peripheries. This constellation of constituencies found expression in the functioning of formal international institutions. The latter comprised a gamut of organizations from the General Assembly of the United Nations, to the Security Council, to the main functional agencies and regional bodies (for example, the Organization of American States, the Organization of African Unity, the Association of South East Asian Nations, the Arab League). Although penetrated by the entangling alliances of the Cold War and by the hegemonic vocations of both superpowers, nation-states remained the predominant political actors (or power-players) in both the global and the regional scene.

Without a bipolar pattern of confrontation the above-described inter-state mode of conflict management came to a sudden end. Despite the practical elimination of the possibilities of all-out systemic confrontation between nuclear superpowers, the emerging structure has been inherently unstable. Major security threats, although basically internal and subsystemic, are today much broader, more unpredictable and more fractal. The global political configuration in the twenty-first century is essentially asymmetrical. Most peripheral states are penetrated political and economic systems with only limited sovereignty. In conventional (military) security terms, this asymmetry is one of loose unipolarism (with OECD and US dominance). The rapid disintegration of other forms of systemic association, such as the East European bloc, the Non-Aligned Movement and the very idea of the Third World in the 1990s left a global vacuum.

On the surface, there is a formal multilateralization of US hegemony in the Western-controlled United Nations system, combined with growing economic polycentrism within the developed world; the latter manifests itself in two directions. One is the emergence of strong economic blocs, namely in Europe (the European Union), in Asia–Pacific (Asia–Pacific Economic Cooperation, the Association of South East Asian Nations), and now in North America (the North American Free Trade Agreement) and South America's fledgling Mercosur. The other is the decline of the United States as an industrial power vis-à-vis Europe, Japan and especially China. However, with Japan's dramatic recession of 1998, and China and India's emergence as global superpowers, this assertion needs to be re-examined.

But this apparent polycentrism is deceiving, as US military and economic might, both within the centre and globally, is still quite formidable, though increasingly ineffectual. Strange (1988) used the term *structural power* to refer to this American paramountcy under a new constellation of global interests, which now includes European, Russian, Chinese and Indian elites. Power in this new world order, other than through the control of resources, is more functional than territorial. Underpinning the geographical poles of growth in Europe, in Asia–Pacific until recently, and even in the semi-peripheries, there is an increasing concentration of force and wealth in the hands of a global ruling class – ironically referred to in the US as "Richistan." In this new order, economic and organizational commonalities are stronger than any traditional definition of, or loyalty to, a single national interest. In fact, transnational integration and national disintegration have gone hand in hand, as in the case of the globalization of production, trade and accumulation. As mentioned earlier, a main consequence of this globalization has been a profound weakening of the sovereignty of most nation-states.

The global political crisis and its manifestations

The contemporary political crisis entails the juxtaposition of two macro processes; both of them posing a threat to the emergence, sustainability and consolidation of democracy. One is the transformation of the global political order at the end of the Cold War, leading to the configuration of a new correlation of forces. The other is a profound alteration of the states themselves as representative mechanisms for conflict management and authoritative allocation of resources. Five major dysfunctional and reciprocating manifestations emerge from the above-mentioned juxtaposition. First is the spread of sub-national "low-intensity" conflict and civil turmoil. Second, the pervasiveness of extreme forms of violence, such as terrorism. Third is the increasingly endemic decline of the rule of law, expressed in soaring rates of crime. Fourth, the breakdown of the nexus between state and civil society, brought about by neo-liberalism and the receiver states (Nef and Bensabat, 1992). Last, but not least, is the rise of fundamentalism, both religious and secular.

The spread of conflict

In an interconnected world, conflicts cannot be easily contained within national boundaries; rather, they have a proclivity to become regionalized and globalized. Almost inevitably such conflicts draw in external actors. Involvement and intervention, especially by paramount participants like the United States or Europe, often mean entangling and costly operations, such as in Kuwait, Somalia, Kosovo, Sudan-Darfur, Afghanistan and Iraq. Peacekeeping, developed to prevent the escalation of local conflicts as contemplated in the specific mandate of the United Nations Security Council in the bipolar era, has given way to a less focused and less transparent, broader and more unilateral notion: the idea of "peacemaking." The latter is a particularly American approach for multilateralizing unilateral actions by means of the legitimation provided by the United Nations Security Council, in which the veto of the former Soviet Union has virtually disappeared.

Not only are interventions brought to the living rooms of the virtual global village through First World "embedded" media, but their repercussions in terms of internal security threats and possible retaliations affect the everyday life of ordinary citizens in very concrete ways. This was the case with the terrorist attacks on New York and Washington (2001), Madrid (2004) and London (2006). As the aforementioned conflicts expand in scope and intensity, they involve theatres other than the primary arenas of confrontation. Even under the restraint of bipolarism, primarily local engagements, such as the Korean and Vietnamese civil wars, the Israeli–Palestinian conflict, civil strife in Central America and power struggles in Afghanistan, showed a tendency to become regionalized and internationalized. Today, without the dangers of unintended superpower head-on collisions, the possibilities of widening local wars have increased. A nearly 15-year-old United Nations report (UNDESD, 1993) gave a sombre perspective on a world at peace but not in peace:

> Civil wars and internal conflicts have become the principal causes of violence, destruction and the displacement of peoples as conflicts between nation States and rivalries among major military powers subside. ... During the period 1989–1990, there were 33 armed conflicts in the world, only one of which was between nation States. Some 2 million people have fled former Yugoslavia as refugees or displaced persons. (Ibid.)

To put these figures in perspective, in the nearly thirty years following World War II there have been over 150 regional wars, with more than 20 million deaths, mostly among civilians (Roche, 1993), without counting more-recent bloody conflicts like Iraq, Afghanistan and Darfur. This suggests that although bipolarism prevented an all-out nuclear confrontation between the Western alliance and the Warsaw Pact countries, it was not as effective in controlling brushfire wars, especially in impoverished regions in the periphery. It also suggests that the incidence of armed conflict has multiplied fivefold in the years following the end of the Cold War. Given the fact that lethality expands with technology, we may expect the number of casualties to grow accordingly.

These conflicts are intensified by external economic and political interests, the search for dwindling natural resources, permeable boundaries, and the pervasive and massive accessibility of arms supplies. The latter "in and of itself increases the instability of unstable situations around the world" (USCR, 1993). The "arms trade constitutes a considerable burden on the already weak economies of developing countries" (Kiana, 1991). Arms imports in developing countries accounted for 80 to 90 percent of the value of global arms imports between North and South two decades ago (SIPRI, 1988). It has gone up ever since. For comparative purposes, although the total volume of arms transfers to developing countries between 1961 and 1980, expressed in constant dollars, was more than 143 billion USD, the total volume of economic aid was about one third of it: 48 billion USD (Maniruzzaman, 1992); a tendency that still persists. With the shrinking of foreign aid, this imbalance has grown even deeper. This transfer has contributed in no small manner to the emergence and perpetuation of repressive regimes and to the tragic and all-too-familiar cycle of dictatorship, rebellion and superpower entanglement in the South.

The wholesale availability of sophisticated arms at discount prices and of equally cheap, accessible and expandable human resources, in the form of mercenaries and "privateers" heightens the prospects of bloody civil and international conflict. The disintegration of the Eastern European armies – especially in the former Soviet Union, in the midst of a collapse of authority, can have deleterious effects on global security. A good deal of military hardware continues finding its way into Azerbaijan, Georgia, Chechnya, Moldova, Tajikistan (Nelson, 1993) and beyond. Conflict regions of Africa and elsewhere are also receiving this influx of military hardware. Civil wars have produced thousands of casualties and created a flow of refugees and displaced persons numbering in the millions. Whether this threat becomes a wider and more painful reality will depend to a large extent on the weak and problematic prospects for peace, development and legitimate government in both the conflict regions and in the supplier countries.

Finally, potentially dangerous scenarios are also evolving from nuclear proliferation among lesser developed countries (LDCs). Western and former Second World technologies have contributed to these trends, as in the cases of India and Pakistan, which are now firmly in the nuclear club and possess a significant stockpile of weapons. This has also been the much publicized cases of Iran and North Korea. But more than the spread of technology, this nuclear drive is the consequence of the breakdown of the checks and balances provided by bipolarism. It is just a matter of time until other governments in Africa, Asia, Latin America or the Middle East follow suit.

Terrorism and counter-terrorism

With the spectre of nuclear holocaust resulting from superpower confrontation gone, non-conventional forms of violent struggle, such as low-intensity conflicts, drug wars and terrorism (Wardlaw, 1989), are increasingly fought on the permeable global stage. Data on terrorist attacks are vague and purposely manipulated. What is clear is that the semantics of terrorism are much more important than the acts themselves. Differences between some of the major producers of data on the subject – the US State Department (USSD), the Central Intelligence Agency, the Rand Corporation and other organizations with various types of affiliations and clienteles – show discrepancies of 300 to 400 percent (Jongman, 1993). For instance, Risk International, a private think tank, recorded a total of 35,150 incidents between 1970 and 1988, whereas the USSD's figure was 13,572 for the period between 1968 and 1991. Such fundamental differences are related to the type of incident recorded, the nature of the group involved, and the political intent of the producer of the data. Between the 1970s and the 1990s, the US government and its agencies consistently attempted to minimize the impact of "wholesale," state-sponsored terrorism by friendly regimes, while over-emphasizing both left-wing terrorism and that taking place in the international arena. As of the beginning of the new century, it emphasized outrages perpetrated by "crazy" states, "Axis of Evil" and the like: Cuba, Libya, North Korea, Syria and Iran. There has also been a proclivity to inflate the incidence of such terrorism in the West by presenting very selective frequencies without reference to population. A USSD (1992) study indicated that between 1983 and 1992, more than 50 percent of the registered incidents occurred in Latin America, 31.5 percent in the Middle East and 7.8 percent, in Europe. The remaining 10.7 percent took place in Africa, Asia and North America.

Until the terrorist attacks of 2001, and subsequent outrages in Madrid and London, most terrorist activity took place in the periphery and involved generally unreported acts of state violence. 9/11 changed the perception of all that: core regions were no longer off-limits to such activities. The perceived security once offered by Western societies has already been rendered porous by dramatic events. Such harbingers of things to come included the destruction of Pan American flight 103 over Lockerbie, Scotland in 1988, and the 1993 bombing of the New York Trade Center. But certainly the emergence of Al-Qaeda, the devastating attacks of 2001 in the US and massive killings in train stations and the subway system respectively in Madrid and London, changed the nature of international terrorism from tactical to strategic.

Historically, terrorism has been a tactical expression of many ideological strains. But ethnic, religious, linguistic and other forms of irredentism are the most frequent sources of terrorist activity. The solution of some of the enduring national and territorial questions (as it happened in Northern Ireland) can bring to an end the violent spate begun in the 1970s. However, without peace in sight, the problem in Palestine continues posing a regional and global security thereat. In a world of disintegrating nation-states, the spectre of nationalist, criminal, radical, vigilante, or government-sponsored terrorism remains an ever-present security threat, with deleterious effects on democracy.

With terrorism moving into a global stage its implications are global in scope.

The menace to democracy posed by the "war of the flea" lies not only with the "disease," as an obscene symptomatic expression of violence. Objectively, until 2001 the numbers of direct casualties resulting from terrorist acts was disproportionately small in relation to the psychological and indirect impact derived from their brutality. The USSD study mentioned earlier indicated that in a nine-year period (1983–1992), fatal attacks involved slightly more than 12 percent of all registered cases; more than half of those were in Latin America. Only a handful of these reported cases occurred in the core countries of Europe and North America: 8.1 and 1.1 percent, respectively. When population is factored in, despite the image of a "world at bay," the relative incidence of terrorism in Western societies has been quite negligible.

Besides very amateurish and utterly unsuccessful attacks in England in 2007, no major attempt has been made in the developed countries since 2001. This is not to say that the systemic impact of terrorism in everyday life is insignificant; quite the contrary – the very logic of terror creates a radically altered social and political environment. This environment changes the dimension of the theatre, from tactical to strategic. Once incorporated in the political system, terrorism alters the very nature of politics, with utterly dysfunctional effects for both political security and democracy.

In this systemic sense, the greatest threat posed by terrorism to political security lies dialectically in its "cure." In many instances, counter-terrorism means hardly more than terrorism with a minus sign in front. It nurtures secrecy and a proclivity to circumvent civil liberties, due process and all those institutions that counter-terrorist measures are supposed to protect (Schmid and Crelinsten, 1993). Peru in the 1980s and contemporary Colombia dramatically illustrate the dialectic of terror and counter-terror. Many policies designed to fight "subversion" have had the unintended effect of multiplying insecurity in both the periphery and the centre. In the lesser-developed societies, anti-terrorism, often in the form of death squads and vigilantism, means the exacerbation of violence and the development of unabashed state terrorism (Chomsky and Herman, 1979). In the West, policies proclaimed in the name of anti-terrorism have enhanced both antidemocratic predispositions and government by deceit. A similar danger can be found in the "moral entrepreneurship" of the war on drugs, and other public-safety campaigns, that today replace the counter-insurgency and counter-terrorist discourse of the past. The globalization of enforcement, combined with the transnationalization of the state, reduces the latter's power and legitimacy. These tendencies increase North–South entanglements and in the long run weaken global and domestic security. In a world closely interconnected by trade, finance, communication and power there is a strong proclivity for mutual vulnerability. The security of the whole, including that of those sectors apparently most protected and affluent, is conditioned by the insecurity of its weakest links. We will return to some of these threats to democratic governance later on, in Chapter 8, where we address the connection between the "securitization" of the state and "undoing" democracy.

Crime and counter-crime

The growing incidence of criminality, violent or otherwise, in the midst of a deepening economic crisis constitutes a related security threat. This expresses itself in two ways. The first is the ostensible erosion of the ethical bonds, trust and consensus that link political systems together. Without these, neither governance nor security or democracy is possible. A true "crime epidemic" appears to have swept many regions of the world, from the poverty-ravaged cities of Africa, to the drug-exporting regions of Latin America and Asia, to the disintegrating societies of Eastern Europe, to North American inner cities. It affects the poorest slums as well as the highest offices. Some of its milder expressions involve increased corruption, venality, abuse, theft and vandalism. Its nastier manifestations include alarming increases in violent crimes in the streets, schools, workplaces and homes.

Violence, especially affecting the relationship between human insecurity and mutual vulnerability, is on the rise. This violence is desensitized, glorified and even legitimized by mass culture and its media. Depressed economic conditions make crime a lucrative opportunity for some and the only opportunity for many, as exemplified in the emergence of gangs in Sao Paulo and El Salvador. Once internalized as a social practice, crime becomes part of the culture and a persistent systemic condition. The drug problem is a case in point. The links that tie the drug trade together begin with peasant producers in remote Third World regions and continue with corrupt officials in the periphery, crime syndicates in both the exporting and the importing areas, functionaries "on the take" (as well as rabid "patriots") at the centre, retailers and First World users, ranging from the destitute to those of higher social standing. Being essentially a consumer-driven market and operating on the purest market logic, its containment requires addressing its social, cultural and economic causes – including the roots of addiction – rather than exclusively treating its symptoms.

The second security threat posed by crime is the way in which criminality is being handled, chiefly through the dramatic expansion in enforcement and containment measures, including authoritarian controls to maintain law and order. As with terrorism, there is a dysfunctional dialectical relationship between the problem of crime and the "technical" solutions to deal with it. Almost as fast as military demobilization was taking place in former war zones and public expenditures in social services were shrinking everywhere, internal-security allotments soared. So has the institutional empowerment of enforcement agencies, both public and private, and vigilantism. In increasingly polarized and fragmented societies, enforcement agencies end up taking sides and becoming politicized. The nature of intervention becomes more and more focused on specific classes or groups of individuals who are labelled as potential lawbreakers (the poor, minorities, the young, people with unconventional lifestyles).

The expansion of internal-security establishments, both public and private, worldwide has more to do with the bureaucratization of social dysfunctions than with their effective solutions. Nor does such growth correlate with a reduction of crime. Without denying the seriousness of the problem and the need for crime prevention in all societies, it is possible to remark that this expansive trend is a wide-ranging threat to democracies. It raises questions of public scrutiny, accountability, uncontrolled red tape, goal displacement, moral entrepreneurship, the emergence of a professionalized siege mentality, corruption, and control by antidemocratic forces.

The above is particularly disturbing, given the worldwide resurgence of racist, ethnic irredentist, and neo-fascist movements, rising precisely from the present crisis and finding themselves in a position to influence enforcement functions (Golov, 1993). Moreover, "law-and-order" issues have often become synonymous with an extremist political stand. This raises the possibility of police states. Important as they are, policing issues are hardly debated at any level of government. Enforcement agencies are sacred cows in contemporary society, with their roles and modus operandi often obscured by secrecy and media manipulation. In fact, breaches of public trust in the name of combating crime are the kind of threats to democracy from which Western societies are not inherently protected.

The action of special agents and paramilitary groups, including the ubiquitous security forces, raise significant questions about procedure, cover-ups, accountability and public safety. The variations of vigilantism and private (or "semi-private") paramilitary organizations are many, varied and growing. They range from the "secret armies" in post-war Europe (e.g. OAS in France), to the para-constabularies of the UDA in Ulster and the death squads in Central America and the Southern Cone in the 1980s, to the Colombian paramilitaries and the US "private" defence contractors of today. The dialectic of crime and counter-crime creates a self-fulfilling prophecy: most social or political activity becomes in one

way or another "criminal." When this begins to happen, the very legitimacy of the enforcement agencies and of the law they attempt to enforce
is brought into question. The consequences are increased personal insecurity, the devaluation of authority, and the perpetuation of corruption,
addiction, alienation and all the other social scourges that crime prevention is purported to address.

Neo-fascism

Last but not least in the list of emerging threats and challenges to political security is the upsurge of neo-fascism (Fakete, 1993); something
more than superficially connected to the above-mentioned paramilitary
and vigilante phenomenon. With pronounced declines in living standards affecting the once secure bastions of the middle-class and blue-
collar sectors in the First World and former Second World, sociopolitical
conditions similar to those of post-World War I Europe have been created. The unemployed, alienated youth, and an economically threatened
middle class constitute a propitious culture for "extremism from the
centre." These symptomatic trends have become more pronounced in
recent years.

Full-fledged Nazi organizations have sprung up as a reaction in
areas of continental Europe that experienced large influxes of immigrants and refugees, chiefly in Germany and Austria. Neo-fascism
is also rampant in the former Eastern Bloc: in the Czech Republic,
Hungary, Romania, Russia, Slovakia and the remnants of the former
Yugoslavia (Fakete, 1993). Established democracies, such as France
and Italy, have seen a recurrence of xenophobic movements, as with
the National Front and the older Italian Social Party, an heir of
Mussolini's fascists, as well as the xenophobic Northern League. The
National Front has fared relatively well at the polls (having increased
to nearly 13 percent of the vote throughout the 1990s), whereas the
Italian Social Party had a poor showing in the 1993 Italian parliamentary elections, after having held 34 seats since 1992. Nonetheless,
the fact remains that neo-fascists have come out into the open as
recognizable contenders in the official arena (Husbands, 1992). In
Germany, the neo-fascist Republican Party won 15 seats in state parliaments in 1992; and obtained 1 seat in federal parliament, and
10 seats in the Frankfurt city council (9.3% of vote in local elections).
The ultranationalist Austrian Freedom Party was the third largest,
with 28 seats in parliament and 20% in Graz's municipal election of
1993. In Italy, the neo-fascist Italian Social Party held 34 seats in parliament in 1992. The xenophobic Northern League won 55 seats in
the same general election (17.5% of the vote in the north) and, except

for Turin, controlled all northern city councils. In France, the ultra-nationalist and xenophobic National Front received 12.5% of the vote in the 1993 election and held 10 seats in the European Parliament. In the 1992 local elections, the National Front elected 239 councillors across France. In Belgium, the ultranationalist Flemish Bloc won 12 seats in the lower chamber and 5 seats in the Senate in the 1991 election, receiving 10.4% of the vote in Dutch-speaking areas. In the Czech Republic, the Republican Party (modelled after the German Republican Party) won 6% of the vote in the 1992 general election. It should be borne in mind that electoral politics has always been but a minor component in previous fascist movements, and therefore a careful analysis of their alternative, extra-parliamentary strategies is essential if one is to ascertain their full potential.

Marked racist and proto-fascist tendencies are also increasingly evident in the Americas, having found a home in a number of fringe organizations with a high capacity to penetrate mainstream movements and public institutions, such as political parties, the bureaucracy, the police and the military. Contemporary fascism is perhaps less nationalistic and more anti-left than its historical counterparts. Nor does it question, as classical fascism did, the tenets of economic liberalism. In this, it largely reflects contemporary globalization and the collapse of communism. Today's fascism is primarily defined by xenophobia, militarism and racism, rather than by a coherent sociopolitical doctrine (such as corporatism) or a national project. It constitutes an appeal to action, especially to the young and to those displaced by economic dislocation, uncertainty, and the trauma resulting from the loss of community and identity (Bunyan, 1993). In this sense, the skinhead phenomenon in Germany, the United Kingdom, and elsewhere deserves particular attention. Most important, though, is the fact, rooted in the historical evidence of pre-World War II Europe, that in periods of crisis the fascist syndrome is more pronounced among the "respectable" white-collar middle classes than in other sectors of society.

These extremist movements are on the rise. Potentially, they have the capacity to affect policy in not only an indirect but also a more direct and forceful way. Key areas are language, education, welfare and especially immigration. In a poisoned political atmosphere, generally moderate governments such as those of Austria, France, and Germany have already been hard pressed, yielding to fringe demands to restrict policies regarding asylum and immigration (Nagorski and Waldrop, 1993). Neo-fascist movements have the ability to come to power in the not-so-distant future in a number of countries, either by themselves or in coalitions. This latter scenario is a significant threat not only to the safety of democracy but also to peace, to the society at large and to global order.

The present global context

With the fading away of Cold War bipolarism, national elites at the Western core, especially in the US, have been enjoying greater room to manoeuvre. But they are also faced with greater uncertainty. The global context has become radically altered. In the case of the underdeveloped societies (and the underdeveloping nations of Eastern Europe), the impact has been dramatic. For the Group of 77, the disappearance of the Second World as an alternative source of support, the debt crisis and a new international trade regime have set the parameters of a more entangling dependency and peripheralization. Although there are fewer constraints on unilateral action than under bipolarism, this untangling is more prevalent in places where the former Soviet Union had a significant presence. Without the restraining influence of Saddam Hussein's former Soviet ally, it may have appeared as an attractive choice for the then Iraqi dictator to attempt to annex Kuwait. There are also fewer constraints on the United States. It was relatively uncomplicated as well for US President George H.W. Bush, largely on account of internal electoral considerations, to assume the role of global United Nations enforcer and only then to seek international consensus. Operation Desert Storm did not face the dangers of escalation resulting from a client relation between Iraq and the other superpower. This lack of constraint also played a significant role in the US involvement in Afghanistan and Iraq after the 2001 terrorist attacks on US soil.

Aggressive peacemaking has substituted for the peacekeeping functions of the past. This approach to collective security entails a globalization and multilateralization of Washington's self-proclaimed role as protector of the Western hemisphere, a policy known as the Monroe Doctrine (Nef and Núñez, 1994). The global policing sanctioned by the United Nations Security Council in the Kuwaiti and the Somali episodes are at odds with the established practices of peacekeeping and conflict management of the United Nations system. Nevertheless, it has become a feature of the present order. The broader implications of this doctrine were seen in President George W. Bush's manufacturing the war against Iraq in 2004.

But the context of contemporary politics goes deeper than a rearrangement of the global configuration. It also manifests itself in the manner in which contradictions between capabilities and expectations and between elites and masses within nation-states are shaped. With the expanding and deepening economic crisis, as outlined earlier, the possibilities for consensual mechanisms of conflict management have manifestly declined. The same is true with the resurgence of acute conflict between diverse social strata. The nature of the state, both at the centre and at the periphery, has changed. It has a greater proclivity for institutionalized repression or for protracted stalemate cloaked in the garments of liberal democracy, elections and the like. Politics runs the risk of becoming ever more crudely an act of elite domination, thinly disguised in the language of legitimacy, while public sentiment against such domination tends to rise whenever elite rule reaches new heights, as the victory of Barack Obama to the American presidency demonstrates. The 2008 US election mirrors similar elections in South America, where political newcomers were elected to the highest office, which demonstrates the general public's discontent with the way politics are done by traditional political elites. Whenever such an election occurs, we witness the recurring strength of the democratic ideal, where ordinary people seek to once more bring rule closer to themselves.

The system's culture

With the end of socialism and the non-aligned hybrids that vainly attempted to straddle ideological bipolarity, one dominant Western worldview, with seemingly universal claims, has emerged triumphant. This is the neo-liberal discourse, with its emphasis on procedural democracy and market forces. Whether its roots are strong or it takes the form of window dressing wrapped in debt management and trade conditionalities, neo-liberalism so far exhibits hegemonic characteristics among the elites in the centre and the periphery. Alternative political cultures are to be found not in the utopias of non-capitalist social orders but in more traditional strains. Ethnicity, culture and religion have substituted for the secular ideological conflict of the Cold War. Despite the disintegration of numerous nation-states and partly as a result of it, nationalism is still a significant force in global affairs. One of its current manifestations is the micro nationalism of once submerged and suppressed nationalities seeking to break free from central rule: the Kurds in Iraq, Turkey and Iran, the Sikhs in India, the Tamils in Sri Lanka, the Croats, Bosnians, Kosovars and others in the former Yugoslavia, and those involved in irreconcilable ethnic strife in Burundi, Rwanda and Sudan. These are among the many instances of violent ethnic insurrections not yet crystallized in formal partitions. Canada and Spain are equally faced with linguistic and ethnic separatism, the long-term outcome of which is still uncertain.

Nationalism is often connected with tribal, ethnic or religious irredentism. In many instances, it can be a reaction to Westernization, widely publicized and misrepresented in the *Clash of Civilizations* (Huntington, 1993). An example of this was the Ayatollahs' Islamic Revolution in post-1979 Iran, with its current projection into Algeria, the Arabian Peninsula and Egypt. Ultranationalism and virulent strains of nationalism based on myths of the past or future grandeur of the dominant ethnic group are also likely to surge at the heart of disintegrating multiethnic states. A probable future pole for strong re-centralizing tendencies is Russia, where ultranationalist tendencies resulted from acute centrifugalism and national decay. Vicious yet more conventional nationalism may re-emerge in the rapidly unified German Republic, in France, and throughout Europe as anti-immigrant and anti-Islamic attitudes rise. It could also emerge in an economically threatened Japan.

The United States itself has never been above flag-waving and aggressive bigotry, especially in the present conjuncture of perceived power deflation. Although it appears ostensibly as the victor of the Cold War, it is experiencing a deep internal and external crisis, accelerated by the traumatic events of 9/11. Should the present economic meltdown and retreat from empire become pronounced and manifest, translating itself into serious unemployment and the threat of domestic turmoil, some US political elites may see fit to resort to extreme chauvinism to avert a crisis of hegemony, as elites have done elsewhere.

In this context, the possible breakdown of Canada, following an eventual separation of Quebec, may provide an enticing invitation for territorial expansion. So might the expansion of a free-trade area in the Americas, or attempts to become involved in the Colombian civil war, encroaching into energy-rich countries in the Andean region. Paradoxically, in a free-trading world where economic blocs such as Europe, North America and Pacific Asia are becoming the very negation of such free trade, imperial proclivities are bound to emerge. Alternatively, the success of the American Democratic Party in 2008 also points to a different scenario, namely a growing awareness that untamed markets and corporate greed might after all not self-regulate and tend toward equilibrium. Rather, the present conjuncture could manifest itself in an ever-more volatile scenario of "creative destruction," threatening social harmony and thus posing a challenge not just to average people and popular rule, but to the political and economic elites themselves – as they are the ones who most rely on stability for the continued pursuit of their economic and political interests.

The structure of the global system

The global political regime is, at best, a loose conglomerate of interactions dealing with local, regional and international conflict management, bound together by limited rules, practices, correlations of forces and institutions. Correlations of forces and institutions make up what can be called the global political regime. International law and organizations, such as the United Nations, the numerous regional arrangements and the now swelling body of international conventions, bilateral agreements, jurisprudence, and regulations give the system a superficial semblance of order and authority. But this image is deceiving, as the real power rests with a small number of national and transnational actors, primarily those among the elite core in the OECD countries. The existing mechanisms for global conflict management, such as the United Nations Security Council, have become tools of the foreign offices of a small number of nation-states, especially the United States.

These institutions of the global regime project the interests of a group of paramount economic elites within the West. In other words, the global political order is ever more subservient to the transnational economic regime, whereas the world is increasingly interconnected, thus producing contradicting forces that bring the world together, while fragmenting it at the same time.

The deregulation of financial markets pushed through under President Nixon in order to gain access to foreign markets brought about the profound liberalization of financial markets and of certain aspects of international trade. These deregulations have exposed the whole world to the manoeuvres of large corporations and to irresponsible actions of some "rookie" and unrestrained stock brokers, trading in derivatives that they do not really understand – or care to understand. The Asian, Mexican, Russian, and the 2007 financial securities crises, as well as the oil and sub-prime mortgage debacle of 2008, all demonstrated that the world is indeed more interdependent than ever imagined. Moreover, problems in one part of the world send ripples through the entire system, sometimes even magnifying the impact at those places that did not cause the problem in the first place, as the case of Iceland demonstrates. Iceland's financial meltdown reminds us of the 1997 Asian crisis, but it demonstrates that such meltdowns no longer only occur in already vulnerable and dependent countries of the third world. To the contrary, a politically disentangled yet economically highly enmeshed international system has increased the vulnerability for all countries, rich and poor alike. The 2008 global financial crisis also points to the tremendous social costs of deregulated financial markets, as the whole world is forced to bear the long-term consequences of greedy executives who were able to take advantage of the opportunities provided by highly complex and grossly deregulated financial markets. Globalization, in other words, has produced an "increased impact propensity" (Held et al., 2005: 69). It has also brought us a world that is at the same time more integrated, yet more fragmented. In it, the benefits of participating in global systems of trade and finance are not only highly exclusionary, but have produced highly unequal results even for those countries able to join in. James Rosenau has referred to this process as one of "fragmegration" (Rosenau, 2005: 223, in Held et al.).

To make matters worse, the IMF, World Bank, and WTO are at the centre of the global political regime and configure a de facto mechanism for global governance without adequately representing the interests of those most affected by their actions – the majority of poor people in poor countries. Despite its most recent reform of internal governance (achieved in April 2008), the IMF is still dominated by representatives of the business world – in the form of representatives from rich countries, or even in the form of restricting its participation to ministers of finance and central bankers, even if they come from poor countries. The IMF, in particular, is an institution where the poor are not represented and are thus not part of its constituency. To them, as Joseph Stiglitz has argued, the IMF represents a case of "taxation without representation" (Stiglitz, 2005: 479, in Held et al.) The recent global financial crisis has highlighted the need to reform these institutions even to such free-market ideologues as George W. Bush, who asked world leaders for a "Second Bretton Woods" meeting to be held in December of 2008, in order to redefine the roles of the IMF and the World Bank. This call to rethink the role of international institutions to make them able to understand, oversee and regulate the international financial markets is indeed pressing and reflects the age-old insight that markets do not simply self-regulate, but rather move from one crisis to the next – if let to themselves. However, despite the recognition that the whole world is affected by the current crisis, President Bush's call to discuss global markets and redefine the role of international institutions was not extended to the leaders of the whole world; not even those sharing a similar economic agenda. Instead, the 2008 "new" Bretton Woods meeting – which now, in addition to the G-7 includes China, India and Brazil, in the so-called G-20- reflects the distribution of power in the world and remains an exclusive club of the rich. Despite its restricted character, this meeting is of utmost importance, as it is within these institutions, and not inside the governing structures of most countries, where effective policies and regulations governing the world order are effectively made. Despite their importance, the public knows next to nothing of such influential institutions as the Bank of International Settlements (BIS), located in Basle, Switzerland, where the world's most influential bankers regularly meet in secret to discuss the international financial system.

All other manners of policy-making formally rest within the confines of the more than 200 heterogeneous states that comprise the official roster of the United Nations General Assembly. Yet most nation-states decision-making power in relevant policy areas is quite limited. The implementation and enforcement of these regulations occur more readily in the "neo-functional" economic realm than in the formal structures of government and international organizations.

The internal structure and operations of states have also been significantly transformed in recent years. With the advent of debt-ridden receiver states, financial decision-making has displaced other forms of "high politics." As we have already noted, the world over, finance ministries, treasury boards, central banks and the like have become the heart of governance, subordinating other functions, ministries and agencies to the role of implementing structural-adjustment agendas for fiscal management. These globalized and eminently technocratic, elitist and undemocratic agendas, rather than national priorities or popular demands, have effective "meta power" to set the rules of the game and determine government policies and their outcomes.

Global processes of continuity and change

With the fading away of territorial sovereignty, persistent centrifugal tendencies (ethnic, linguistic, or sub-regional) are more pronounced, and the political process has become increasingly fragmented. Sub-national conflict is at the same time endemic but also highly transnationalized. This generates overall systemic instability. Many nation-states have shown unequivocal signs of disintegration and territorial secession. The most dramatic and multisided examples are those of the former Soviet Union – with the subsequent fracturing of many of its former republics, Yugoslavia, and today Iraq. To these one should add the peaceful, but definite, division of Czechoslovakia, along with the possible cases of other multicultural states, which are exhibiting strong centrifugal tendencies.

As conflict becomes more acute, the prospects for consensual solutions to long-drawn confrontation are diminished. The policy process becomes diffused and progressively devoid of effective checks and balances, and meaning. This translates into deadlock, mixed with superficial consensus and an entrenchment of the socioeconomic status quo above and beyond the short-term equilibrium of shifting correlations of forces. In the new configuration, indecision and paralysis prevail. Disillusionment and alienation with politics on the part of the public is a common feature in both the developed and underdeveloped worlds. This is happening in the Western democracies, and in the post-communist societies of Eastern Europe, in the post-authoritarian regimes of Latin America, and in the chaotic complexity of Africa, parts of Asia, and the Middle East. Rates of electoral abstention are over 60 percent in the United States, as is the case in Colombia, and the trend of deteriorating civil confidence and alienation increases practically everywhere.

Insecurity under muted unipolarism

These developments are likely to have a long-term impact on human security, and democracy, well beyond the sphere of the political.

Environmental security, economic security, social security and cultural security are equally at stake. One way of looking at these consequences is to concentrate on human rights. Even though their specific content is changing and evolving, the political trends discussed so far point to a deterioration of human dignity on a planetary scale, irrespective of the standards of measurement. Whether it's ethnic "cleansing" or killing fields, torture chambers, discrimination, or oppressive conditions that deny people their humanity, the picture is far from optimistic. An assessment made over fifteen years ago is still descriptive of the global predicament:

> In every region of the world, it seems that human rights are being rolled back. Frustration and bitterness are fuelled by economic policies, which make the rich richer and the poor poorer. And governments seem unwilling or unable to do anything about it. ... But they are prepared to go to great lengths to cover up their crimes. They know that a blood-stained human rights record will damage their international relations. ... Some turn to "arm's length" ways to achieving their aims. They set up or back death squads and civilian defense forces to do their dirty work. Long standing democracies such as India, and newer ones such as the Philippines, proclaim the sanctity of human rights while in the streets people are being extrajudicially executed by government, or government-backed forces. Every year thousands of people are assassinated in Brazil and Colombia – even children whose only crime is their homelessness. (Sané, 1993: December 10)

Democracy needs human security as ground upon which liberty and equality can be constructed. Under conditions of extreme insecurity and whenever fear becomes the reigning principle of communal life, the pursuit of hope becomes impossible and democracy faces a severe challenge. Human insecurity is caused in part by the increased fragmentation and heightened impact propensity caused by increased interaction among states. As such, it is an unintended by-product of increased interdependence, but it also results from deliberate political choices by all those favouring the politics of deterrence and "security" over the politics of negotiation, trust-building, and peace. Human security, to the contrary, will not result by default, as a by-product of growing interdependence; nor can it be constructed from mutual threats. It requires deliberate, dedicated, courageous and concerted action and it demands that some nations take the risk of taking the first step, as human security ultimately relies on mutual cooperation and trust. Wherever the politics insecurity prevails, democracy is at peril.

Chapter 6

Poverty, Inequity and Democracy[2]

As we have stated in the previous chapter, democracy cannot be enjoyed if the security of the population is threatened. One particular aspect of insecurity which has a direct bearing for democracy, and its absence, is poverty. The term poverty here is not limited to the notion of relative or absolute deprivation: it also connotes the idea of inequity and skewed distribution of assets and liabilities. In fact, since sociocultural, economic and political inequities are closely interconnected, lack of democracy and political insecurity in general are closely and structurally related. The limitation of capabilities to satisfy expectations tends to raise the level and intensity of conflict among various sectors of society, enhancing the prevalence of authoritarian and abusive modes of conflict management, as discussed at the beginning of this book. Economic security, broadly defined as "non-poverty" is a necessary but not sufficient condition for the functioning of consensual popular rule. The key issue here is not solely equality and inequality of outcomes, important as they are, but access to the process whereby resources and possibilities are allotted. This chapter will thus take a closer look at poverty and inequity and how they impact democracy, challenging its meaningfulness and importance.

The political economy of poverty conditions the nature of policies addressing poverty, and such policies, in turn, have an effect on growth and distribution. In this sense, the *World Development Report 2006* specifically noted that

> [t]he interaction of political, economic, and sociocultural inequalities shapes the institutions and rules in all societies. The way these institutions function affects people's opportunities and their ability to invest and prosper. Unequal economic opportunities lead to unequal outcomes and reinforce unequal political power. Unequal power shapes institutions and policies that tend to foster the persistence of the initial conditions. (World Bank, 2005: 20)

Conventional ways of conflict management centred on maintaining and re-enforcing the status quo, far from delivering public capabilities to extricate the poor from their predicament have generally excluded them from partaking in the share of valuables, especially power and decision-making. In addition to intentional policies, this exclusion is the result of both pre-existing internal structures that preserve economic insecurity and the nature of the global economic regime that manages and nurtures such conditions. Even the most reputedly democratic polities rest upon less than democratic social structures and oligarchic economic systems.

Broadly speaking, poverty is a situation in which people experience "a fundamental deprivation – a lack of some basic thing or things essential for human well-being" (CPRC, 2005: 5). The adjective global applied to economics means here

> the increasing integration of economies and societies, not only in terms of goods and services and financial flows but also of ideas, norms, information and peoples. In popular use...the term...has come to mean the increasing influence of global market capitalism or what is seen as the increasing reach of corporate and financial interests at the global level. (Birdsall, 2002: 2)

The nature of poverty

Why has poverty such a conditioning impact on democracy? The answer to this question has to do with the very nature of poverty. Amartya Sen has provided the most helpful formulation of this relationship, by introducing the concept of "capabilities." According to Sen (1992),

> capability is, thus, a set of vectors of functionings, reflecting the person's freedom to lead one type of life or another.... This freedom, reflecting a person's opportunities of well-being must be valued at least for instrumental reasons, e.g. in judging how good a 'deal' a person has in the society. But in addition...freedom may be seen as being intrinsically important for a good social structure. (Sen, 1992: 40f)

Sen thus elaborates a new foundation for the study of individual behaviour and its connection to freedom, choices and democracy. It is Sen's insight that investing in an individual's capabilities also has a positive effect on markets, as these freedoms will very likely be used to produce and trade. What matters, according to him, is thus the range of capabilities individuals have so that they can live the kind of life they deem worth living. Among those choices, democracy ranks high – but so does the freedom to barter and trade, as well as the ability to live safely and without shame because of one's lifestyle, culture, social orientation and the like. Poverty, then, represents a diminished capability to live as one wants to live and as such, it reduces the amount of freedom available to those individuals and communities affected by it. At the same time, poverty is the most visible manifestation of economic insecurity. It is often related to other symptoms such as low or stagnant growth, large and inextricable indebtedness, deteriorating terms of exchange, food scarcity, bad health, and unemployment. Many lay people and experts alike see poverty as the principal economic and social problem in the world; and *the* main developmental challenge. Underdevelopment is much more than the size of GNP, GDP per capita or the rate of growth. It involves basically the question of "what's happening to poverty?" (Seers, 1977). Perhaps the most ironic paradox of our time is that poverty is persisting and spreading in the most prosperous age in human history. For the problem of deprivation is not one of wealth-creation, but squarely one of distribution. Fifteen years ago, the UNDP report (UNDP, 1993) noted that the wealthiest 20 percent of humanity received 82.7 percent of the world's income. One year later, in 1994, the last year these comparative statistics were systematically published in a comparable manner, the upper percentile had increased its share to over 90 percent. Though more recently, neo-liberal intellectuals have made claims regarding a decline of inter-national disparities; the long run historical trends (1960–1994) are quite revealing (Dwivedi et al., 2007: 45). Also revealing is the apparent tendency for within-country disparities to increase in recent years, even under conditions of apparent reduction of disparities among countries (Milanovic, 2006: 7). These trends point at an entrenched structural bias in the material distribution of assets and liabilities in the world system. As we mentioned earlier, the global middle sectors have been shrinking considerably: the 20 percent that could be called the world's middle class received only 11.7 percent of the world's wealth (Robinson, 1994). In the words of Geoffrey Garrett: "globalization...has squeezed the middle class, both within societies and in the international system" (Garrett, 2004: 84). In the first years of the twenty-first century, global profits grew at an unprecedented rate, while workers' incomes dropped accordingly.

On the other hand, well over one-half of the African population has lived in a state of destitution for decades. These societies did not fare much better under the assistance of IMF and World Bank inspired Structural Adjustment Policies (SAPs): their condition of pervasive poverty has become imbedded. In addition, the drastic restructuring of the transitional Eastern European economies – that is, the movement to capitalism in the formerly centrally planned economies – has resulted in declining material productivity, unemployment, dropping living standards and unequal distribution of income (UNDESD, 1993; Milanovic, 2005), even under formally more "democratic" regimes. About one-half of the poor in the North today live in Eastern Europe and in the territories of the former Soviet Union. These post-communist poor include social categories virtually nonexistent scarcely a decade earlier: homeless people and beggars. Nevertheless, a comparative World Bank study using the Gini index to measure income inequality in the late 1990s and early 2000s suggests that the former socialist countries' income distribution profiles were less unequal than that of Latin America (GDR, 2006: 200–201).

Reiterating a previous observation, poverty is not just a question of material deprivation and limited accessibility to wealth and opportunity. It is essentially a multi-sided problem of disenfranchisement and exclusion, generally rooted in powerlessness and exploitation. Ultimately it is sanctioned by force. This state of insecurity and "ill-being," juxtaposes material want with numerous socioeconomic, cultural and above all political, circumstances. These reinforce and maintain people in a vulnerable and demeaned condition of unsustainable livelihoods, where political, economic and social insecurity are closely interconnected.

The various structural manifestations of insecurity, in turn, are maintained and reproduced by a culture – one could call it "pedagogy" – of insecurity. Culture here is understood as a set of shared psychological orientations towards the self, others and their circumstances (Almond and Verba, 1989), which involves more than the values, myths and beliefs of the poor. It includes the adaptive/learning processes by which poor people cope with, and rationalize their poverty. Popular sayings like "it has always been this way," "we can get only what God gives us," or "we have our children," provide a mantra of quiescence and fatalism. It is also and primarily reflective of the ideologies and doctrines, hegemonic and otherwise, by which the privileged few justify and generate poverty for the many. As socially-constructed representations, attitudes such as cultural atavism, racism, class and gender biases, or "technical" categorical imperatives (such as prevailing economic theories), reproduce, rationalize and justify the material and political conditions underpinning poverty. We can often hear the perpetrators of deprivation rationalize the predicament of their victims in terms of: "they've always been lazy – they just don't want to get ahead"; "they're just happy working with the soil – close to the earth, living with their families"; or "they never know how to handle money when they have it anyway."

The dimensions of poverty

Superficially, poverty appears as a situation of low income. Many use terms like "living on less than a dollar a day," or "people below one-half of the median income." However, while low income is an important indicator of the actuarial valuation of deprivation, the main issues lying underneath low income are distinctively material, social, and above all, political. These refer to substandard quality of life and inadequate cap-abilities to sustain livelihoods. Most significantly, these inadequacies entail very limited accessibility and coverage, as well as low quality of resources and capabilities to sustain livelihoods. In other words, the material indicators of poverty involve a series of interconnected symptoms. These comprise among others: short life expectancy, high infant mortality, hunger and malnutrition, stunted anatomical growth, disease, unemployment and underemployment, inadequate housing, unsanitary conditions, absence of safe and clean water, environmental deterioration, lack of and under-access-to education, and exposure to multiple manifestation of violence (Sen, 1993). Galtung has referred to these symptoms as structural violence (Galtung, 1969).

There are also "social" liabilities that are both contributors to, and consequences of, poverty: discrimination, exclusion, stigmatization, abuse and hopelessness. All these have also distinctive political overtones. Low income is merely the tip of the iceberg of economic insecurity. It correlates strongly with all these manifestations of deprived well-being, but of itself the concept of low income fails to portray the complex, dynamic, and multi-sided nature of the poverty phenomenon. National accounts are often unable to convey the essence and depth of poverty. Not only is it hard to capture material, behavioural and social situations in one single economic measurement, but also its measurement presents some significant technical problems of data acquisition and computation.

Estimates put the world's poor at over 1.39 billion, out of a population of 4.97 billion in 2005 (CPR, 2005: 9). This is slightly over 28 percent of the world population. Historical analyses, such as those undertaken by Surendra Patel (Meier, 1964), have suggested that in the period between 1850 and 1960 the development gap between industrial and non-industrial economies expanded with progress. For most of the twentieth century, the gulf between rich and poor, as well as between "rich" and "poor" nations, has continuously increased. This gap, resulting from the expropriation of surplus by colonial powers and their central and peripheral elites helped to pay for the West's Industrial Revolution. In recent years, neo-liberal economists and ideologues have questioned the growing gap hypothesis. The fact remains, however, that since Gini indexes were first calculated, until systematic reporting ceased, there has been ample evidence of this polarization. Recent corrections, assisted by statistical refinements and the surge of India and China as trading giants, stand against a long-run historical trend.

Some analysts have distinguished three groups of populations with regards to the dynamics of poverty and poverty transition. The first is the non-poor, made-up of those who remain above the poverty line – from the super-rich to those who merely get by, and who, short of a societal dislocation, are generally secure. The second group is the transitorily poor, fluctuating between occasional poverty and non-poverty and who are relatively vulnerable. Finally, the most vulnerable are the chronically poor, including those who are permanently poor, and those usually poor. "Chronic" poverty here refers to the poorest of the poor: people who are in extreme, persistent and often inherited poverty. These three categories correspond to levels of vulnerability regarding food and health security (Nef and Vanderkop, 1989: 2). Pauperization is a process by which people who are transitorily deprived fluctuate in and out of poverty, experience severe downturns, and always face the risk of falling into chronic squalor.

Estimates for the early 2000s put the global number for the permanently and endemically poor between a low figure of 298.3 million and a high one of 421.7 million; a range between 24 and 34 percent of the world population. Although poverty and wealth are often seen at opposite ends, the dynamics of wealth and poverty generation are more complex than a simple linear relation. Poverty in terms of the quantum and intensity of deprivation can move at a different rate and direction to those of income generation. Although under conditions of economic deterioration the absolute and relative numbers of those unable to afford a basic "basket" of goods and services can, predictably, increase, absolute and relative poverty also expands under conditions of economic growth. For instance, during the recoveries of the mid- and late 1980s and the mid-1990s in North America, employment creation failed to keep pace with economic reactivation. This type of recovery without employment gains is also noticeable in Latin America, after the so-called lost decade. The deleterious impact of pauperization is felt harder by sectors already vulnerable (like women, the young, the elderly, minorities, the unemployed), as it is more strongly associated with existing income disparities and powerlessness than with composite levels of prosperity.

The average global per capita income in constant dollars by the end of the twentieth century was over US$5,000 per annum in constant purchasing parity dollars; this is 2.6 times that of 1950 (UNEP, 1999). In 2005, the GNP per capita had risen to $8,753. "The year 2004 was a milestone in the world economy, which grew 5.1 percent – the fastest in nearly three decades" (Jimenez, 2005: 1). However, world poverty has not been reduced, either proportionally or absolutely. The number of those below this threshold in 1993 was around 1.3 billion people; about a quarter of the Earth's population. The ratio has remained roughly the same.

Despite rapid economic growth, income disparities are increasing across regions and within countries. As world output doubled during the last two decades, income inequality worsened within 33 countries.

With one in every five people in the world surviving on less than $1 a day, poverty continues to afflict significant parts of the world population. (Ibid.: 3)

Since 1961 the lesser-developed economies of Africa, the Americas, Asia and the Middle East have gone through at least four United Nations-sponsored "development decades." However, for most people not much development, let alone catching up, has taken place. From a long-run historical perspective, it appears that periods of generalized prosperity are indeed abnormal and that economic crises, volatility and uncertainty are more the rule than the exception. This has a most immediate effect in the political economy of world poverty: by and large the process of accumulation with deprivation creates conditions that weaken democracy. In turn, lack of democracy contributes to policies that worsen poverty by increasing concentration of wealth and power, by skewing distribution in fewer hands.

The largest absolute number of the world's poor (almost 1 billion) inhabits the Asia-Pacific region, a densely populated area. Yet, the highest proportion and the fastest growing rate of poverty have occurred in sub-Saharan Africa, where at the turn of the twenty-first century half the population was estimated to be poor. In Latin America, estimates made in the early 1990s put the figure at well above 100 million, and growing. In Eastern Europe and the former Soviet Union, a decade ago, the "new poor" had risen dramatically to 120 million people. Most significantly, in the industrialized countries of Europe, North America and the rest of the G7 nations and the OECD, during the same period, 80 million people remained below the poverty line (UNDP, 1997). In the US, the proportion of the population living under that line has fluctuated between 12.5 and 14 percent. Income distribution figures are quite revealing: "In 1979, the top 1% of the US population earned, on average, 33.1 times as much as the lowest 20%. In 2000, this multiplier had grown to 88.5" (Hogan, 2005: 1).

Globalization, maldistribution and poverty

As suggested earlier, the relationship between globalization, development, poverty and politics is by no means a simple and uncontested one. Rather, it is pregnant with ideological implications. This is further complicated by the fact that the very concept of globalization has become an all encompassing, almost metaphysical idea-force representing both "progress" and Western-style development. Two basic schools of thought have produced diametrically opposite theses regarding this relationship. The debate continues about the merits and drawbacks of market-led globalization for the poor (Birdsall, 2002: 2). Opinions have relatively sharp demarcation lines.

> One side includes most mainstream economists, international finan-
> cial institutions, globalized financial managers, government elites
> (ministries of finance and central banks), and the development estab-
> lishment of experts and consultants. They generally support the
> proposition that globalization is not to be blamed for any increase in
> world poverty and inequality. On the contrary, they advance the the-
> sis that globalization has closed international inequalities and the
> poverty gap. They argue that it is the people least touched by global-
> ization, living in rural Africa and South Asia, who are the poorest in
> the world. (Ibid.)

The other side of the debate includes "most social activists, members of non-profit civil society groups who work on environmental issues, human rights and relief programs, most of the popular press, and many sensible, well-educated observers" (ibid.). For this group, there is clear and conclusive evidence that globalization benefits the rich – both coun-tries as well as rich people within rich and poor countries. There is also evidence that it has deleterious effects upon the bulk of the population in poor countries, and especially for the most vulnerable sectors in both the South and the North.

Scholarly backing for the pro-globalization thesis and the neo-liberal policies associated with it is provided, among others by the works of Sala-i-Martin (2001), Dollar and Kraay (2002) and especially Firebaugh and Goesling (2004). The core of their thesis centres on three assertions: (a) World-wide income inequality has been declining steadily since at least the mid-1970s; (b) This decline is due to a great extent to the indus-trial globalization of large once-extremely poor countries, like China and India; and (c) Poverty has been reduced as a consequence of such globalization. A report commissioned by the Norwegian government (Melchior et al., 2000) echoes in general terms the tone of the poverty-reduction hypothesis, and argues for the adequacy of using country differentials and purchase parities as a good way to adjust conventional measures of inequality.

On the other side of the debate, Milanovic (1999), the UNDP (2002), Weller and Hersh (2002), and Wade's critique of Firebaugh and Goesling (2004), challenge the above assertions. Broadly speaking, the "anti-globalization" counter-thesis centres upon three arguments: (a) Given the sheer size of India and China, overall GNP per capita increases there would affect the distribution *among countries*. Thus, changes in the Lorenz curve (measuring skewed income distribution) are more the result of the incidence of large populations in rapidly industrializing countries than improvements of real income disparities; (b) While income differentials among countries may have shown a small decline in recent times, this does not mean that *internal* income disparities within countries have decreased, nor that all people in these new emerging powers have equal incomes. For instance, income differentials have grown significantly within China, in all of Latin America, in the former socialist countries of Eastern Europe, as well as in North America. The proponents of the critical view argue that neo-liberals overvalue the decrease of international disparities among countries at the expense of in-country inequities; (c) Finally, as Nobel Laureate in Economics Amartya Sen has noted, globalism should not be judged by small changes in income inequality but by its ability to provide the poor with a fair share of growing planetary resources (Sen, 2002; *Atlas of Global Inequality*, 2005: 6).

Sen, as well as Birdsall (2002), suggests also a broader way of looking at the conundrum. In their opinion, even if there may be evidence that global inequality was not rising, the reduction is at most slight, and the historical legacy of distributional skewness so prolonged, high, and entrenched as to produce and sustain poverty. Thus, the record is at best not sufficiently unproblematic to assert that globalization has had a beneficial impact in reducing either maldistribution or, most importantly, poverty. The corollary is that without policies, regulatory and redistributive efforts, globalization – and market liberalization – are unlikely to have a direct positive impact in reducing poverty; especially its worst and chronic manifestations. From this perspective, globalization, even if in the best-case scenario not clearly being part of the problem, certainly is not part of the solution. This is especially the case since the rules of the game and public policies are stacked against the poor, and the powerful create and use them to benefit themselves (Birdsall, 2002: 6). It is those rules and the state and global formations that generate those policies that need to be changed to allow the poor to improve their lot.

The drivers of poverty and unequal distribution

Besides the above-mentioned rules of the game, there are numerous factors that drive and perpetuate poverty. According to those emphasizing the negative aspects of globalization, the most common factors are: low investment, low productivity, resource scarcity, large and short-term boom-and-bust cycles, indebtedness and conditionalities, deteriorating terms of trade and exchange, a hostile international environment, structural unemployment, environmental collapse, induced natural disasters, political instability, widespread violence, corruption, and especially lack of democracy. Stress on livelihoods comes from acute and often combined manifestations of these factors.

Since at least the World Depression of the 1930s, a most repeated and ubiquitous belief has been that economic security, measured by poverty-reduction, is attained through growth. However, short of a radical redistribution of wealth and income, the standard recipe for such growth has been enhancing the wealth of nations (capabilities) through increases of the marginal capital/output ratio. This means essentially domestic savings or foreign investment. In fact, development theory and specifically modernization theory were constructed on the inextricable and causal relationship between the expansion of per capita income and the improvement of sociopolitical conditions, eventually leading to democracy. Conventional wisdom also postulated that once the society's overall level of goods and services increased in relation to population, a form of automatic "trickle down" of benefits was bound to occur. Given their level of income, the rich in this equation have a built in greater propensity to save (or not to consume), than do the non-rich, whose income largely goes into need satisfaction. In theory, assuming that savings equals investment, this would eventually translate into more expansion, more jobs, more and better salaries, and improved social and overall living conditions. The latter, in turn, would reduce social antagonisms and bring about a stable democratic order.

This mode of reasoning took for granted that wealth and poverty were at opposite ends of the economic continuum, each being the reciprocal value of the other. Thus, if wealth, defined as per capita income increased, poverty would decrease accordingly. So would all its negative social and political consequences. The practical experience of the post-war boom appeared to corroborate this reasoning. The Marshall Plan and most of the induced development and international assistance schemes since 1947 would reflect this mode of thinking about development; a corollary of which was the oft-repeated "trickle-down" effect. Between the late 1940s and the late 1970s, most industrial economies experienced a prolonged period of prosperity and low unemployment and a consumption boom. North America, Europe, the South Pacific and parts of Asia led the way. The global demand for raw materials triggered a unique pattern of commodity-based expansion in the peripheral former colonial regions. In Latin America, the post-recession import-substitution industrialization (ISI), boosted by the war and reconstruction-driven export expansion, brought about rapid and sustained growth.

Yet, this allegedly normal scenario of prosperity proved to be the exception rather than the rule. It applied mostly to those countries with significant infrastructure, high urbanization and population density, a strong social safety network and relatively pluralist and open political systems. Since the 1970s, the ever more integrated Bretton Woods global economic order created in 1944 began moving from crisis to crisis, revealing the persistency of widespread poverty, increasing misdistribution and unstable growth. Even in the shorter interludes of economic expansion, poverty grew in scope and intensity. Development, globalization, and the bulk of the managerial, endogenous and external, bilateral and multilateral schemes to deal with poverty had proven not to be class, gender, or ethnically neutral. These inner contradictions were less apparent and acute when economic capabilities expanded. If capabilities grow to meet or surpass expectations, distributional conflicts between "haves" and "have-nots" will tend to decrease.

However, disguised under the Keynesian induced consumption boom, the benefits and the burdens had not been equally distributed among various socioeconomic groups. Nor did the development and globalization game occur on a level playing field. Rather, the rules of the game, as was the case with the Bretton Woods system, turned out to be biased in favour of some actors at the expense of others. Without continuous growth, a situation which is altogether unsustainable, conflict under the above circumstances is inevitable. This is where politics, as conflict management, and democracy, come in.

Poverty as an obstacle to democratic governance

One common claim, rooted in the end-of-history and globalization theses, has been that of a post-Cold War world of expanded democracy. The issue of democracy, or rather lack of democracy, is of fundamental importance for poverty reduction. Neither policies not the automaticity of hitherto invisible hands and trickle-down effects can create equity by themselves. Globalization, far from bringing universal democracy, has meant by and large a process of gradual (and at times sudden) disenfranchisement, corporatization and de-democratization: to paraphrase Michels, a kind of global "iron law of oligarchy" (Michels, 1915). As discussed earlier, many states have become increasingly dependent on external constituencies and conditionalities; thus undermining sovereignty and the responsibility of their governments to their constituencies, and to majority rule, as will be discussed in greater detail in Chapter 7.

Contingent labour, job and income insecurity, the persistence of regressive redistribution and taxation, and the decline of labour power and solidarity have brought about pauperization in areas of the world where labour absorption through outsourcing from abroad has not been possible. Meanwhile, globalization has at least temporarily benefited regions where the pool of labour is massive, cheap and relatively well-educated (such as in China and India). Not even Mexico, Central America, Central Asia and Eastern Europe are now viable alternatives. On the whole, outsourcing as a way to increase profits by slashing the cost of labour has largely resulted in a "race to the bottom" regarding wages and salaries. This downward trend in popular influence is inscribed in the new social contracts.

In the developed world, chiefly in the US, outside the protection of a still-robust but weakening welfare state and particularly the neo-imperialist role of the military industrial complex, blue and white-collar workers have been hit hard. In most semi-developed countries, after the illusion of *maquiladora*-like outsourcing employment faded away (as in the US Sunbelt, Mexico and Central America) job losses, unemployment and income declines have been the order of the day. In the last analysis, the lure of development and the benefits of globalization have remained illusive to a significant majority of the world population. Despite Gini index fluctuations and minor inequity reversals among nations, the net effect has so far been greater concentration of wealth among the very rich and deepening inequality throughout.

This is not to say that globalization and development will necessarily result in benefits for the few and great losses for the majority. What is apparent is that the current modalities and style of management of development, globalization and *intentional policies* contain dysfunctional characteristics. Once again, the issue of regulation, both national and international needs to be re-examined in the light of the costs and benefits – especially whose costs and whose benefits – of the above-mentioned form of globalism.

Again, the last two decades have been characterized by a bimodal pattern of crisis and recovery. Between the early 1980s and the 1990s the world economic system experienced a phase of decline and disarray. As said earlier, stagflation, unemployment, indebtedness and shrinking opportunities were traits commonly associated with a state of generalized crisis. This crisis has had profound de-democratizing effects. Although the world economy experienced a significant upturn after 2000, this failed to translate into a widening and especially deepening of democracy. The driving force of this recovery was decisively led by the expansion of two Asian giants: China and India, accounting between them for nearly 40 percent of the world population. Even during the preceding contraction, when the world economy was experiencing low and negative growth rates, both economies were outperforming all other countries, with annual growth rates of 10 percent for China and 5 percent for India. First sluggishly and then at a faster pace, the global GNP has steadily increased. In the developed world and particularly in the Americas and the new Eastern Europe, the financial speculative sector reaped the bulk of the benefits at the expense of labour and the more productive sectors. Irrespective of the rate of expansion, in both the sluggish and faster periods, accumulation of wealth has continued unabated and popular rule has not expanded accordingly (if at all) in the new global power-houses; or in the world at large. In the mid-1980s a new global oligarchic regime of economic management was in place, the hub of which was the World Trade Organization (WTO).

However, despite greater institutionalization, many of the features of crisis persist for most of humankind. Growth, prosperity, and the domestic and global economic order, appear to have worked to the advantage of those who control capital, production and political power. Economically, the world is utterly undemocratic and this has political implications for popular rule in both the international and domestic fronts. At any rate, one should bear in mind that the impact of expansion and recession does not affect an entire population in the same way. Rather, since inequalities are cumulative and economic vulnerability affects various sectors of the population differently, development and underdevelopment tend to be class, gender, age, ethnically, and regionally sensitive.

Poverty: cycles of expansion and contraction

The 1970–1990 recessive phase of the global economy exhibited two principal features. One was the slowing down of the rapid economic expansion of the post-war years, since the late 1940s. The other was an entrenched structural crisis. Since 1974 there have been four recessions. The first two, in 1974–1976 and 1980–1981, were a direct result of oil-price increases. During these years, rates of growth in personal income dropped sharply worldwide but remained on the positive side. The 1990–1992 and 1998–2000 recession, resulting from broader structural transformations in the industrial and post-industrial economies, were deeper, and much more severe than their predecessors. The 2008 crisis has to do more with the incompetence of greedy financial and energy sectors, combined with the bursting of the speculative bubble of the real estate market and its financial institutions in the US. Because of the global connectivity of all financial markets, the crisis has had, and continues to have, far reaching implications. Between 1990 and 1992, the average global growth rate in per capita income in fact not only slowed down but even became negative: an annual average of 1.1 decline of the GNP per capita for 1990–1992 (Brown, 1993). As the 2008 crisis has occurred in the midst of a contraction of the labour market, it is likely to have deeper and long-lasting implications, bringing about a combination of stagnation and inflation – and unemployment – the likes of which the world has not seen since the 1930s.

The decline in per capita rates of income growth in Africa and Latin America during worst years of the so-called "lost decade" (1991 and 1992) were, respectively, 0.9 and 0.8 percent. In Africa, per capita incomes were lower in 1992 than in 1971, and in Latin America they were worse than a decade earlier. In terms of the pace of deterioration, however, the once relatively affluent centrally planned economies of Eastern Europe were the most severely affected by the downward spiral. A 2003 report by the World Watch Institute noted that

> [t]he global economy has grown sevenfold since 1950. Meanwhile, the disparity in per capita gross domestic product between the 20 richest and 20 poorest nations more than doubled between 1960 and 1995. Of all high-income nations, the United States has the most unequal distribution of income, with over 30 percent of income in the hands of the richest 10 percent and only 1.8 percent going to the poorest 10 percent. (WWI, 2003: 88–89)

This distributional bias certainly has enormous implications for the kind of political process and public policies characteristic of the country. It also has an overwhelming impact upon client states and the increasingly unipolar global order.

All in all, aggregate figures fail to convey the disparate regional and intra-societal impacts of reduced incomes. For instance, the international Gini coefficient, used to measure income disparities in a range between 0 and 1, rose from 0.69 to 0.87 between 1960 and 1989, "an intolerable level that far exceeds anything seen in individual countries" (UNDP, 1992). Dramatic as they are, these numbers do not show the pre-existing and expanding enormous inequalities. Nor do they show the actual growth of poverty since, as mentioned earlier and contrary to widespread developmental mythology, such poverty is not just the reciprocal value of wealth, but dialectically intertwined with wealth creation.

The incidence of international indebtedness

A related major contributing factor to macroeconomic insecurity has been expanding and insurmountable indebtedness. In 1970, according to World Bank figures, the total external debt of all debtor nations was equivalent to 14 percent of their GNP and 142 percent of their annual export earnings. In 1987 these figures had climbed to 51.7 and 227.9 percent, respectively (IDRC, 1992). Debt crises directly affect employment, consumption and credit in the less affluent countries. In industrialized states, the exposure of lending institutions has led to uncertainty and severe internal dislocations. Financial institutions, attempting to reduce exposure, normally transfer the debt burden to the public sector through government-sponsored insurance schemes or simply pass on losses to their customers at home. Most of these meta-power transactions occur outside parliamentary and democratic controls, but set the rules of the political game and, above all, its outcome. Ultimately, the burden falls on the shoulders of salaried taxpayers, those who cannot take advantage of the shelters created to protect the business elites. Most countries have debt burdens (the bulk of them to foreign creditors) larger than their annual GNP, and many of them cannot generate enough export earnings to pay principal, interest, and maintain basic imports.

As a liquidity problem, the foreign-debt crisis in the periphery translates into equally burdensome indebtedness and growing vulnerability and exposure in the centre. This is a manifestation of mutual vulnerability. As credit tightens or as economic recession sets in, material production tends to decline. Bankruptcies of the most heavily indebted firms ensue, bringing about a chain reaction: more defaults, unemployment and shrinking consumer demand. This, in turn, feeds the spiralling productive downturn. The consequences are extreme concentration of income and wealth and economic decay. An overextended public sector is frequently singled out as the major cause of public indebtedness. Whereas irresponsible spending and misdirected use of public funds are probably a direct and manifest cause of indebtedness in most countries, its root causes vary considerably. For instance, in the case of the largest debtor country, the United States ($7.85 trillion, or $26,500 per capita) the huge government deficits (between $294 billion and $368 billion for FY 2005, and projected to be $482 billion in 2009) can be traced back to the combination of deep tax cuts for the corporate sector, extensive overspending in wars, arms races and huge military budgets (Samuel, 2005: 1). Such inherited encumbrances set significant constraints upon policies and choices. This latter combination, incidentally, drove the former Soviet Union into material bankruptcy in the late 1980s.

In other countries, increases in the cost of basic imports (such as oil), growing interest rates on borrowing, declines in the value of exports, sunk costs in existing projects, and government inefficiency, secrecy and corruption, played a major part. Likely the debt problem is a combination of all these. Yet the debt crisis is specifically the consequence of national revenues', especially exports', being unable to keep pace with increasing interest rates (IDRC, 1992) and imports. In a way, the debt crisis was created by high-interest-rate monetary policies in the developed countries – policies that were designed to fight the stagflation of the late 1970s and early 1980s (Sheppard, 1994).

Another side of the debt crisis was the use of credit policies by Western elites and their governments to turn the tables against the newly found "oil power" of the Organization of Petroleum Exporting Countries and the commodity cartels it inspired throughout the Third World. The West "won" the "credit wars" of the 1980s; credit resulting from recycled

petrodollars generated by the 1970s "oil crisis." The enormous profits
created by soaring prices between 1973 and 1980 had accumulated in the
hands of transnational corporations, the likes of Exxon, Texaco, Shell,
BP, and Standard Oil, and the ruling sectors in the oil-producing countries: Brunei, Indonesia, Iran, Kuwait, Libya, Mexico, Nigeria, Saudi
Arabia and Venezuela. Petrodollars were transformed into long-term
deposits in major Western banks, which in turn peddled them at low, yet
floating, interest rates. Third World political and economic elites in both
the oil- and the non-oil-producing nations were particularly enticed by
the availability of easy international credit. High indebtedness was the
consequence of expanded financial availability. When oil prices sharply
fell in 1981–1982, on the eve of the Iran–Iraq war, borrowers were sad-
dled with unmanageable debt burdens.

The inability to meet debt payments resulted from the double impact
of declining export values for primary commodities, including oil, and
higher interest rates. Credit restriction by means of high interest rates,
geared to fight inflation, was the trademark of a new monetarist policy
relentlessly pursued by the central banks in the major industrial nations.
This manoeuvre had tangible short-term financial and political benefits
for the ruling sectors in the West. It had, however, disastrous systemic
consequences. It further destabilized an already vulnerable periphery,
bringing about severe balance-of-payment deficits. The tight money
policies also wreaked havoc among middle and lower-income earners in
the centre. The credit squeeze sent a second shock wave against salaried
sectors barely recovering from the earlier impact of high energy prices
and stagflation. This economic onslaught facilitated the restructuring of
labour relations and the overall implicit Keynesian "social contract" in
place since the Depression and World War II.

The debt crisis was construed by Western elites and their associates
very much as the "oil crisis" of the 1970s was: as a pretext to increase
accumulation at an unprecedented scale. The crisis justified an economic "state of exception": belt-tightening for the majority of the
population, anti-labour and pro-business policies. The emergency was
used to rationalize the imposition of massive structural-adjustment
packages in both the North and the South, not to mention the former
East. What all this adds up to is the breaking down of labour's share
of the economic "pie," generalized unemployment, and a concomi-
tant process of transnational accumulation of capital. It has also
facilitated a major revamping and concentration of the global power
structure. The dismantling of the foundations of a yet unborn "new
international economic order," a more equitable trade regime based
on price stabilization for basic commodities for producing countries
enhanced the historical trend of deteriorating terms of trade extant in
traditional export economies (Todaro, 1989). The relationship among

terms of trade, debt, poverty and underdevelopment has been noted by analysts:

> The long term deterioration in terms of trade is deeply entangled in the debt situation in a process of mutual causation. A fall in the terms of trade dampens the growth of purchasing power of exports and increases the need to borrow for necessary imports, and a rise of debt puts downward pressures on export price and the terms of trade through devaluation and other measures of forced exports. (Singer and Sakar, 1992)

Poverty, unemployment and underemployment

It has been estimated that the effects of the above-mentioned terms of trade accounted for about 357 billion USD of the debt in less developed countries in the mid-1980s. By the end of that decade, it had risen to about 500 billion USD. "More than 70% of this increase can be explained by a deterioration of the terms of trade of LDCs" (Singer and Sakar, 1992). But this long-term and structurally conditioned tendency has in the long run also negatively affected ever increasing numbers of people elsewhere. Unstable commodity prices and unfavourable terms of trade in the lesser developed countries (LDCs) not only have created depressed living standards for the majorities there but, most importantly, also reduced the capacity to import. This has had a negative effect for manufactured exports in developed countries, resulting in loss of jobs and marginalization at both ends.

The transnationalization of production and the displacement of manufacturing to the semi periphery, on account of the comparative advantages brought about by depressed economic circumstances and the low-wage economy, results in import dependency in the North. This import dependency does not imply that developed countries become dependent on LDCs for the satisfaction of their consumption needs. Because most international trade takes place among transnational corporations, all that import dependency means is that First World conglomerates buy from their affiliates or from other transnationals relocated in peripheral territories. The bulk of the population at the centre, therefore, becomes dependent on imports coming from core firms domiciled in investor-friendly host countries. Via plant closures and job losses, such globalism reproduces depressed conditions in the centre similar to those in the periphery.

Manufacture evolves into a global *maquiladora*: off-shoring undertakings, operating in economies of scale and integrating its finances and distribution through major transnational firms and franchises. Abundant and, above all, cheap labour and pro-business biases on the part of host governments and their supporting alliances are fundamental conditions for the new type of productive system. Because many peripheral areas have easy access to inexpensive raw materials and have unrepresentative governments willing to go out of their way to please foreign investors, a decline of employment and wages at the centre will not necessarily create incentives to invest or increase productivity. Nor would it increase "competitiveness." Because production, distribution and accumulation are now global, it would rather evolve into a situation of permanent unemployment, transforming the bulk of the blue-collar workers – the working class – into a non-working underclass. In the current global environment, production, distribution, consumption and accumulation are not constrained by the tight compartments of the nation-state, national legislation or responsible and representative governments. On the contrary, regulation has become anathema. Rather, deregulation becomes the elite's way to regulate labour by keeping wages down and profits high. The implicit social contract articulated in the system of labour relations and collective bargaining in the industrialized countries has become invalidated by transnational business. The new correlation of forces is one in which blue-collar workers have lost, and lost big, while agricultural workers have remained permanently outside this franchise. Persistent unemployment and underemployment have been increasing by leaps and bounds in Western and in the less "competitive" countries, as a proportion of total unemployment (OECD, 1991, 1992). This means endemic and inescapable poverty.

Poverty as an ingredient of the global economic regime

The present world economic order is, by far, more centralized, concentric, and institutionalized at the top than it has ever been. Its fundamental components are trade, finance, and the protection of the proprietary rights of international business. Rules, actors and mechanisms constitute a de facto functional and non-democratic system of global governance, with core elite interests in the centre and the periphery increasingly intertwined. As the Bush Sr. administration was ostensibly vetoing a global environmental regime at the 1992 Rio Summit, its representatives, in conjunction with their counterparts in the Group of 7, were giving the final touches to an international trade and financial regime. This mechanism to replace the General Agreement on Tariffs and Trade (GATT) would come into being a year later: the WTO.

The historical and structural circumstances of this new economic order are defined by three fundamental contextual parameters, the common denominators of which are global macroeconomic restructuring and de-democratization. One of these parameters was the end of the Cold War and the collapse of the socialist Second World, construed as a victory for capitalism. Another was the disintegration and further marginalization of the Third World. Last but not least was a process of economic globalization, at a scale and depth unprecedented in human history.

But harmony and predictability at the level of the transnational core do not necessarily translate into security at the base. Nor, in the last analysis, do they make the core itself more secure. As production, finance, and distribution in a rapidly globalizing economy become transnationalized, so does mass economic vulnerability. After the worldwide prosperity of the 1960s and the 1970s, and even during the prosperity bubbles of the 1990s and early 2000s, instability and exposure have become endemic. The effects of economic insecurity, manifested in poverty, unemployment and sheer uncertainty, are felt by the bulk of the population in both the centre and the periphery. After all, a system whose ethical, operational and political foundations are inequality and exploitation would have substantial difficulties in reducing the self-induced cycle of powerlessness and poverty it creates.

In sum, poverty poses a serious challenge to democracy. At the core, poverty excludes. It prevents poor individuals from satisfying their most basic needs, thus threatening their very existence and imbedding social and political marginalization. We cannot even start talking about democracy in the presence of such a basic denial of effectiveness. Still on the individual level, poverty excludes those affected by it from "living the lives they deem worth living" (Sen) and hence, it excludes them from their full exercise of their rights as citizens. The poor run the risk to become at best second-class citizens and at worst pariahs vis-à-vis the more affluent, as the latter tend to capture crucial resources and monopolize access and opportunities to collective goods and public institutions – most importantly to the state itself. If poverty affects one part of a population but not the other, those not affected by it tend to "privatize" the state and use it to advance their own ends. The same is true for the inter-state and global level. In a community of states, the richer ones have privileged access to the resources and institutions that should serve all communities alike. The "public good" ceases to be public and becomes a privatized commodity. The skewed decision-making and interest-laden actions of such institutions as the World Bank, the IMF or the UN Security Council illustrate this point. In most international organizations, the poor and the disenfranchised have only weak representation and the constituents of most of these organizations are made of members and representatives of what Joseph Stiglitz (2005) has termed "the financial world." Poor individuals and nations alike thus suffer a great risk of not having a say in the decisions and the making of rules that affect them, of remaining invisible and being silenced by those whose affluence allots them with more agency and, at times, the power of agenda-setting. Instead of being able to influence the frameworks and structures that affect their lives, the poor run the risk of having to play along in a game where they cannot win, or change the rules, other than by violence. Poverty, then, decreases agency and increases human vulnerability and insecurity – Sen's human capabilities – and it thus undermines the very foundation upon which democracy must rest: autonomy. If poor individuals, or entire nations, are not recognized as equal players, the game can never be fair and will never produce equitable results. In this basic sense poverty and inequality remain perpetual threats and obstacles to democracy. Without shared equity and equal access to opportunities, democracy becomes a mere façade; without democracy, the possibilities of social, educational and economic equity become largely illusory.

Chapter 7

Global Regimes, Governability and Democratization[3]

The late-twentieth-century phenomenon often referred to as globalization involved a drastic reshaping of the overall structure of world politics, from rigid bipolarity to diffuse unipolarism. The East–West divide was replaced by a hub-and-spokes configuration whose centre was the United States and the other Group of 7 nations and whose periphery was a heterogeneous conglomerate of underdeveloped Third World and former Second World nations. The conventional view of three worlds of development, with an East–West and a North–South axis, had been replaced by a single but highly stratified conglomerate. This uneven neo-imperial system, which President George H. W. Bush christened the "New World Order," (1991) meant a fundamental rearrangement of international regimes. It increased the ongoing erosion of national sovereignty, reducing the scope of the UN system and multilaterality in general, while enhancing the hegemonic role of the global financial institutions that define the rules of world politics, economics and culture skewed in favour of Western interests.

This shift had profound implications for the nature of interactions both among and within nation-states and for civil society itself. In this sense, it decidedly changed the context in which democratization and de-democratization would take place. A crucial effect of globalization upon the nation-state relates to the above-mentioned loss of sovereignty. This is the growing difficulty of upholding democracy as a means of asserting the popular will and majority rule in policy making. This chapter will attempt to trace the factors, processes and implications of the challenge posed to democracy by the so-called global age. In this sense, we will undertake the task of sketching a series of conjectural explanations regarding the effects of global regimes and neo-liberal reforms on the emergence, development and consolidation of "governable" and limited democracies. We will also examine the extent to which such governability relates to democratization, or lack of it.

What is globalization?

Historically, globalism, which represents the end stage of a process of globalization, is by no means without precedent. Leaving aside the Hellenistic project of Alexander of Macedonia (336–323 BC) and *Pax Romana* (27 BC to 180 AD), since the emergence of the modern-world system in the seventeenth century we have been living, one way or another, in a "shrinking" and increasingly integrated world. Portugal, Spain, the Netherlands and England developed colonial empires of undeniable global reach, in which "the sun never set." So did Ghengis Khan, the Ottomans and the Han Dynasty, to name just a few. However, what makes the present conjuncture special is the intensity and the peculiar character of its driving forces. Its structure and dynamics are rooted in changing and interconnected circumstances that could be grouped into three main categories. One such circumstance refers to the far-reaching changes brought about by expanding technology (Nef, Vanderkop and Wiseman, 1989). This specifically refers to the multiple and profound innovations that have occurred since the end of World War II, resulting in a reduction in time, space and cost of communications. Another set of circumstances refers to changes in the ideological-political matrix defining the cultural/ideological polarities in the system. In particular, we are talking about the sudden disappearance of the Marxism–Leninism of the Cold War and the emergence of the hegemonic discourse of neo-liberalism. The third cluster of circumstances has to do with changes in the economic fabric of the world order: the shift from essentially international transactions among countries and states to *transnational* transactions among firms.

Central among the factors that drive globalization is the rapid development of technology. In the past 50 years this development has been exponential, and it has affected the nature of the world system in two ways. One is the impact of technological innovation upon the instruments of war, both hard (weapons) and soft (organization and operations). The other is the dramatic improvement in the speed and reach of communications and transportation, accompanied by a significant reduction of their cost. Information, finance, goods and people have become more mobile than in any previous era of human history. The development of military and industrial technology since World War II has reduced the time and space boundaries of world politics.

What once were international relations, understood as "politics among nations," have progressively and unavoidably become a post-Westphalian form of global politics (Castells, 2000). In this context, domestic concerns have become so intertwined with "external" factors as to make the distinction between "national" and "global" merely semantic. Some authors even use the term "glocal" (Escobar, 1995) to refer to the intersection of the world with the community. The long-range effects of technological permeability on the territoriality of nation-states and upon the very idea of sovereignty have been far-reaching.

However, even more important than the technological changes just mentioned have been transformations in ideology. Religious conflict, central in the Protestant Reformation (1517–1648) and the Catholic Counter Reformation (1560–1648), evolved into dynastic rivalries during the late seventeenth and eighteenth centuries, just to mutate into national competition for markets and raw materials during the high noon of imperialism (1883–1914). As Hobson and later Lenin noted, the struggle for colonies where raw materials could be obtained, and surplus production and population could be dumped paved the way for planetary confrontations fuelled by aggressive nationalism; as was the case with World War I and II. The post-war period between 1945 and 1989 was defined by a clash of two cultures with universal claims: liberal capitalism and state socialism. The semantic foundations of this binary worldview conveyed an inescapable logic – alignment as either friend or foe. Its corollary was a rigid ideological bipolar standoff between two incompatible camps – the East and the West – that permeated national boundaries.

The emergence in 1955 of Third World nationalism "from below" in Bandung was a reaction against this sharp ideological schism. But nonalignment and attempts to separate North–South issues from East–West confrontations paradoxically increased a proclivity for clientelism, entangled alliances and ultimately facilitated the transnationalization of peripheral states (Nef, 1986). Foreign aid, the international transfer of technology, manpower training, planning and administration, as well as the all-pervasive presence of military assistance during the Cold War, all have had the effect of increasing the reliance on external constituencies. Peripheral elites were integrated into a global structure by means of manifold linkages of complex dependency – military, ideological, political, and economic (Nef, 1983). Conversely, the bulk of the population and the very idea of the "popular will" were marginalized and increasingly excluded from the political process. A patron–client structure was created by both power blocs, generating structural conditions that survived the demise of the USSR. Bilateral relations of subordination, irrespective of who occupied the centre, have had a tendency to persist. External constituencies, especially in the penetrated systems of the periphery, became an intrinsic part of the political alliances partaking in the internal public policy process; as was the case with conditionalities attached to economic reforms.

There have also been multilateral forms of transnationalization resulting from the development and expansion of international law and international organizations. Furthermore, the legacy of collective defence and collective security, not to mention a complex body of international contract law based on trade, further limited state autonomy. Elite nationalism was displaced by elite internationalism. Correspondingly, in an increasingly unipolar world, a global ideology with hegemonic pretensions gained predominance among the core sectors within the Group of 7 (now, with the inclusion of Russia, Group of 8) countries. This ideology is trilateralism (Sklar, 1980) – another name for neo-liberalism, as articulated by the Trilateral Commission and now the World Economic Forum (the Davos Forum). Substantively, the cultural software of this "New International" is distinctively conservative, elitist, and espouses a non-democratic pro-business stand. The trilateral view has wide appeal for the affluent, globally integrated, and modern elite sectors in what used to be called the Third and Second Worlds. Its intellectual antecedents lie partly in nineteenth-century Social Darwinism and partly in the messianic universalism of neo-classical economics.

The two central polarities that emerged after World War II among *national* actors – between North and South, and between East and West – have been replaced since 1989 by a single core-periphery axis of relations. The Western core, the First World, remained as it was: an interdependent and stratified bloc of dominant trading partners made of the advanced capitalist economies. But the other two worlds collapsed into a complex set of actors, including the "newly industrializing," "developing," "poor," and "transitional" societies of the former socialist camp. The core-periphery conflict persists as a form of interaction, but it occurs mainly not between nations but *between social sectors* within both developed and less-developed societies. It takes place between transnationally integrated and affluent elites and their related clienteles and a large and fragmented "mass" of subordinate sectors at the margins of the modern and integrated global society (Slaugther, 2004). This divide along lines of powerlessness and inequality gravitates against democracy.

The impacts of globalism

The sociopolitical consequences of this new order are quite visible. Reiterating an observation made in the previous chapter, poverty is spreading dramatically in the most prosperous age in human history and the problem is squarely not one of production but of distribution. While there were 157 billionaires and about 2 million millionaires in 1989, there were also 1.2 billion inhabitants of the planet living in absolute poverty, including 100 million living without shelter (Brown, 1993). A 1993 United Nations Development Program report noted that the wealthiest 20 percent of humanity received 82.7 percent of the world's income. The historical trend is even more revealing. While in 1960 the income differential between the better-off 20 percent of the world population and the bottom 20 percent was 30 to 1, in 1991 the distance had more than doubled to 61 to 1 (UNDP, 1992: 34; 1994: 35).

As indicated earlier, one and a-half decades ago, with less pronounced concentration of wealth as compared to today, the global elite controlled over two-thirds of world trade, nearly the entirety of credit, two-thirds of all domestic savings and a similar proportion of world investments. It also consumed nearly two-thirds of the planet's energy, and most of its metals, timber and food supplies. This skewed concentration of wealth, consumption and power has had the effect of shrinking the global "middle class," which has ended up losing its share of assets in a global scale (Robinson, 1994).

As mentioned, over one-half of the African population lives in a state of permanent destitution. Indeed, in the 1980–1990 decade "average per capita incomes fell by about three percent per year in Sub-Saharan Africa and by about 1.3 percent in the highly indebted countries" (IDRC, 1992). The cumulative figures of economic decline for the decade are 25 percent for Africans and 10 percent for Latin Americans. In addition, there is the drastic restructuring of the "transitional" Eastern European economies. The transition to capitalism in the formerly centrally planned economies of the East resulted first in declining productivity, dropping living standards and an extremely unequal distribution of income (UNDESP, 1993). Only in the beginning of the twenty-first century, income levels in Russia would go back up to pre-1990s levels, but then with dramatic increases in inequality. About one-half of the poor in the northern hemisphere now live in Eastern Europe and the territories of the former Soviet Union, and include new forms of destitution unknown less than two decades ago.

This dispossession is not just a Third World, or "transitional economy" phenomenon. In North America, where a radically regressive distribution of income has been underway since the 1970s, the proportion of the American population living below the poverty line has been steadily growing to reach about 12 to 15 percent. In some years, poverty has increased at annual rates of around 5 percent. The Gini coefficient measuring income inequality in the US has increased dramatically, from 0.39 in 1970 to 0.47 in 2008; one of the most skewed in the developed world. In Canada, between 1973 and 1997 the ratio in order of magnitude of income between rich and poor reportedly jumped from 31 to 1 to 314 to 1 (*Toronto Star*, 22 October 1998). The 2008 recession – induced by orthodox economic policies – has had a devastating effect upon low and medium-income earners and is accelerating social inequalities and income concentration.

The myth of the global society

There has never been a real global society, especially for the vast majorities of the poor and disenfranchised. What does exist is a social construction: an image of social interactions encapsulated in terms such as the "global village." The process of globalization expresses itself in an increased velocity of elite circulation and communications across national boundaries conveying and strengthening that image. Perceptions of the global village are grossly distorted by unique First World experiences. For most of the world population, despite claims of an emerging cosmopolitanism, the globalization of social life means hardly more than the virtual reality of canned media and the advertising of products. Thus, when we talk about the global village, we are referring to a relatively small portion of humanity: the affluent, the powerful and the informed, which really possess a transnational character. The bulk of the world's population, while affected by the planetary character of communications, production, distribution and accumulation, does not partake of the benefits of a new social regime. The negative consequences of transnationalization have a greater impact on the lives of most people than the promises of a unified and supportive global social order.

When asked whether globalization was really a euphemism for Americanization, Francis Fukuyama (1999) candidly replied:

I think that it is, and that's why some people do not like it. I think it has to be Americanization because, in some respects, America is the most advanced capitalist society in the world today, and so its institutions represent the logical development of market forces. Therefore, if market forces are what drive globalization, it is inevitable that Americanization will accompany globalization. (Ibid)

While internationalization has meant increased freedom of movement for capital and for those who possess it, labour mobility is not an intrinsic characteristic of the present system. For most workers and for the unemployed, globalization means hardly more than the old notion of an international division of labour: capital "shopping" for cheaper wages in various national markets and relocating there as a function of lower costs. It is much more likely for the affluent to go to the global South than for those in the periphery to visit the centre or even be allowed in, other than through the fortuitous routes of illegal immigration and exile. A myriad economic, political, legal, regulatory and security factors (as well as prejudices) militate against their doing so. Thus, the idea of a global social order – let alone a global civil society and citizenship – remains, at best, an ideological illusion.

There are, nevertheless a number of interconnected factors that constitute material global tendencies affecting the quality of social life in otherwise eminently national and sub-national settings. Globalization manifests itself in a number of interrelated trends: population growth, hyper-urbanization, the decline of communities, migration and refugee flows. What seems to be taking place all over the world is a transnationalization of elites side by side with a growing disintegration of national societies and local communities. The internationalization of the low-wage economy has increased the marginalization, polarization and social disintegration of the wage-earning and salaried sectors while, conversely, facilitating the formation of a new global power elite. Beside the manifold linkages provided by international networks, international integration is facilitated by the aforementioned developments in communications technology, global finance, trade and transportation.

On the other side of the equation there is the decimation of organized blue-collar labour; in most places the social base of people's power. This tendency follows a generalized pattern of de-industrialization of the centre and internationalization of a new form of transnationally-integrated manufacturing, without any of the externalities resulting from unions, collective bargaining or a protective veneer provided by labour legislation. Meanwhile, as the pressures by wealthy taxpayers for restructuring the administrative state, the educational establishments and the workplace multiply, white-collar, middle-class sectors are also declining. To a large extent, the processes of globalization and structural adjustment have brought about the demise of the middle class and the "mesocratic" values associated with it, namely the centrality of the family, nationalism and "civic duty."

Paraphrasing Antonio Gramsci, the challenge to democracy posed by globalization consists in that the old is dying and the new cannot be born. We are indeed far from Fukuyama's concept of a "global democracy," that would allow for the establishment of some kind of regulatory framework of global reach, involving both processes of production, as well as of distribution. As Habermas (2001) has explained, dismantling the Bretton Woods system of fixed exchange rates and barriers to international trade and finance did not require concerted action, but was driven by the need of advanced capitalist states to find new markets. The liberalization of international trade and finance thus occurred as a side effect of unilateral action taken by the major players. However, constructing a global, integrated system would require coordinated, positive action by all affected states and it would furthermore rely on the construction of a global citizenry in order to legitimize such a system. Yet despite the recent global financial crisis, which severely undermines the legitimacy of the current political system as it demonstrates how ineffective our current structures of global governance really are, it is highly questionable if it is even theoretically possible to construct global solidarity in a system based on competition. Indeed, the immediate response to the global recession caused by "lenders gone wild" was one where nationalism triumphed over global concerns. Instead of devising instruments to increase global governance, which would entail giving more power to international and regional institutions, such as the

United Nations and the EU, and pressing the few international institutions able to regulate international monetary flows, such as the Bank of International Settlements, to become more transparent and pro-active, most countries responded to the crisis by putting their national interests first. To the US, as well as to the EU member states, increasing regulation first and foremost means "taming globalization" instead of regulating and controlling it through an increased investment into transnational institutions.

Furthermore, it is also not clear if such a system of increased concentration of global political power would be desirable for the ruling elites within the developed world, given all the risks and uncertainties it would bring, including the risk of a "tyranny of the majority" on a global scale. At the beginning of the twenty-first century, we are thus confronted with a highly fragmented system, whose foremost characteristic, so far, has been one of dismantling institutional boundaries and liberating the forces of capital.

Increased vulnerability

The implications and causes of social breakdown are global, though their manifestations are quite specific to each local society. Acute disintegration of existing structures and the weakening of solidarity make smooth social adaptation to externally induced changes extremely difficult. The legacy of economic restructuring is an acute social decomposition with profusion of symptoms in the centre and the periphery: marginalization, addiction, alienation and crime. For those unable to acquire extraterritorialities, the quality of life tends to decline substantively: poverty and personal insecurity become endemic. This climate is hardly conducive to democracy.

As discussed earlier, the formal decision-making structures of the emerging global regime are a recognizable and seemingly decentralized "apolitical and technical" conglomerate of international institutions dating back to Bretton Woods (1944). They confer a multilateral aura to what are essentially bilateral and even unilateral arrangements. Such mechanisms encompass the General Agreement on Tariffs and Trade (GATT) and its subsequent mutation into the World Trade Organization (WTO), the IMF, the World Bank, the various regional banks, the Organization for Economic Cooperation and Development (OECD), the Group of 7, and the already established major trading blocs: the European Union (EU), the Association of South East Asian Nations (ASEAN), the North American Free Trade Agreement (NAFTA) and Mercosur.

The Multilateral Agreement on Investment (MAI) (Clarke, 1998), derailed by massive protests in 1998, was meant to be another complementary set of rules: a charter of rights for finance capital. This global structure finds its correlate in the internal mechanisms of macro-economic management within nation-states mentioned in previous chapters: ministries of finance, treasury boards and central banks; the majority of which are removed from basic democratic scrutiny. The formal linkage between global and domestic management is provided by international agreements and external conditionalities attached to fiscal, monetary and credit policies, especially those for debt management. In turn, this linkage is reinforced by common ideology and professional socialization on the part of national and international experts. Through these devices, world economic elites manage their interests and negotiate regulatory structures to serve their common interests and maximize profits. As Huntington (1993: 16) rather cynically put it:

> Decisions...that reflect the interest of the West are presented to the world as...the desire of the world community. The very phrase "the world community" has become the euphemistic collective noun (replacing the Free World) to give global legitimacy to actions reflecting the interest of the United States and other Western powers.... Through the IMF and other international economic institutions, the West promotes its economic interests and imposes on other nations the economic policies it thinks appropriate.

But harmony and predictability at the level of the transnational core do not necessarily translate into security at the base. As production, finance and distribution in a rapidly globalizing economy become transnationalized, so does economic- and political-vulnerability for the vast majorities of the people. After the worldwide prosperity of the 1960s and the 1970s, instability and exposure have become endemic and more and more people are starting to realize that the kind of "world community" that global capitalism can create is no real substitute for the real communities it constantly destroys. As globalization under the banner of shock doctrines and restructuring advances, the proportion of those in the "other world" increases. And so does the probability of human insecurity and mutual vulnerability. Driven by the irrationality of a system that promises prosperity and happiness yet delivers empty consumerism, people experience increased risk, uncertainty and alienation resulting from the destruction of community life, while striving to acquire possessions they are unable to pay for. Once fulfilled, this induced dream of "having" condemns consumers not only to struggle in order to meet their debt payments; it also brings them to live in monotonous suburban landscapes where urban encounters are made almost impossible and the neighborhood is substituted by the artificiality of the shopping mall.

Yet, despite the inherent contradictions of the brave new world created by unleashed market forces, highlighted by the free fall of the global recession sparked by a failing war and accelerated by the sub-prime landing and oil crises of 2008, there is still a great deal of optimistic triumphalism among those who espouse the current mode of globalization. From the perspective of its supporters, the inherent universal superiority of this project has been "demonstrated" by the collapse of Eastern Europe, the disintegration of African societies, and Latin America's "lost decade." Yet, the sharp schism between two worlds – "this" and "the other" – and the conflict between an expanding Western elite project and an increasingly fragile, unstable and besieged global and domestic periphery, offers a scenario of acute future confrontation.

The growing squalor of the many that makes possible the prosperity of the few has intrinsically destabilizing effects; it is a direct threat to everyone's security. The world's reciprocating and multiple environmental, economic, social, political and cultural dysfunctions point in the direction of a more severe emerging global crisis potentially much larger and deeper than the global meltdown of the 1930s. Its gravity is determined by a condition of mutual vulnerability: in a highly interdependent world, the strength and resilience of the total configuration is largely conditioned by its weakest links. The evidence gathered so far on the unfolding Asian, East European, and Latin American crises in the 1990s and the current implosion in the first decade of the twenty-first century indicates that the world's core nations, and in particular those sectors that lack the power and the resources to shelter themselves from unemployment, are very much at risk. This means most people.

Since social safety nets, already stressed by budget cuts and structural adjustment, are insufficient to accommodate the white and blue-collar workers who are falling by the wayside, this means that the overwhelming majority of the population is exposed. The "Fordist" social contract, based upon a system of mass production and consumption to attain sustained economic growth and widespread material advancement in highly developed economies, has finally broken down.

At the same time, the prevailing ideological software, with its fixation on automaticity, "natural" self-correction, and its glorification of greed precludes decisive intervention to prevent and reverse the tide. The anti-planning bias is an ideological cul-de-sac, one that privileges and serves the interests of those espousing the kind of short-term Social Darwinism that brought about the crisis in the first place. It also serves as an ideological justification for the ultimately self-destructive proclivities of a predatory and objectively unproductive speculative sector. The paradox is that there exist intelligence and planning mechanisms – a social "hardware" of sorts – at the national and international level for policy and program planning capable of overcoming the crisis. What does not seem to exist, and this is likely the Achilles heel of the present global order, is the conceptual "software" and political determination to take the bull by the horns. It seems that in their enthusiasm for tearing down the authoritarian enclaves of "really-existing-socialism" those who talked about freedom and the open society demolished the foundations of democratic planning and social equity. In so doing, as Soros has denounced, they brought about another kind of arrogant economic determinism: "really-existing-capitalism." It is against these tendencies that the anti-globalization movement from Seattle to Genoa, to the *Via Campesina*, has to be understood. The same goes for the reactions of the global elites challenged by the very possibilities of an emerging international civil society and popular power at home.

Between governance and governmentality

Michel Foucault coined the term "governmentality" (*Gouvernementalité*) to characterize a situation where governments increasingly control people instead of representing their interest. As said earlier, democracy is no gift from the elites. In every instance the popular classes had to wrestle it away from the owners of capital, wealth and privilege. As with the tension between liberal capitalism and unionism, which gave room to the emergence of democracy, today's neo-liberalism presents a challenge to democracy. The difference is that, under the presently ever more labour-unfriendly circumstances, the tide is flowing in favour of the business elite. In the more developed societies, supply side economics has transformed the implicit social contract, bringing an end to the welfare state and redistributive (as well as distributive) policies. Political neo-conservatism has gone hand in hand with neo-liberal economic policies, based upon deregulation, privatization and overall social exclusion. The impact of these developments on democratic processes was to denude bargaining and mobilization in favour of demobilization, de-unionization and de-industrialization. Concentration of capital, information and power, has shifted the nature of politics into an increasingly elitist, ritualistic and basically meaningless process, in which democracy is an empty shell. This phenomenon referred to earlier is what Duverger called, several decades ago, "democracy without people" or "Pluto-democracy," which will be further discussed in Chapter 8.

In the peripheral countries, the conditionalities of Structural Adjustment Policies (SAPs) attached to debt relief schemes brought to an end import substitution and induced developmental policies and transformed the states into transnationalized and weak receiver states (Nef, 1985), whose major function is debt collection and the management of fiscal bankruptcy. With limited and ever diminishing capabilities to accommodate popular demands, and a penetrated state responding to external constituencies, consensual forms of conflict management are increasingly problematic. Instead, short of stalemate, the decision-making process becomes either more repressive, or decidedly confrontational, as hitherto latent and institutionalized social conflict escalates.

A key issue here is governance – the ability to steer with legitimacy and attain results – in polarized societies. The capacity to govern involves solving conflict and moving ahead by means of peaceful, basically non-violent, compromises and equilibriums. This means critically learning about the issues to be solved and about the governmental structures established to address these problems. Governance presupposes some degree of basic equality: a level playing field. A distinction needs to be made here between this capacity for "good government" in an Aristotelian sense, and simple governability: the ability to impose a decision even by arbitrary rule. A potentially antidemocratic trend throughout the globe is the effort by socioeconomic elites and their institutional intellectuals to circumvent established democratic traditions and make politics "governable." The trend of creating "limited," or what Held calls "legal," democracies (Held, 1987: 243–253), responsive to market (that is elite) forces, constitutes an attempt to reduce participation and depoliticize politics. The challenge presented by the 1975 report, *The Crisis of Democracy* (Huntington et al., 1975), was how to reconcile democratic politics, built on the premise of equality, with market economics, centred precisely on the opposite: the idea of free and unrestricted private accumulation, leading to monopoly.

The neo-liberal solution has been to limit the role of the state and the minimal sphere of what is public, to facilitate private accumulation while reducing the scope and salience of popular participation, as well as strengthening enforcement – all in the name of an essentialized notion of freedom. Elite politics offers very few real distributive options, other than repression or the status quo, transforming the state's social safety and welfare functions into mere symbolism. Without the legitimizing trappings of welfare provision, a strong connection develops among neo-liberal policies, the above-discussed deepening of law-and-order concerns, and the possible emergence of police states. One disturbing contemporary trend is the emergence of a minimalist state in terms of social services combined with an all invasive state in terms of accumulation, enforcement and punitive security. In it, neo-liberalism and national security blend into a plutocratic and authoritarian solution.

The implementation of this project essentially involves redrafting the implicit social covenant among the various actors. Such covenant basically regulates the pattern of labour relations (and income distribution) in society. It also relates to the definition of which social actors, especially non-elite actors, are considered legitimate. The neo-liberal project is distinctively exclusionary and heavily biased in favour of business elites, foreign and domestic. It constitutes an act of popular surrender. The so-called leaner but meaner state resulting from structural-adjustment and debt-reduction policies has built-in limitations to prevent possible redistributive policies resulting from allegedly "irresponsible" majority demands and "over participation." The choices of citizenship are stripped of substance. Monetarist economic policies and those referred to as macroeconomic equilibrium are effectively taken away from public debate. They become enshrined in binding supranational treaties and rules, and in autonomous mechanisms charged with the management of these rules. Prime directives and overriding commands remain confined within "acceptable" limits by means of transnationalized regional trading agreements, central banking mechanisms and bureaucratic expertise. This elitist project to facilitate the "governability" of democracies reduces the governments' capacities for governance as an expression of sovereign national constituencies. It also produces an effective loss of citizenship.

A crucial ideological trait underpins the present allegedly "apolitical" model; one predicated under a revised "end of ideology" thesis (Bell, 1960). This is the pervasiveness of a hegemonic and homogenizing discourse, and "cultural software." Neo-conventional economic thinking has substantively displaced democratic politics: it is a type of scientific capitalism. Most important, however, are two intrinsic underlying traits. One is the entrenchment of inequality and the devaluation of labour as guiding principles of economic life. The other is the transfer of sovereignty from "the people" at the national and local level to a transnational global compact and to the security apparatus. This compact constitutes a network of reactionary coalitions (Moore, 1967: 433–454) without borders. This configuration links the various centres among themselves, with flows of capital, information and power; connecting also these central nodules with their semi-peripheries and peripheries across the world through a multiplicity of overlapping regimes. These regimes in fact constitute the current world order, at the centre of which are extremely dynamic commercial, financial, extractive and industrial cosmo-corporations. Important international non-governmental (or semi-governmental) organizations like the World Economic Forum (the Davos Group) or the Trilateral Commission provide a domain for discussion and policy generation. Such bureaucratic regulation (under the guise of de-regulation) confers upon the regulators – and the groups they represent – a form of relational control, or meta-power, to alter the nature of social interactions by setting and changing the rules of the game. This has been done largely behind close doors and with little debate and scrutiny.

In the last analysis, practices like those described here create a situation in which the only possible outcome is the creation or maintenance of an inequitable socioeconomic status quo. Attempts to resist the "inevitability" of this regressive order expressed through a "shock doctrine" (Klein, 2007) are confronted with arguments along the lines of Margaret Thatcher's famous "there is no alternative (TINA) principle." Failure to perceive this persuasion as reality may bring in the seamy side of democracy: the management of silence by a highly concentrated media, and the application of "authorized" force and intimidation as an insurance policy against dissent. Critics and dissidents end up being labelled "subversives" and are subjected to numerous security measures. In the words of a perceptive analyst, "the neo-liberal policy package is inconsistent with democracy because an informed majority would reject it. The main reason it cannot win popular support is that it neither assures employment opportunities nor provides any other way to ensure that lower income groups can participate in economic growth" (Sheahan, 1987).

In fact, the economic policies charted under this economic doctrine have been best suited for authoritarian political regimes – such as Brazil under the generals (1964–1985), Pinochet's Chile (1973–1990), or some of the Asian "miracles" in Singapore, South Korea and Taiwan – than for any substantive kind of democracy. The juxtaposition of economic "freedom" with political repression is the essence of the formula known as authoritarian capitalism, which preceded the so-called democratic opening in Latin America. There is a definite solution of continuity between the authoritarian and the electoral phase of neo-liberalism in the latter region. As the national security regimes that forcefully altered the rules of the game made an orderly retreat into their barracks, restricted democracies with neo-liberal economic agendas emerged, with the encouragement of the US government. The most ostensible of these reform packages was the above-mentioned Washington Consensus of 1987, with its orthodox free-market prescriptions promoted by the International Monetary Fund (IMF), the World Bank and the US Treasury Department. A similar trend towards liberalization took place in most of the former socialist republics of Eastern Europe. Many of these emerging and re-emerging democracies are for all intents and purposes countries in a state of receivership, with restricted participation and a peculiar consociational arrangement: a pact of elites geared to preserving the status quo. The key role of this state is to secure macroeconomic equilibrium, private accumulation, privatization and deregulation. Above all, the prime function of this type of state is to act as a debt collector, transferring the payments of the national debt to transnational creditors. These states are also charged with the execution of the conditions attached to the negotiation of such debt.

However, receiver states are not circumscribed to the periphery of the Third and former Second Worlds. Nor is a large foreign debt one of their intrinsic characteristics. Western elites have been entrenching a similar political agenda in their own societies. Its manifestations have been Thatcherism, Reaganomics and the supply-side policies applied in Canada by Conservative Prime Minister Mulroney in the 1980s and continued by the Liberals and the Conservatives into the twenty-first century. Australia and New Zealand have also developed their own version of these policies. The latter have been rationalized on grounds of keeping inflation down, reducing the tax burden, or, more recently, the fiscal crisis of the state. Economic "restructuring" and new elitist social contracts are their programmatic expressions.

Removing the electorate and, broadly speaking, "the people" from crucial aspects of policymaking and making the state accountable to external supports and constituencies has reduced the scope and depth of citizenship. In most places this has happened without much resistance. With highly concentrated media outlets in the hands of the same economic groups benefited by the reforms, combined with the atomization of labour and control over expert opinion, protest and opposition have been kept at bay. A consequence of this has been passive alienation and apathy. In the more developed societies of Western Europe, North America and Oceania disillusionment with politics as usual has been an outcome of the effective loss of citizenship. Consumers are not citizens; nor are disenfranchised workers. This disillusionment has begun eroding the consensual foundations of the political system, and the pluralist structures of brokerage and representation, such as political parties and interests groups. In recent years, war has once again become both a diversion and a call to suspend criticism and rally around the government. Conservative administrations, like those of George W. Bush and its British, Canadian, and until recently (2007) Australian counterparts have used war as a major diversion from domestic concerns.

A similar, though even more acute crisis of representation has become manifest in the relatively less-developed societies of Latin America and the Caribbean. However, the long range consequences of the crisis may well be to de-legitimate the receiver state, its supporting reactionary coalitions, and the structural adjustment policies which define its *raison d'être*. With the crisis of brokerage and representation, new potentially democratic forces have emerged into the forefront. These forces are essentially the hundreds of grassroots social movements to rise as restrictive democracies imploded: landless peasants, unemployed workers, citizens' organizations, indigenous movements, environmentalists, women, youth and the like.

In turn, in the much poorer and less institutionalized societies of Africa, and parts of Asia and the Middle East, state failure has become an ever more present prospect. Even the very maintenance of "order as usual" has become unattainable. The hopes of development and democracy in post-independence Africa, even the most promising experiments of decades ago such as those in Ghana, Nigeria, Uganda, Kenya, Zambia and, above all, Zimbabwe and Tanzania's version of African socialism, are paralysed or have fallen apart. Pre-existing centrifugal tendencies rooted in the nineteenth-century colonial scramble for Africa played a significant part; but so did corruption, mismanagement or outright authoritarian rule. Foreign actors and the Cold War contributed to further destabilization. From the 1960s through the 1980s, the West and the Apartheid regime in South Africa performed a most destructive and destabilizing function. Simultaneously, Cuba with Soviet backing contributed to the turmoil, by counter balancing US, Western and South African influences, as with the independent movements and subsequent civil conflict in Angola and Mozambique. This "revolutionary solidarity" also resulted in propping up extremely authoritarian regimes, like that of Colonel Mengistu (1976–1991) in Ethiopia, or Robert Mugabe in Zimbabwe.

The Middle East is a region where democracy, even its merely formal manifestations, has failed to take root. Turkey's military modernizer, Mustafa Kemal Attaturk unleashed a republican and Westernizing revolution between 1923 and 1938. However, despite the fact that popular government was part of his movement's agenda, Kemalism was by far more successful in dismantling the old Caliphate, Europeanizing the society and introducing numerous secular Western-style political institutions, than in establishing stable and deeply rooted democracy, let alone a social revolution. For decades Turkey has remained a country gripped by praetorianism: its pro-Western and conservative military establishment intervenes from time to time to re-arrange the political scene as they see fit. Yet Kemalism has persisted as a potent model of modernization, nation and state-building for the entire region. It influenced in no small manner the various nationalist secular movements from the 1950s to the 1970s in Egypt, Syria, Iraq and Libya.

Traditional autocracies in Saudi Arabia, Kuwait and the United Arab Emirates have feared secular republicanism in its Egyptian Nasserite (1954–1970), Ba'aht Syrian (1963 to the present) and Iraqi (1968–2003) varieties, as well as in Gaddafi's Libya. National secularism with revolutionary and populist overtones has also been influential in the early stages of the Palestinian Fatah movement. Nevertheless, with the Iranian Revolution and the Soviet invasion of Afghanistan in 1979, religious fundamentalism, with Western encouragement, began to replace secularism as a source of pride, identity and ultimately resistance. Traditional and conservative Arab regimes have begun to foment their own fundamentalist version of Islam of the Sunni and Wahabi varieties to countervail both secularism and socialism, and the upsurge of Shiite Moslems. Even secular countries and movements in the Middle East and North Africa, like Lebanon, Syria, Tunisia, Algeria, Turkey, and the Palestinian

Liberation Organization have experienced serious challenges from increasingly religious forces. The civil conflict between Hamas and Fatah over control of the Palestinian territories in 2006–2007 is a case in point. It illustrates the acute polarization between secular and modernizing Arab nationalism, inspired by Nasserism, and more religious and sectarian forms of nationalism. The US, Israel and the Shiite government of Iran, not to mention Saudi Arabia, have taken advantage of these contradictions to divide and rule, extending their influence throughout the region by supporting various factions engaged in this bitter struggle.

The situation with the Arab nations throughout the Middle East, which emerged from the dismantling of the Ottoman Empire and the European Mandates following World War I, has persistently been problematic. A legacy of British and French colonialism and their artificial boundaries, regional and religious factionalism and traditional allegiances, compounded by Western interests in oil, a persistent Palestinian question, and superpower politics during the Cold War, have created an explosive mixture. The consequences have been a continuous state of war, both international (e.g. Arab–Israeli and Iran–Iraq) and civil strife combined with terrorism. The contextual circumstances have been less than salutary for effective governability, let alone democracy. In the entire region, only one or at most two countries exhibit democratic traits: Israel and Lebanon – though the latter has been at the verge of bloody disintegration since the 1980s. The Iranian Revolution that toppled the largely secular pro-American and tyrannical regime of Shah Mohamed Reza Pahlevi (1954–1979) was indeed republican and popular, but it fell short of creating a democratic order. A theocratic state filled the vacuum in the form of an Islamic Republic. This regime was intent in wiping out less fundamentalist and left-leaning tendencies, such as the People's *Mujahedin* of Iran (PMOI) and other revolutionary groups. The same could be said of the Syrian and Iraqi version of Ba'aht socialism a decade earlier: despite their ideological appeal to "the people" democracy was circumvented in favour of authoritarianism. In sum, deficit democracy in the Middle East has complex historical and structural roots that go much deeper than foreign induced economic restructuring. Acute internal conflict, combined by foreign intervention – the USSR in Afghanistan in 1979 and the US in Iraq since 2003 – have exacerbated conditions inimical to popular rule.

If we examine all the different regions briefly discussed here, in all these cases, democratic processes have been compromised, or more precisely, derailed. Despite claims of a final stage of history characterized by global democracy, the outcome today is at best uncertain. If democracy was ever thought to mean a benchmark of political development in nation and state building, the contemporary situation appears to be one of de-development and turmoil. Most certainly, democracy – whether liberal or collectivist – cannot be imposed on the people by foreign intervention and the force of arms. This was something the Russians learned at high cost in Afghanistan and their US counterparts are beginning to realize – yet not quite learn – in their involvements in Afghanistan and Iraq.

International constraints to democracy and democratization

The 1970s late transitions to democracy in Southern Europe, as well as their subsequent consolidation, illustrate the crucial role that a favourable international milieu can have in this process. The transition in Portugal, following the death of fascist Prime Minister Oliveira Salazar in 1973, was significantly assisted by the EEC and the Council of Europe. This experience was not unprecedented. Rather, it built upon the experience of democratization with reconstruction in Western Europe, following the end of World War II. It also worked because a number of political parties on the left, including the Socialists and the Communists and other politically progressive and liberal groups in the country, possessed a wide array of international and regional connections.

This continental and global network, together with European encouragement, created a most favourable climate of quiet and positive engagement, as well as incentives for democratization. The Spanish and Greek processes were slightly longer and more convoluted, but equally unfolded in a very favourable international environment. In all these instances, the governments of the EC countries allowed significant leeway for internal forces to lead the process, using persuasion – heavy at times – while staying away from ostensible clandestine and security operations. In these transitions the antidemocratic forces walked away unscathed and still with sufficient time and latitude, and the interests of the classes and sectors they represented remained untouched. Yet they had to make concessions. Most important, in a post-Watergate period the US government remained in the back, supporting the process but without direct involvement or heavy-handiness. The transition was gradual, but in less than a decade democratic benchmarks had been achieved.

The Latin American situation, by contrast, was far more patchy, incomplete and haphazard. Although some European government and political forces (for instance the Social Democratic and Christian Democratic International) played a supportive role in providing forum for discussion and mediating the peace accords in Central America, the main player was the United States, especially the ultraconservative Reagan administration. Historically the US had a dismal record in fostering and building democracy by and for people shedding an authoritarian legacy.

From Cuba to the Philippines in the nineteenth century, to Panama, Nicaragua, Haiti, Guatemala, Iran, Cuba again, Congo, Indonesia, Vietnam, Laos, Cambodia, Ecuador, Brazil, the Dominican Republic, Argentina, Uruguay, Chile, Panama and Granada in the twentieth, US interventions – despite declared intent and rhetoric – have largely been inimical to democratization.

The predominant pattern in all these cases has been precisely, at one point or another, one of forceful de-democratization by imposition. This translated into interventions to prevent popular forces from gaining control of their countries. In this clearly counter-revolutionary role, Washington has had a direct involvement in toppling popular, potentially democratic, or fully democratic regimes, by either direct invasion with occupation, economic and political destabilization, or remotely-controlled coups d'état by military structures subservient to their interests.

However, US military occupation, followed by polity-forming efforts, did prove successful in Europe and Japan. In the cases of Italy and Germany, democratization, under the auspices of the Marshall Plan for European reconstruction was an essential component for a subsequent containment strategy to countervail and turn the tide against the Soviet Union. In these three cases internal and basically conservative political forces also performed a crucial role in shedding fascism and creating parliamentary forms of liberal democracy. Beyond these examples, including post-World War II Greece, Washington's role has not only been central in the demise of democratic possibilities, but one of continuous and often enthusiastic support for military dictators. The list is long: the Somoza dynasty, the Shah of Iran, the Greek Colonels, Mobutu in Congo, Tieu in Vietnam, Lon-Nol in Cambodia, Batista in Cuba, Zia in Pakistan, Suharto in Indonesia, Pinochet in Chile, Videla in Argentina and other authoritarian regimes throughout the world. Worse, most of the US intellectual establishment – both conservative and liberal – has remained oblivious of this fact. This record can only compare with that of the former Soviet Union.

Throughout the nineteenth and early twentieth century, there has been persistent US intervention in Central America and the Caribbean. The rationale has always been the Monroe Doctrine: the self-appointed and unilateral role of the US as a defender of the Hemisphere. The venue has ranged from gunboat and dollar diplomacy, to clandestine operations, to coups d'état. The justification has varied depending on the international conjuncture: fighting possible European intrusions, communist penetration, or terrorism. This pattern of intervention has been a major contributor to instability and to the inability for democracy to develop and set roots. In this historical context, the current failures in Iraq and Afghanistan constitute more the rule than the exception.

Other than brief periods in history, such as Franklin D. Roosevelt's Good Neighbor Policy (1934–1947) and Jimmy Carter's concern for human rights (1975–1979), the US government has persistently micromanaged and hijacked the democratization process, and not allowed internal forces to occupy central stage. The problem lies not only in the fact that "democracy-forming" US style is overridden by powerful interests from plutocrats at home and the military-industrial complex, but that the Madisonian polyarchical model is intrinsically flawed. It does not account for the multiple variations of political and cultural experiences of the alien civil societies it is supposed to serve. It is also intrinsically conservative and biased against significant social change. Historically, this is not a successful track record. Worse, if we look at the current political predicament of the Republic, it is not working well in the contemporary context. As an observer, writing about Washington's heavy reliance on unilateral coercive power, noted: "American superpower is primarily the power to destroy and, at the extreme, to create chaos but not necessarily to assure compliance with its will, even after it proclaimed military victory" (Caraley, 2004: ii).

Besides the presence of internal structural conditions gravitating against democratic development, there are external or global circumstances that impede effective democratization. These represent the specific manifestations of a world order. We will briefly discuss the nature of such order. The idea of world order presupposes the existence of regimes, or mechanisms of governance with structures of decision-making, rules and influence (Keohane and Nye, 1975; Hopkins and Puchala, 1978). Unlike institutions or "international organizations," which assumes the existence of differentiated, formally sanctioned norms and mechanisms of governance, regimes constitute the actually existing arrangements for handling particular clusters of issues: environmental, economic, social, political or cultural. Regimes are subsystems of the larger global system. Some are highly institutionalized, have clear boundaries and enjoy a notable degree of concentricity. Others are loose and without a recognizable authority structure. Regimes also vary considerably in terms of how effectively they manage the issues in their areas of concern.

Power and governance

One important empirical aspect of the analysis of regimes is ascertaining who governs, as real power structures in complex regimes are often neither clearly formalized nor transparent. Power, understood as the ability of one actor or cluster of actors to induce compliant behaviour in others (Dahl, 1970), is the very essence of the global system and its constituent regimes. So is powerlessness. But such ability and inability are essentially dynamic and multidimensional. For one thing, power entails a fluid and changing relationship between ends (what for) and means (with what) and is much more than the sum of the resource capabilities, or even possible resource commitments, of an actor or an alliance. In the last analysis, effective power can only be assessed in terms of outcomes vis-à-vis objectives pursued and resources deployed. In this sense, authority in the Weberian sense of legitimated power (Weber, 1947) requiring minimal amounts of coercion (or conversely, rewards) is an efficient and effective element in regime governance. The latter essentially involves the ability of both the government and the governed to manage conflict with limited use of violence or coercion.

Another important aspect in the analysis of regimes is to differentiate between power, as defined above, and relational control, or metapower (Baumgartner et al., 1977). The latter is the ability to affect the outcome of decisions, non-decisions, actions and inactions in a given regime by altering the regime's rules and protocols. Metapower can be associated with three fundamental concepts representing diverse intellectual traditions in political analysis. One is the idea of legitimation, based on tradition, charisma, or legal-rational calculation, as developed by Weber; the second is Gramsci's notion of hegemony (Cox, 1978); and the third is Crozier's (1964) observation regarding the relationship between power and uncertainty. Very few actors at any given time possess legitimacy, can articulate hegemonic discourses or have established control over the sources of uncertainty. More often than not, those who can affect the outcome of an interaction, both within specific functional or regional regimes and in the global system, are elite sectors inside the core, in alliance with their counterparts in the global south.

The global political regime

Since the end of World War II, the world system has been undergoing a rapid transition from the rigid bipolarism of the Cold War (1947–1989) to a form of highly stratified yet unipolar globalism, with US paramountcy. In it, micro politics coexists with conventional interstate relations, as well as with trade arrangements, and collective defence and security arrangements. The result of the restructuring has been greater volatility and an increased impact propensity, caused by the deregulation of trade and financial markets, which, in turn, was made possible by new technologies, especially in the area of communication and transportation. As production is becoming more global, it is putting increased pressure on the existing systems of regulation and distribution. A "run to the bottom" has already begun; and to stop it, governments would be confronted with the need to coordinate their actions and, sometimes, forsake their competitive advantages. Under the current political situation, that is the lack of global democratic system, this is highly unlikely.

The challenge to democracy that grows out of globalization and the externalization of networks of constituencies is thus probably the most severe of all challenges we have discussed so far. Since the end of the Bretton Woods system in the 1970s, market forces have conquered more and more ground and pressed for more and more deregulation. At the surface, this "great transition" at the global scale has created jobs and introduced mechanisms of global competition, which ultimately favour consumers – at least according to orthodox economic theorizing.

However, participation in this global economic system is restricted to only a partial "civil society." It has been highly skewed and the "big players" have been able not only to take disproportionate advantage of the new global opportunities. They have also made sure that the rules of the game remain under their control and continue to work in their interest. In a world of global markets, those with the biggest assets, the best access to information, the quickest means to process information, and the ability to make global moves – be it in the form of transferring money, making foreign direct investments, or simply being able to change their physical location to take advantage of new opportunities thousands of miles away – have benefited greatly from this new scenario. The rest of the world, including countries, regions, but also individuals and families, is stuck. Whereas the global jet set is able to make millions in the blink of an eye, the majority of the world has to suffer through the effects of this "casino capitalism" as they are unable to sell their houses after the "players" have taken a gamble on their mortgage securities. The global economy, in short, requires the freeing up of assets in order to follow the rhythm of global markets. To some extent, this has already happened. Jobs are as flexible as ever and job security is quickly becoming a thing of the past. Finance is already globalized, with several trillion dollars circulating the globe every day. Trade is also global. People, on the other side, are the least mobile, especially those without gold club memberships. To the advocates of globalism, people have thus become the sand in the machine of globalism and we are facing the absurd situation where people are asked to conform to the requirements of markets on an unprecedented scale for the sake of achieving increased market efficiency. Instead of a human-driven development, we are on a path to market-driven development that bears the great risk of dismantling our notions of place, having a "home" and living in a community and we have not yet found even a theoretical way out of the pervasive challenges to democracy everywhere.

Chapter 8

Democracy, Authoritarianism and De-democratization

Democracy, as we have argued in the preceding chapters, is not a good that can be easily achieved, inherited or even purchased. To the contrary, democracy is a constantly evolving social artefact: an idea posing new challenges and raising the bar of our expectations. At the same time that the democratic concept is evolving, real-life democratic practices are constantly being challenged within, outside, above and below the institutions of the state. This challenge occurs both at the macro and micro levels: in the international system, in communities, the workplace, and in face-to-face primary groups. How close we come to the ideal varies greatly and there certainly is no "golden path" to guarantee a workable and resilient democracy.

As suggested by the very limited participation in the classical Greek *polis* and the railings of American political leaders like Alexander Hamilton and James Madison in the *Federalist Papers*, many versions of democracy have fallen short of including all of the people in the political formula. Rather, they sought to incorporate only some of the body politic. In a more contemporary reinstatement of the same argument by Hayek, "unless the *demos* is constrained in its actions by general rules, there is no guarantee that its commands will be good or wise" (Held, 1987: 274). For "democracy is not an end in itself; rather it is a means, a 'utilitarian device' to help safeguard the highest political end: liberty" (ibid.: 249). Although the myth of government by the people and participation is now widely peddled as part of the pretended newly arrived age of "democratization for the world and democracy for all," the practice is far different from the discourse.

As mentioned in Chapter 6, fewer and fewer of the lower strata are part of the decision-making process, not only in the impoverished global South but in the North as well. If, as many American scholars and political leaders proclaim, US liberal democracy is the global model for democratization, a careful analysis of its actual functioning suggests severe contradictions (Grenson and Ginsberg, 2002). Until at least the 2008 presidential campaign and the Obama phenomenon in the USA, an ever shrinking pool of the non-elites has been participating in the formally democratic process, as voter turnout plummets and an ever shrinking proportion of registered voters even bother to go to the polls. Fraud, exclusion and manipulation are not rare occurrences, as illustrated by the 2000 US presidential election. This, combined with manifest episodes of blatant corruption, foments a public mood of alienation, apathy and cynicism, whose effect is to further the gap between politics and people, even under the mantra of change. Moreover, outside the electoral arena, other forms of participation are even thinner. Yet whenever elite-rule becomes more and more ingrained, the democratic ideal finds new strength even under adverse conditions, as protest movements and mass mobilizations challenge and weaken oligarchic rule. Resistance and defiance increase the chances of democratic change by developing ways and practices to crack the sanctuary of exclusion and authoritarianism.

Nonetheless, this chapter will focus upon three persistent threats to democracy that, in addition to systemic challenges addressed earlier on (expanding violence, erosion of citizenship, poverty and inequality, structural and ideological globalization, and loss of sovereignty) have been undermining popular rule. These developments are largely domestic, "from within" but occurring on a worldwide scale and having a global impact. One is the concentration of the power of the media and its negative effects upon democracy.[4] Another threat is the growing "securitization" of politics, resulting from the pervasiveness and expansion of security establishments, at the expense of people's rule. The third challenge is the crisis of democratic brokerage. The latter refers to the ever growing problematic intermediation and representation – both articulation and aggregation – between state and civil society provided by structures such as political parties, interest groups and social movements.

Media concentration and oligarchy

One of the central societal places where a persistent erosion of democratic quality is taking place is in the field of communication. The same way that "free and fair elections" is often perceived as a visible benchmark of democracy, so is the existence of a free, plural, and critical system of social communication. Its role is crucial in creating the flow of information necessary to maintain a minimal degree of interaction and in generating and providing a vehicle for public opinion. All things considered, the predominant characteristic of contemporary democracies is one of diminishing participation and declining opportunities for non-elite influence in the political process. This feature is particularly notable with reference to the media, going hand in hand with a dramatic increase of corporate concentration and influence. Michels' observation about the "iron law of oligarchy" at the turn of the twentieth century is starkly applicable as a descriptor of a globalized and transnationalized world, especially regarding communication. These developments towards greater oligarchy have taken place despite the massive diversification of users provided by the internet. Deconstruction of the citizen, atomization and trivialization of opposition and dissent, monopolistic and manipulative communication, as well as government by deceit, lead to popular alienation from politics.

Freedom House (2008), a conservative think tank, which has monitored press freedom since 1980 has presented a fairly pessimistic outlook:

> Press freedom declined on a global scale in 2007, with particularly worrisome trends evident in the former Soviet Union, Asia, and sub-Saharan Africa. This marked the sixth straight year of overall deterioration. Improvements in a small number of countries were overshadowed by a continued, relentless assault on independent news media by a wide range of actors, in both authoritarian states and countries with relatively open media environments. Unsurprisingly, many declines – such as those in Pakistan, Bangladesh, and Georgia – took place in the context of broader political crises that led to crackdowns on the media. A number of these crackdowns appeared to focus on newer forms of media, such as satellite television and internet-based news outlets, which are helping to provide more diverse and independent sources of information in otherwise restrictive media environments. (Karlekar, 2008)

The velocity of innovation in telecommunications technologies has increased at an exponential rate since their emergence in the last century, and it is still expanding at a much faster pace than actual demand. For instance, during the late 1970s and the 1980s international satellite communication, measured by traffic in half-voice circuits, increased in less developed countries by an average of 40 percent per year. In the developed countries, including the former Soviet Union, annual growth was nearly 48 percent (Pelton, 1981). A 2006 report by International Communication Union (ITU) "reveals that considerable progress has been made to bridge the digital divide;" in at least half of the 50 developing countries:

> teledensity has more than doubled in the majority of least developed countries since 2000 with some of them boosting connectivity by as much as 20 times, due to rapid growth in the deployment of mobile technologies. The race towards universal access has been mainly led by Small Island Developing States such as Cape Verde, Maldives and Samoa, as well as small-to-average sized countries such as Gambia, Lesotho, and Mauritania, some of which have achieved teledensities

of up to 44 lines per 100 inhabitants surpassing many developing countries. (ITU, 2006)

In the last two and a half decades quantitative and qualitative changes like those mentioned above have been unimaginable. These developments build on – and further globalize – the already vast and expanding realm of radio, telephone, television and communications in general. But communications technology, irrespective of its extensive coverage, and its potential for creating alternate channels of communication, is neither neutral nor freely available. It is a highly concentrated, vertically integrated business, run by a small oligopoly of conglomerates and companies with interlocking directorates. These mega-conglomerates are prone to mega-mergers, leading to more concentration. Neither the existence nor expansion of such technology is a clear sign of freedom of information. As the often friendly relationship between global internet providers and authoritarian regimes (e.g. China) suggests, profitability and censorship can go hand in hand. Moreover, Western think tanks tend to decry censorship as government control over private-sector media, not as the control of social communication by private monopolies.

US and worldwide media concentration

In the US case,

> [c]entralization within the top tier was substantially increased by the post-World War II rise of television and the national networking.... Pre-television news markets were local, even if heavily dependent on the higher tiers and a narrow set of sources for national and international news; the networks provide national and international news from three national sources, and television is now the principal source of news for the public. (Herman and Chomsky, 1988: 5)

Since the late 1990s and early 2000s, thanks to aggressive de-regulation by the Federal Communications Commission (FCC), eight media giants controlled most of the communication industry. In 2006, these corporations included Disney (Market value of $72.8 billions), AOL ($90.7b), Viacom ($53.8b), General Electric ($390.6 billion), News Corp ($56.7b), Yahoo ($40.1b), Microsoft ($ 306.8b), and Google ($154.6 billion).

Three decades ago, of the top 10 information and communication enterprises, which virtually controlled the technology and research and development (R&D) of global communications and informatics, two were American (IBM and AT&T), four Japanese (NTT, Matsushita, NEC, and Toshiba), one German (the state-owned *Deutsche Bundespost*), one

Dutch (Phillips), one British (British Telecom), and one French (France Telecom). Their volume of annual sales was more than 266 billion USD. Likewise, of the top 10 media enterprises that dominated the bulk of global newsprint and broadcasting, eight, including the top two, were American-owned, with annual sales of 24 billion USD. The remaining two were an Australian and a German conglomerate (Frederick, 1993).

By 2001, the top ten included: AOL Time-Warner (US, over $36 billion revenue), General Electric (US, $126 billion), Viacom (US, $20 billion), Walt Disney (US, $24 billion), Liberty Media (US, a spin off from AT&T, $42 billion), AT&T (US, $66 billion), News Corporation (US, Rupert Murdoch's, $11.6 billion), Bertelsmann (European, $16.5 billion), Vivendi Universal (US–European, $37.2 billion), and Sony (Japan, $53.8 billion). All these transnational companies were multisided operations (including television, radio, internet, books, sports and other), and formed a virtual communications cartel, with interlocking memberships. Their combined income was over $433 billion a year; a 60 percent increase in eight years. On the other hand, the number of international telecommunications firms has declined from some 50 by 1985, to the above-mentioned ten in 2001, to nine in 2006.

In individual countries and regions the same type of conglomeration and concentration is taking place, with hyper forms like those owned by Rupert Murdoch (News Corp/Fox), or until recently by Conrad Black/Hollinger, having truly multi-national control in the US, the UK, Canada, and Australia. American firms are at the centre of the international media operations, but powerful monopolies like Bertelsmann AG, Sony, the Lagardère Group, and John Fairfax Holdings have a significant market share. The above-mentioned tendency of interlocking boards of directors re-enforces integration and centralization at the top.

The political implications of such economic and technological concentration and integration are dramatic. Not only do these mega corporations control the manufacturing of ideology and information, but they effectively wield enormous political power. In places like Korea and more so Italy they not only make public opinion, but also make and unmake governments. The most blatant case is that of Silvio Berlusconi and his family news empire. His being a media mogul has constituted the foundation of his political machine, political party, and his two-decade career as Prime Minister.

Global and national deregulation and liberalization, under the spell of the prevailing economic orthodoxy have contributed to greater concentration. Deregulation has also favoured an almost perpetual state of takeovers and mergers, and to the cartel-like structure of their operations. Ownership concentration is closely interconnected with informational and power concentration, congruent with plutocratic forms of government. Though the economic compacts that control the media wield a significant amount of influence, and have identifiable right-wing political preferences, they do not make their conservative political preferences public. Instead, their more common strategy is by means of indirect control, rather than open censorship. This gives media conglomerates an aura of "freedom of the press" and the determination of what is newsworthy, referred to by some as the "management of silence." (E.g. what US third party candidates have had to say, such as Kucinich and Nader, generally goes unreported.) However, from time to time, such preferences become quite open and manifest, as in the case of Murdoch's, Black's or Berlusconi's unabashed support of a generally conservative and at times ultraconservative political agenda through outlets of global reach.

Over the last decades, a combination of political, economic, cultural and technological forces has "moved the international mass media industry towards more competition and less regulation on a global basis" (USDC, 1993). This has meant a disappearance of state-owned public information systems and their replacement with highly concentrated private international consortia that rely heavily on imported materials. This has been the case especially in Eastern Europe, Latin America and even Western Europe. While on the surface this development could appear to favour greater diversity and freedom of information, in practice it has meant a highly stratified global information order, in fact more oligarchic than the global economic regime discussed in previous chapters.

In 1986, only five countries – China, India, Japan, the (then) Soviet Union and the United States – imported less than 10 percent of their television programming. Today the number has dropped to three. Most of the others are heavy importers. The lower layers/larger users in the communications order are those countries whose cultural imports ranged from 10 percent to complete dependence on imports for their programming (Mowlana, 1986). In the years since these studies were conducted, the system has become even more stratified and porous to external forces regarding content and control. Only Japan and the United States remain at the top.

The development of the news and entertainment industry has meant an unprecedented explosion of cultural imports practically everywhere. This is most important when it comes to the construction of hegemonic discourses (and ideology for public consumption), especially when media expansion is mainly unidirectional. The centre of the dissemination is clearly the United States (specifically its socioeconomic, informational and political elite), where the fastest growing industry, in addition to financial services, is cultural products. It is important to notice that both are essentially intangibles, whose relevance is precisely in the ability of finance and the media to set the parameters of the aforementioned relational control of (or metapower over) images, words and figures.

In 1991, foreign sales accounted for 39 percent of US film and television revenue, a 30 percent increase in five years; a tendency even more pronounced in the first decade of the twenty-first century. Between 1987 and 1991, global net exports in this sector doubled: 7 billion USD, surpassing the previous benchmark of 3.5 billion USD. In addition, the export of American records, tapes, and other recordings (excluding software) moved from 286 million USD in 1989 to 419 million USD in 1991; an increase of 47 percent in two years. In 1998, it was estimated that the musical industry alone had grown to about 20 billion USD in annual sales, 70 percent of it coming from abroad (Hamelik, 1998). To this, one must add the ever-expanding computer-software market. By 2008, the market share in all these items, including software (which was hardly developed a decade ago) has nearly doubled.

Media programming, especially in radio and television, shows marked uniformity, in addition to unidirectionality. In general, the structural content of world media has maintained a fairly consistent pattern over time: on average of 20 percent of broadcasting time and space is dedicated to news and information; four percent goes to advertising; and more than half is devoted to entertainment (UNESCO, 1987). The importance of "soft" and indirect political socialization through entertainment and other repetitive rituals upon the popular (folk and common sense) culture is cardinal. It constitutes a crucial vector of public arousal and quiescence (Edelman, 1967: 172). To appreciate the phenomenal impact of externally produced entertainment, one must keep in mind that most countries are located in the lower tiers of the global information and communications order, where 40 to 60 percent of all television broadcasting time is filled with imported materials (US movies, soap operas, sitcoms). The effects of this homogenization and uniformity are particularly strong among the young, who are the main target audience of the entertainment industry.

Because of the production and dissemination of information technology flow from North to South, it is "quite possible that the external impulse transmitted is so powerful that all forms of national information converge towards a small number of common and hence universal types" (UNESCO, 1982). One such type is an emerging dual cultural pattern. On the one hand, there is an elite managerial culture, "both a set of attitudes, values and behaviour models, and a set of forms and models of organization" (UNESCO, 1982) centred on the market and the myth of achievement. Another related mode is a passive consumer culture, geared towards apathy, de-politicization and obedience (Milgram, 1963, 1974). Its mass ideological correlates are the culture of consumerism in its mainstream and pop versions. *Time Magazine, Newsweek, Reader's*

Digest, U.S. News and World Report, and *The Economist,* but more so CNN, Fox, and *Much Music,* are the conveyor belts in the transmission of a common neo-materialist and hedonistic worldview. Its foundations are inserted in the same possessive individualism and competitiveness of classical liberalism; yet, this time the message is geared to a global consumer audience conditioned by a massively marketed coating of pop culture. The elite doctrines underpinning this apparently random ideological veneer of mass appeal are a *mélange* of neo-liberal and neo-conservative discourses, neither of which is imbued with a democratic ethos. The consumer and the owner replace the citizen. In the new culture, "cyberpunk" and market economics blend in a complex amalgam, reproduced by a mantra of informational distortion and alienation.

However, as in the case of the globalization of society and the illusion of the global village, the communications revolution is equally a hyperbole: there is a phenomenal gap between a minority accessing the technology and a majority at the receiving end experiencing "digital inequity" and above all socioeconomic and political inequity. Those who control the political effects of the technology constitute an even smaller elite. According to a 1992 report by the International Telecommunication Union, when the world population was 5.7 billion, there were about 1 billion telephones in the world. Yet, only 15 percent of the inhabitants of the planet had access to over 70 percent of the main global lines. At the same time, 50 percent of the people of the world reportedly had never used a telephone. This exclusionary divide has become even more extreme in the present century, despite growing availability. "Lower income countries (where 55 percent of the population lives) have access to less than 5 percent of the telephone lines. While the high-income countries possess 50 telephone lines for every 100 inhabitants, many low income countries have less than one telephone line for 100 inhabitants" (Hamelik, 1998).

Media concentration and growing homogeneity make "freedom of the press" an empty slogan. This is especially the case when the bulk of the media is not really free and independent, but as presented earlier, is controlled by oligopolies and oligarchies with a proclivity for advancing their hegemonic interests. Certainly, the actually-existing structure and function of the media, whose role is to advance a corporate agenda and manufacture consent (Herman and Chomsky, 1988), is in practice not a facilitator, but a hurdle for popular participatory democracy. Fragmentation and trivialization of dissent as well as disinformation, not debate and deliberation (the internet "revolution" notwithstanding) are common features of the current information and misinformation order.

One of the results of the concentration of media power is that the reach and accessibility to the political process in most contemporary governments has become distinctively plutocratic. Increasingly "the government" appears as something remote and unable to provide services to the public. Meanwhile more "imperial" decision-making and hints of autocratic rule and denial of basic constitutional rights have emerged as national security considerations are becoming paramount in the post-9/11 world. This world relies heavily not only on managing silence, but also on disinformation. We will briefly examine these challenges in the section below.

The dangers of "securitization"

Towards the end of Chapters 5 and 7 we made reference to a persistent and serious challenge for democracy. This is the growing importance of entrenched techno-bureaucracies, and especially the expanding power of the security and intelligence apparatus upon the quality of political life. This brings us to the thorny issue of national security and the state; something that precedes 9/11 and the rhetoric on the "war on terror." In his farewell address in January 17th 1961, former US General and Republican President Dwight D. Eisenhower warned: "In the councils of government, we must guard against the acquisition of unwarranted influence, whether sought or unsought, by the military-industrial complex. The potential for the disastrous rise of misplaced power exists and will persist" (Eisenhower, 1961, 2006).

In this speech he was recognizing a fact that had been a continuous feature in the expanding empires of France, England, Germany and Japan since the latter part of the nineteenth century. The concept refers to a triangular relationship and circulation among arms manufacturers, the military establishment and the government that supplies taxpayers' money to feed into this alliance. The profound influence of such alliances in two of the four above-mentioned countries undoubtedly had had a most negative effect upon democratic development and world peace. In the US case, C. Wright Mills' study of the power elite (Mills, 1956) and Seymour Melman's Pentagon capitalism (Melman, 1970) have provided a glance at the entangling linkages between politicians, bureaucrats, business, academia and the military, and their ability to circumvent democratic controls; creating a de facto parallel government and state.

During the Cold War, the arms race between the US and the USSR created conditions for powerful military conglomerates in both sides, exercising their influence domestically and on a global scale. The Cold War also created conditions of bipolar military and security clientelism and highly autonomous military and security bureaucracies across the globe. This autonomy of the military and security apparatus referred mainly to internal constituencies. These security structures in their Third

World manifestations, until the demise of the Soviet empire, remained penetrated by – and subservient to – both global hegemonic powers. Those who control the supply of hardware, training, and ideology (and doctrine) for the local security forces, not the national governments, have relational control over those forces. This development was, and continues to be, a persistent threat to democracy and political institutionalization. Former Dominican President Juan Bosch captured the essence of this danger in his *Pentagonism: a Substitute for Imperialism* (Bosch, 1967). For him,

> [t]he old imperialism – exploitation of raw materials and of colonies has been replaced by a new kind of imperialism: the ... mother country exploits her own people in order to insure the aims of an economy permanently geared to war. The people are exploited as a source of labour and of taxes, which in turn assure that men and war material will be wasted in an endless cycle which profits only the military-industrial-complex. (Ibid.)

Its heavy dependency on the war economy, in the context of the arms race, had the effect of bankrupting the Soviet economy as a whole, paving the road for the end of the USSR. This event had a significant impact in dismantling the centre-periphery linkages built between the then Communist superpower and its client regimes in Cuba, Eastern Europe, Africa, the Middle East and Asia. However, there was no symmetrical disengagement regarding the relationship between the US and its military satellites, although the end of the Cold War made these linkages less crucial in the exercise of metapower.

With the Cold War over, Trilateralism, and the theory of "complex interdependence" (a.k.a. regime theory), based upon the primacy of economic interactions (Keohane and Nye, 1975), displaced security networks as a prime vehicle for exercising international power. But this displacement was only partial, as economic clout and "soft" power did not replace them altogether. Rather, the two mechanisms coexisted, with security playing a backup role. Since the terrorist attacks of 2001, security considerations have once again become paramount in the US and among its closest allies and client regimes. The security bureaucracies and the military-industrial complex have acquired, once again, what President Eisenhower referred to as "unwarranted influence," all the way down to its own extra constitutional legal, judicial and penal system. This new context, under the ideology of the "war on terror" poses a potentially larger threat to democracy than the previous Cold War configuration. Beyond its defence of democracy discourse, the practice of counter-terrorism has created a dangerous retro-feeding system, inimical to civil liberties and popular rule.

The crisis of brokerage and representation

The challenges outlined so far – those related to globalization, inequality, the prevailing economic model and the dangers emerging from bureaucratization and praetorianism – are in a sense extrinsic to democratic governance. The problems of inadequate brokerage and representation are instead intrinsic to the nature of democracy, though by no means disconnected with media concentration and securitization. Government by the people means essentially that there is an identity between those who rule and the governed, whose will is supposed to shape authoritative decisions and actions. In a democracy it is also the governed that must provide feedback to those in office about the direction and effects of public policies.

Thus, the key element in a democracy, as well as its government in general, is the articulation and aggregation of interests in the "input" side of the political process. This is especially the case in political systems as modes of conflict-resolution based upon representation and consensus building, as discussed in Chapter 1. The main venues for such representation are agents such as interest groups and political parties. At times government institutions (as in the aforementioned case public bureaus and the security apparatus) influence the political process as interest groups do. At other times, especially when party and interest group brokerage fail, social movements can erupt into the political arena. Massive demonstrations and anomic protests can articulate demands and support (both positive and negative) from the civil society into the political process.

However, parties and interest groups remain the main "normal and customary" venues for societal expression in a democracy. In fact, it is impossible to talk about democracy nowadays without reference to rather specialized social groups that put together and present policy platforms and options, influence the government, and also develop practices to select leadership to contend for political office. In fact, there is not always a clear distinction between parties and interest groups, for influencing policy and putting incumbents in offices are just two sides of the same coin.

For Duverger, political parties and party systems, more than constitutions and the form of government, played a fundamental role in defining, strengthening or weakening a democracy. Most analysts concur in that democratic politics involves to a large extent interest groups and party politics, providing brokerage between people and government. For the sake of simplicity, we can distinguish two fundamental dimensions or perspectives to address political brokerage. (a) One of these is the micro perspective, concentrating on the nature – goals, structure, resources, modus operandi – of individual agents. (b) The other is more macro in intent, and focuses on the brokerage system as a whole. In it, specific brokers interplay among themselves, as well as with the larger civil society and the institutions of government, exercising influence on the policy process and determining who governs.

The Nature of brokers in a democracy

The impact of individual brokers on democracy is contingent upon the extent to which political agents – "parapolitical" organizations mediating between state and civil society – contribute to the establishment and maintenance of an open and inclusive political system. Agents transform specific interest and resources into programs, leaders and policy proposals, providing the public with coverage and accessibility to the policy process. Individual agents' brokerage manifests itself in several non-exclusive patterns.

(1) One pattern is groups or parties representing broader class or social interests and platforms. This often takes the form of the brokers advocating for conservative, liberal or radical agendas, along a loosely class-based continuum of right-centre-left, representing the upper, middle and blue-collar (popular) classes. Business associations, farmers' and rural groups, professional organizations, and labour unions, as well as parties representing these interests, are examples of class-based agents. (2) Another type of broker is that representing single issues, whether pragmatic or based on fundamental adherence to principle. These organizations tend to have a lifespan limited by the attainment of their issue-related goal and its salience. (3) A third pattern refers to organizations that represent persistent "clienteles," ethnic or territorial interests or grievances. (4) There are also personalized organizations clustered around the character of a leader, essentially based upon charismatic appeal. (5) Finally, and most important, there are brokers whose main goal is to function as machines to get people elected into office.

As politics becomes more bureaucratized and dependent upon massive publicity campaigns, with heavy marketing and mega expenditures, broader social interests, specific issues, and personality-based groups tend to move into the background. In their stead, political machines, many linked to patronage and sponsorship, become predominant. A net effect is to privilege experts and heavy financing – the means of politics – over substance. In the long run this implies goal displacement. Politics and candidates are commodities that must be sold to consumers; and power, and access to it, can equally be bought...and sold.

This logic and practice raises the issue of buying favours, conflicts of interest, and corruption. The type of brokerage discussed above has a devastating effect upon public probity and ultimately democracy, as the latter rests upon trust; something that has to be gained, not purchased. The fundamental practical and ethical question is how to differentiate between private and public interests while maintaining public trust. At present and in most of the world, this balance has hardly been achieved. A long-run impact of this crass type of politics is to devaluate the prestige of politicians and the public sphere in general, generating an anti-political attitude among the populace. The politics of anti-politics, in turn paves the way for authoritarian solutions.

But political machines are not the only type of broker with a potentially dysfunctional effect upon participatory democracy. Territorial, ethnic and charismatic representations pose a challenge too. In this case, the ethnic and territorial mode of articulation tends to fragment the political process, while often deepening existing divisions in civil society. Charismatic representation, in turn, tends to substitute Bonapartist-style leadership and messianism for political compromise. Brokers in a democracy, while representing the general divisions and cleavages extant in society, can also offer ample room for negotiation, accommodation and compromise. As the historical record suggests, charismatic leadership can rarely perform this task in a persistent way.

Democracy and the system of brokerage

While individual agents and brokers influence the democratic process in undeniable ways, the system of brokerage as a whole has a most decisive macro impact on democracy. We are referring here to the configuration, or structure, of brokerage and mediation between polity and society. One important dimension of this system is its polarity. This refers to the number and strength of the various actors engaged in brokerage. In this sense one could use terms like unipolarity, bipolarity and multipolarity, with their respective qualifiers.

Unipolar brokerage

Unipolarism here refers to the monopoly, de facto or induced, of one actor taking in the role as principal or exclusive conduit between polity and society. In this case, one party, organized interest, or a combination of the two controls the gateway to politics, becoming, for all intents and purposes an integral part of the state. Any situation in which, despite attempts at inclusivity or good intent, a dominant agent defines the domain of, and accessibility to, the system and (the very meaning of who are the people), is inimical to democracy. This has been historically the case with many revolutionary and national unity parties, including most traditional communist and populist movements. Though most revolutions in their insurrectional phase are inherently popular and democratic, the dynamics of acute conflict tends to generate greater concentration of power; as was the case with Castro, or Mao. This concentration, as Brinton suggested in his classical 1938 study, generally includes a terror phase, and above all a Thermidorian (conservative) reaction observable when authoritarian rule prevails (ibid.: 205–235).

In addition to the USSR, its former East European allies, China, North Korea, and Cuba, examples of this monopoly are Mexico's PRI (1917–1994), the various nationalist movements in the Middle East (the Arab Socialist Union in Egypt and the Ba'ath parties of Syria and Iraq), and Africa (ZANU in Zimbabwe, ZANU-PF in Zambia and TANU in Tanzania). Some of these, especially in the Middle East, became entrenched dictatorial devices for single party and/or authoritarian rule. After the demise of the USSR and the collapse of the Third International and the Soviet model of people's democracies, most East European countries evolved into multiparty and multi-broker systems, while many Central Asian nations regressed into local and dynastic autocracies. Others, as was the case in Tanzania and Zambia, mutated from single-party to multi-party rule; yet others, as in the case of Mexico, opened the gates to competitive elections.

Besides the two African cases mentioned above, an interesting example of transformation from non-authoritarian single party rule to a highly competitive system is the case of India.

> The 1989 general elections marked the beginning of a new era in the Indian national party system.... The Indian National Congress Party that once used to command formidable majorities in the ... lower house of the Indian national legislature, lost its hegemonic position in the party system. Although returning to office in 1991 to form a minority government, the party had clearly ceased to be the natural party of government in India. (Nikolenyi, 1998: 367–380)

Despite the fact that the Congress Party experienced a slight resurgence two decades later, it has not yet regained its once hegemonic position.

Bipolar brokerage

Bipolar brokerage refers to an essentially binary government and opposition configuration in which alternation of ruling clusters, or minority–majority coexistence, allows for bargaining and compromise. The most referred-to example is that of the United States, in which the bipolar mould has effectively become institutionalized as part of the formal political process to the virtual de facto exclusion of real or significant third alternatives. To some extent, Great Britain and its English-speaking former colonial offspring constructed upon the Westminster parliamentary model – Canada, Australia, New Zealand, and a number of West Indian countries – all based upon majority electoral systems with single member districts, also exhibit a largely bipolar structure of party brokerage. This involves constellations of interest groups connected with the dominant political parties. In all these cases, there is either Liberal–Conservative, or Labour–Conservative loose bipolarism, with other smaller third-party actors. Few if any forms of bipolar brokerage exhibit the highly structured and overwhelming Democratic–Republican bifurcation present in the American case. Nor do they possess the intricate and powerful clusters of lobbies that accompany the Washington model.

There are many other examples of political bipolarism. In the German case, the Social Democratic SPD and the more conservative Christian Democratic Union occupy centre stage. Both parties have client interest groups and organizations in their orbit. In Greece, the major historical divide is between Conservatives (New Democracy) and Socialists (PASOK); with clusters of related associational and other types of interests groups (e.g. industrialists and labour unions) operating on a centre-right versus a centre-left split. Even in the Greek, Spanish and Portuguese example, as is also the case with Britain's Liberal Democrats, Canada's Liberals and Conservatives and its "lesser" New Democrats and Parti Quebecois, there are still smaller parties of some significance. Meanwhile, in Germany, the left-leaning *Grünen* (Green Party) and the conservative and more regional Free Democrats in effect partake in coalition-forming and policy decisions.

A variation of bipolarity is found in a number of Latin American countries. One example is the social-democratic National Liberation versus the loose centre-right coalition known as Unity (*Unidad*) in Costa Rica, one of the region's most enduring democracies. Another example is the White (conservative) Red (liberal) split in Uruguayan politics since the beginning of the twentieth century until the victory of the left-wing Wide Front, third-party government of Tabaré Vásquez in 2004. There are also examples of contrived bipolarism. One is the traditional liberal–conservative split in Colombia, at times maintained under manipulated treaties securing parity and alternation. Another is Venezuela's "fixed point" agreement between the Democratic Action (ADECO) and the Christian Democratic (COPEI) parties (early 1960s to mid-1990s), until these two parties collapsed in the 1998 election, which brought populist Hugo Chávez to power. Since the gradual withdrawal of the Pinochet dictatorship in 1989, Chile has experienced a rather artificial transformation of its once vigorous multiparty system into an emasculated de facto two party system, based on a right–left split: the centre-left

Concertación and the rightist *Alianza*. The new system, designed by the dictatorship before stepping down, included a binomial, first-past-the-post electoral system geared to isolate and minimize the left (especially the Communists), while guaranteeing the preservation authoritarian enclaves and privileges to the right. Though the country has been governed by a centre-left coalition since 1990, policy decisions have been stalemated by the right to secure the continuity of the socioeconomic order moulded by the dictatorship.

Seen in historical and structural context, bipolar brokerage presents some undeniable association with democratic rule. However, this relationship is constrained by the extent to which the bipolar configuration reflects *real* and not purely mechanical political forces and options. In many of the cases mentioned here, bipolarism is an often manipulated, mere superstructural and meaningless feature behind which oligarchic interests are paramount. In this case, despite appearances, both poles represent basically the same elite interests. The central issue is not the number of brokers, or if voters are given a choice between one and the other. The issue is whether both poles represent basically the same class and socioeconomic project. In North America at least, the crisis of democracy has become a crisis of bipolarism. In it, different party labels end up representing basically the same cluster of interests (or "products"), in the final analysis structured around an entrenched power elite, economic, military and political.

Multipolarity, polarized pluralism and stalemate

Theoretically at least, the greater range of inclusiveness and representation is provided by the countervailing forces of multipolarity. But there is a big gap between theory and practice. The presence of a wide array of civil society constituents would suggest that a multi-broker configuration could allow for issue and multi-class coverage and accessibility in the input side of the political process. Nevertheless, in many cases the spectrum of opinion is closely connected to a narrow base, and often with operational and ideological rigidity of the individual brokers. What we are suggesting is that multipolarity often reproduces at the level of political agents underlying deep fractures on the society, with polarizing cleavages and little room for compromise.

Sartori (1976), reflecting on the case of Italy in the 1970s referred to these as polarized pluralism: a situation of perpetual zero-sum games leading to protracted stalemate. This situation, as we discussed in Chapter 1, has not been uncommon in pluralistic democracies experiencing acute social and economic stress, when capabilities are unable to keep pace with expectations, with precarious sovereignty and with

limited elbow room to manoeuvre. The resulting stalemate is a manifestation of lack of consensus and compromise, and any kind of centrist politics is often a feedback of extreme tendencies, not a sign of agreement or
moderation. The net effect of the politics of stalemate, as mentioned in
Chapter 1, is to weaken democracy generally paving the road for rebellions and repressive forms of conflict management.

Examples of this precarious form of democracy have been abundant
in the twentieth century. The German Weimar Republic (1919–1933), its
Spanish counterpart (1931–1939), Austria in the 1930s, France during
the Fourth Republic (1946–1958), Italy between the end of World War II
and the 1980s, Greece from 1949 to 1967, Australia and the United
Kingdom in the 1970s, as well as Chile in the years preceding the 1973
coup by General Pinochet, are instances of highly polarized and bitter
pluralism.

A number of these instances of what Sartori (1969) called "polarized
pluralism" ended in right-wing and fascist military takeovers, in most
cases abetted by a foreign power. Yet a few others have been able to pull
away from the brink. A rare example was Italy in the 1970s and 1980s in
which, despite left and right-wing terrorism and coup plotting, and even
secret armies, political meltdown did not take place. The fact remains
that as the tensions between and among capabilities and expectation,
elites and masses, and sovereignty and dependence grow, so does the fragility of democracy. For contrary to popular belief, democracies are the
result of delicate balances, the nature of which has to be nurtured and
consciously preserved and redrawn time and time again; not of homeostatic automaticity, or fail-safe mechanisms.

Besides subordination to foreign interests, a reactionary and concentrated media, and penetration of the security apparatus by extraneous
and undemocratic forces, the Achilles heel of democracy lies in a fundamental internal factor. This is the mode of articulation between politics and society performed by the system of brokerage. In the delicate
balance between support and opposition, capabilities and expectations,
elites and masses, is where democracy is challenged, negotiated and re-
invented every day. Its success and resilience does not depend on a fixed
formula or "magic" combination, and its conditions for survival operate
within a very limited range.

Conclusion: The Crisis of Democracy Re-visited

This exploration into what MacPherson (1966) termed "the real world of democracy" undertaken in the previous chapters suggests two possible generalizations. One is that democracy, especially substantive as opposed to merely showcase democracy, poses a challenge to the conservative nature of most socioeconomic regimes. This is the radical and revolutionary character of democracy. If democracy is not a fetish used to justify the status quo, the very equalitarian traits of "popular rule" would have a levelling effect on systems of socioeconomic inequity. In this sense, democracy as a social practice may contribute to the creation of a deliberative level playing field, chipping away at authoritarianism and arbitrary rule, leading to social and economic justice. Of course, the socioeconomic impact of democracy is dialectically conditioned by the multiplicity of circumstances we outlined in Chapter 1:

(a) One is the existence of an adequate economic surplus to be distributed on the margin, vis-à-vis the aggregate level of social expectations.
(b) Another is the historical and structural brokered pattern of mass–elite relations, permitting (or impeding) a sustained degree of accommodation and compromise between "haves" and "have-nots." Cultural factors such as an acquired proclivity for consensus and legitimation also play a role.
(c) Last, but not least, is the issue of sovereignty versus subordination. Distribution of surplus is possible to the extent that the ruling elites have some control over those resources that can be distributed. This sovereignty, in turn, re-enforces legitimacy, facilitating the consensual compliance of rules.

These conditions are indeed rare, and at any rate not persistent, in the real world. In practice, they constitute more the exception than the rule. For that reason, actually-existing, as opposed to limited and low-intensity democracy remains so improbable despite its alleged global "triumph." Most ruling elites see real, as opposed to fictional, popular and participatory democracy as a threat, more than a challenge. That is why the same forces that claim to possess a monopoly of the idiom, and try to impose their own truncated vision as a global panacea, have such a murky record of impeding people's rule. In this context, it is reasonable to expect that such democratic initiatives will be contested by these very same elites, and will likely fail to bloom.

The other and opposite generalization is that there are powerful un-democratizing challenges faced from within existing democratic practices. This trend points towards the paradox presented by the anti-popular and at times reactionary potentials of democracy. Particularly relevant in examining this "seamy side" of democracy are the effects of both neo-liberal and national security policies on democracy. In this case, democracy is not a challenge (unless seen from the perspective of authoritarian enforcers and profiteers); rather, democracy as a practice is challenged and smothered by the bureaucratic and class nature of the state and the socioeconomic regime it supports. In many developed societies, increasing deregulation and economic liberalization (which is nothing but regulation with a minus sign in front) combined with "securitization" have reduced majority rule to a simple electoral ritual, not only without equalizing effects, but with outright regressive distribution of wealth and power.

Under these auspices, a great deal of economic policymaking takes place outside the democratic process, hijacked by entrenched domestic and international interests. It becomes an exercise of relational control or metapower (Baumgartner et al., 1975: 417–440), with elites retaining the ability to alter the rules of the game, turning democratic practices into un-winnable "games" for most people. Short of revolt, and with the support of corporate media, the result is turning off the electorate and transforming citizens into apathetic subjects, with limited access to an otherwise plutocratic state.

Its counterpart in the so-called called developing world is the receiver state (Nef, 1994), whose very essence is serving the interests of a transnational constituency through the conditionalities attached to debt-service policies. In essence this has been the type of regime that flourished throughout Latin America following the transition from the bureaucratic authoritarian states of exceptions of the 1970s. These receiver states involved a mixture of limited, "low-intensity," democracy (Gills et al., 1993) and neo-liberal economic management, along the lines of the Washington Consensus we discussed in previous chapters. It was the unravelling of these pacts of elites that opened the floodgates to the popular mobilizations and "people's coups" (Vilas, 2004) started on the eve of the twenty-first century, bringing forward a new strain of populism.

National security has always been a harbinger of both deficit democracy and outright authoritarianism. The experience in South and South East Asia, Latin America, and the United States points unequivocally to the erosion and downsizing of popular rule and civil liberties extant in the militarization and securitization of politics. However, this authoritarian trend does not always go unchallenged. There are signs of a reviving democratic spirit whenever democracy reaches its nadir, as the broad mobilization and participation in the 2008 US presidential election demonstrates. The post-9/11 syndrome has become the West's version of the same restricted democracy model, with potential and actual deleterious effects; this time in a different and more convoluted context than that of the Cold War. The crisis of democracy needs to be re-examined, not in terms of subversion or excessive demands, but in the light of these challenges of and to popular rule.

Seen from the perspective of neo-conservatives and neo-liberals, the crisis of democracy, as we have discussed in earlier chapters, is undoubtedly a crisis of governability resulting from over-participation, raising the spectre of resistance. That is, majority rule and political democracy pose the threat of systemic overload, diminishing the ability of elites to rule, rendering them exposed and accountable and, above all, vulnerable. The prescription is also simple: substitute markets for politics and consumers for citizens; reduce and retrench participation to a minimum and make democracy essentially formal and contingent on electoral rituals. This requires political venality, "domestication of the citizen" and media concentration. From the standpoint of National Security "theologians," too much democracy is a nuisance limiting the state's ability to fight the enemies that define the very essence of the security establishment and the state itself, à la Carl Schmitt (1932, 1996). As Barach and Botwinick (1992: ix) observed more than a decade ago with reference to the United Sates:

> While wealth and power are increasingly concentrated in the upper classes and in the giant corporate oligarchies, the lower strata have suffered a depressed standard of living and a growing sense of powerlessness. The widening gap between the powerful few who rule and the alienated many who are ruled threatens the very existence of American democracy.

This could well describe the predicament of today, though the dysfunctional traits are even more severe. From our critical perspective, the crisis of democracy is rooted precisely on lack of participation and the absence of people from the political process. Its contemporary dimensions are unequivocally connected to the encroachment of the National Security state and the alienation of popular sovereignty to the plutocratic and oligarchic practices of unrestricted markets. From this point of view, the crisis can only be overcome by deepening democracy in all the other economic, social and cultural spheres of the regime, not just its politics. This deepening involves the democratization of civil society in its macro and micro-representations, from the market to the workplace, making the government more accountable and responsible, and engaging wider grassroots constituencies.

Looking back at the various themes explored in the previous chapters, we have been searching for the common roots and circumstances of the crisis of democracy. If one accepts the crisis as one of governability resulting from over-participation, it becomes apparent that there has been a purposeful deconstruction of the popular component of democracy and its replacement with Pluto-democracies, (Duverger, 1967). Our analysis also calls into question the thesis that there is no alternative to the prevailing liberal, free-market model of democracy that is being peddled as the last and highest stage of political-economic development. The root of the crisis, far from being over-participation on the "demand side" of the political process has remained basically on the "supply side." Taking a systemic and long-run perspective, it seems that the once heralded optimism related to democratization and re-democratization of the 1980s and 1990s needs to be re-examined in the light of eroding democracy, de-democratization, social exclusion and growing threats to civil liberties.

Is this democratic retrenchment a manifestation of a historical "pendulum," or a sign of dystopic and almost inevitable things to come? As we mentioned at the beginning of this exploration, this riddle is not easy to resolve. One thing is clear: democracy is not an object that once acquired remains resilient and unchangeable. Rather, it is a summation and multiplication – but also subtraction and division – of attributes requiring continuous practice and nurturing. In this "pedagogical" sense, it is something requiring the collective and constant learning by people engaged in the practice of citizenship. From this perspective, democracy is by its very nature an incomplete and unfolding project. It is not an end-product conditioned by a mythical end of history; and this is its greatest strength and hope. If new vistas on democracy are to be charted, there are numerous democratic practices that need to be critically and systematically explored and developed.

Accordingly, special attention needs to be devoted to social movements, past and present in opening participatory gates and in removing structures of inequity. As an observer noted, "radicals on the left do have another direction..., to the new social movements, such as... feminism, ecology, peace, or human rights" (Giddens, 1994: 3). These agents occupy the place of the historical proletariat. However, with the exception of the Greens, these movements are not proposing broadly ideological and "totalizing" images of the future (ibid.). The vast experience with social movements south of the Rio Grande needs to be closely examined; from the Zapatista assemblies in Chiapas and across Mexico, to the numerous grassroots organizations in Central America, to the landless peasants' movements in Brazil, Ecuador and Bolivia, to the largely non-violent "people's coups" in Argentina, Ecuador and Bolivia that toppled unpopular governments, to the emerging community movements in North America, including the immigrants mobilizations of 2005–2006 and the anti-globalization movement. There is also a need to study systematically the emergence and consolidation of numerous governments in the South with policies that question the prevailing development and security orthodoxy.

Despite the current trend of "undoing democracy" the above-mentioned new forms of popular rule might provide ways for the common people to retake control of their destiny through the practice of self-empowerment. At this stage, a fundamental tenet of this exploration is the need to re-affirm in the light of the preceding analysis that democracy is not a teleological "aesthetic" and static, one-size-fits-all architectural construct, but a living form of association. In this sense, it is a process where real people define and practice equity and freedom by themselves and for themselves. This is the very essence of human dignity.

Notes

1. Some of the ideas contained here, as well as in Chapters 7 and 8 are based upon our earlier work in Nef *Human Security and Mutual Vulnerability. The Global Political Economy of Development and Underdevelopment*, Second Edition. Ottawa: IDRC Books, 1999.
2. This chapter draws on our chapter on "Poverty and Sustainable Livelihoods," in O.P. Dwivedi, Renu Khator & Jorge Nef. *Managing Development in a Global Context*. Basingstoke, UK: Palgrave-Macmillan, 2007, pp. 44–72.
3. Our reflections on the theme were first presented in a sketchy form as "Globalization and the Crisis of Sovereignty, Legitimacy and Democracy," *Latin American Perspectives*, Issue 125, Vol. 29, No. 5, September 2002, pp. 59–69.
4. This section on media is an updated and revised treatment of cultural insecurity and media in the abovementioned *Human Security and Mutual Vulnerability*... (1999), pp. 93–95.

References

Abers, Rebbeca. 2000. *Inventing Local Democracy. Grassroots Politics in Brazil*. Boulder, CO: Lynne Rienner.

Almond, Gabriel and Sydney Verba. 1989. *The Civic Culture: Political Attitudes and Democracy in Five Nation*. Newbury Park, CA: Sage Publications.

Anderson, Benedict. 2006 [1991]. *Imagined Communities*, 3rd edn. New York: Verso.

Andrews, George Reid. 2004. *Afro-Latin America 1800–2000*. London: Oxford University Press.

Arato, Andrew and Jean Cohen. 1995. *Civil Society and Political Theory*. Cambridge: Cambridge University Press.

Arblaster, Anthony. 1987. *Democracy*. Minneapolis, MN: University of Minnesota Press.

Arendt, Hannah. 1970. *On Violence*. New York: Harvest Books.

_____. 1966. *The Origins of Totalitarianism*. New York: Harcourt Brace & World.

Aristotle. 1986. *The Politics*, translated by William Ellis, first published circa 335 BC. Buffalo, NY: Prometheus Books.

Avritzer, Leonardo. 2002. *Democracy and the Public Space in Latin America*. Princeton, NJ: Princeton University Press.

Bachrach, Peter and Aryeh Botwinick. 1992. *Power and Empowerment: A Radical Theory of Participatory Democracy*. Philadelphia, PA: Temple University Press.

Balibar, Etienne. 2004. *We, the People of Europe?: Reflections on Transnational Citizenship*. Princeton, NJ: Princeton University Press.

Barber, Benjamin. 1984. *Strong Democracy: Participative Politics for a New Age*. Berkeley, CA: University of California Press.

Barry, Brian. 1979. "Is Democracy Special?" in Laslett, Peter and James Fishkin, eds. *Philosophy, Politics, and Society*. Oxford: Blackwell.

Bartlett, John. 1919. *Familiar Quotations a Collection of Passages, Phrases, and Proverbs Traced to Their Sources in Ancient and Modern Literature*. Boston, MA: Little, Brown and Company.

Baumgartner, T., Burns, T. R. and DeVille, P. 1977. "Reproduction and Transformation of Dependency Relationships in the International System. A Dialectical Systems Perspective," in *Proceedings of the Annual North American Meeting of the Society for General Systems Research*: 129–136.

Beiner, Ronald, ed. 1995. *Theorizing Citizenship*. Albany, NY: SUNY Press.

Bell, Daniel. 1960. *The End of Ideology: On the Exhaustion of Political Ideas in the Fifties*. Glencoe III: Free Press.

Benhabib, Seyla. 1996. *Democracy and Difference: Contesting the Boundaries of the Political*. Princeton, NJ: Princeton University Press.

Birdsall, Nancy. 2002. "Asymmetric Globalization: Global Markets Require Good Global Politics," The Carter Center, Development Cooperation Forum Conference on Human Security and the Future of Development Cooperation, Center for Global Development, *Working Paper* No. 12 (October): 2.

Birdsall, Nancy and Richard H. Sabot, eds. 1996. *Opportunity Foregone. Education in Brazil.* Washington: Inter-American Development Bank.

Bobbio, Norberto. 1987. *The Future of Democracy.* Minneapolis, MN: University of Minnesota Press.

Bosch, Juan. 1968. *Pentagonism. Substitute for Imperialism.* New York: Grove Press.

Bossuet, Jacques-Benigne. 1987 [1709]. "Politics Derived from the Words of Holy Scripture," in *The Old Regime and the French Revolution*, Keith Michael Baker Ed. Chicago, IL: The University of Chicago Press: 31–47.

Brinton, Crane. 1965. *The Anatomy of Revolution.* Revised and expanded edition. New York: Random House.

Brown, Lester. 1993. "A New Era Unfolds," in *State of the World 1993: A Worldwatch Institute Report on progress to wards a sustainable society*, Brown et al. (New Center for Global, Regional and International Studies (CGRIS). 2005. *UC Atlas of Global Inequality*. 2005. Santa Cruz, CA: University of California at Santa Cruz, York: WW Norton. *http://ucatlas. ucsc.edu/income/debate.html*)

Bunyan, Tony. 1993. "Jeux sans frontières: it's a lockout" *New Statesman and Society*, 6(277): 23–26.

Caraley, Demetrios. ed. 2004. *American Hegemony: Preventive War, Iraq and Imposing Democracy.* US: The Academy of Political Science.

Castells, Manuel. 2000. *End of Millennium.* New York: Wiley-Blackwell.

Castro, Juan E. de. 2002. *Mestizo Nations.* Tucson, AZ: The University of Arizona Press.

Chalmers, Douglas. 1972. "Developing in the Periphery: External Factors in Latin American Politics," in *Contemporary Inter-American Relations. A Reader in Theory and Issues*, Yale Ferguson, ed. Englewood Cliffs, NJ: Prentice-Hall: 11–35.

Chambers, R. and G. Conway. 1991. *Sustainable Rural Livelihoods: Practical Concepts for the 21st Century*, IDS Discussion Paper, No. 296, Brighton.

Chomsky, Noam. 1995. "Noam Chomsky on Anarchism, Marxism & Hope for the Future." Originally in *Red and Black Revolution* No. 2 (Ireland), Interview by Kevin Doyle. *http://flag.blackened.net/revolt/rbr/noamrbr2.html*

Chomsky, Noam and Edward Herman. 1979. *The Political Economy of Human Rights.* Montréal, PQ, Canada: Black Rose.

Corwin, Edward. 1925. "Constitution v. Constitutional Theory." *The American Political Science Review*, 19(2): 290–304.

Crenson, Matthew and Benjamin Ginsberg. 2002. *Downsizing Democracy. How America Sidelined Its Citizens and Privatized Its Public.* Baltimore: The Johns Hopkins University Press.

Crozier, Michel. 1964. *The Bureaucratic Phenomenon.* Chicago, IL: Chicago University Press.

Dahl, Robert. 1956. *A Preface to Democratic Theory.* Chicago IL: The University of Chicago.

Dahl, Robert. 1961. *Who Governs? Democracy and Power in an American City*. New Haven, CT: Yale University Press. Series: Yale studies in political science, 4.

_____. 1973. *Regimes and Oppositions*. New Haven, CT: Yale University Press.

_____. 1989. *Democracy and its Critics*. New Haven, CT: Yale University Press.

_____. 2003. *Modern Political Analysis*, 6th edn. Upper Saddle River, NJ: Prentice-Hall.

Diamond, Larry. 1999. *Developing Democracy: Toward Consolidation*. Baltimore: Johns Hopkins Press.

Diamond, Larry, Juan J. Linz and Seymor M. Lipset. 1995. *Politics in Developing Countries. Comparing Experiences with Democracy*. Boulder, CO: Lynne Rienner.

Dollar, David and Art Kraay. 2002. "Growth Is Good for the Poor." *Journal of Economic Growth*, 7(3): 195–225.

_____. 2002. "Spreading the Wealth." *Foreign Affairs*, 81(1).

Dubois, Laurent. 2006. *A Colony of Citizens: Revolution & Slave Emancipation in the French Caribbean, 1787–1804*. Chapel Hill, NC: The University of North Carolina Press.

Duchacek, Ivo. 1973. *Power Maps: Comparative Politics of Constitutions*. Santa Barbara, CA: ABC-Clio.

_____. (1973b). *Rights & Liberties in the World Today: Constitutional Promise & Reality*. Santa Barbara, CA: ABC-Clio.

Durkheim, Emile. 1997 [1893]. *The Division of Labor in Society*. New York: Free Press.

Duverger, Maurice. 1966. *The Idea of Politics: the Uses of Power in Society*. New York: Methuen.

_____. 1967. *La démocratie sans le peuple*. Paris: Editions du Seuil.

Dwivedi, O. P, Renu Khator and Jorge Nef. 2007. *Managing Development in a Global Context*. Basingstoke, England; New York: Palgrave Macmillan.

Easton, David. 1957. "An Approach to the Analysis of Political Systems." *World Politics*, 9(3): 383–400.

Edelman, Murray. 1967. *The Symbolic Uses of Politics*. Urbana and Chicago, IL: University of Illinois Press, Illini Books Edition, 1967.

Eisenhower, Dwight D. 17 January 1961. *Public Papers of the Presidents*, Dwight D. Eisenhower, Washington, DC: Office of the Federal Register (OFR) 1960: 1035–1040.

_____. 2006. *The Military-Industrial Complex: With an Introduction by Jesse Smith*. Portland, OR: Basementia Publications, 2006.

Escobar, Arturo and Sonia Alvarez. 1992. *The Making of Social Movements in Latin America*. Colorado: Westview Press.

Escobar, Arturo. 1995. *Encountering Development: The Making and Unmaking of the Third World*. Princeton, NJ: Princeton University Press.

Evans, Peter. 1995. *Embedded Autonomy*. Princeton, NJ: Princeton University Press.

_____, ed. 1996. *State-Society Synergy: Government and Social Capital in Development*. Berkeley, CA: University of California Press.

Fakete, L. 1993. "Guide to the Fascist Labyrinth." *New Statesman and Society,* 6(277): 23–26.

Fiorina, Morris and Theda Skocpol. 1999. *Civic Engagement in American Democracy.* Washington, DC: Brookings Institution Press.

Firebaugh, Glenn and Brian Goesling. 2004. "Accounting for the Recent Decline in Global Income Inequality." *American Journal of Sociology,* 110(2): 283–312.

Foucault, Michael. 1995. *Discipline and Punish.* New York: Random House.

_____. 2000. *Power.* New York: New Press.

Frank, Andre Gunder. 1966. *The Development of Underdevelopment.* Boston, MA: New England Free Press.

Fraser, Nancy. 1989. *Unruly Practices: Power, Discourse, and Gender in Contemporary Social Theory.* Minneapolis, MN: University of Minnesota Press.

_____. 1997. *Justice Interruptus.* New York: Routledge.

_____. 1998. "Heterosexism, Misrecognition and Capitalism: A response to Judith Butler." *New Left Review,* 228 (March/April): 140–149.

Freedom House. 2008. *Global Press Freedom 2008: A Year of Global Decline.* Washington DC: Freedom House. *http://www.freedomhouse.org/uploads/ fop08/FOTP2008Charts.doc*

Fukuyama, Francis. 1986. "The End of History?" *The National Interest,* 16: 6–18.

_____. 1989. *Have We Reached the End of History?* Santa Monica, CA: Rand Corp.

_____. 1992. *The End of History and the Last Man.* New York: Free Press; Toronto: Maxwell Macmillan Canada; New York: Maxwell Macmillan International.

Fukuyama, Francis and S. Marwah. 2000. "Comparing Asia and Latin America: Dimensions of Development." *Journal of Democracy,* 2(4): 80–94.

Galtung, Johan. 1980. *The True Worlds: A Transnational Perspective.* New York: Free Press.

Ganser, Daniele. 2005. *NATO's Secret Armies. Operation Gladio and Terrorism in Western Europe.* London: CASS.

Garrett, Geoffrey. 2004. "Globalization's Missing Middle." *Foreign Affairs,* 83(6): 44–96.

Gellner, Ernest. 1983. *Nations and Nationalism.* New York: Cornell University Press.

Giddens, Anthony. 1994. *Beyond Left and Right: The Future of Radical Politics.* Stanford, CA: Stanford University Press.

_____. 1998. *The Third Way. The Renewal of Social Democracy.* Cambridge, UK: Polity Press.

_____. 2000. *The Third Way and its Critics.* Cambridge: Polity Press.

Gills, Barry, Joel Rocamora, and Richard Wilson, eds. 1993. *Low Intensity Democracy. Political Power in the New World Order.* London: Pluto Press.

Habermas, Jürgen. 1973. *Theory and Practice,* translated by John Viertel. Boston, MA: Beacon Press.

_____. 1975. *Legitimation Crisis,* translated by Thomas McCarthy. Boston, MA: Beacon Press.

Habermas, Jürgen. (1984/89). *The Theory of Communicative Action*. Boston, MA: Beacon Press.

_____. 1998. *Between Facts and Norms*. Cambridge: MIT Press.

_____. 2001. *The Postnational Constellation*. London: Polity.

Hamelik, C. 1998. "Tecnologías digitales y desarrollo. D+C: Desarrollo y Cooperación." 3 (May–June): 9–14.

Harding, Sandra. 1993. *The Racial Economy of Science*. Bloomington, IN: Indiana University Press.

Hasenbalg, Carlos and Nelson do Valle Silva. 1988. *Estructura Social, Mobilidade e Raça*. Sao Paulo: Vertice e IUPERJ.

Hayek, Friedrich. 1960. *The Constitution of Liberty*, paperback edition 1978. Chicago, IL: University of Chicago Press.

_____. 1978. *Law, Legislation, and Liberty*, Vol. 2: Chicago, IL: University of Chicago Press: 108–109.

Held, David. 1987. *Models of Democracy*. Stanford, CA: Stanford University Press.

_____. 1996. *Models of Democracy*. Stanford, CA: Stanford University Press

_____. 2004. *Global Covenant: The Social Democratic Alternative to the Washington Consensus*. Cambridge: Polity Press.

Held, David, A. McGrew, D. Goldblatt and J. Perraton. 1999. *Global Transformations: Politics, Economics and Culture*. Stanford, CA: Stanford University Press.

_____. 2005. *The Global Transformations Reader: An Introduction to the Globalization Debate*, 2nd edn. New York: Polity.

Herman, Edward S. and Noam Chomsky. 1988. *Manufacturing Consent. The Political Economy of the Mass Media*. New York: Pantheon Books.

Hinich, Melvin and Michael Munger. 1997. *Analitycal Politics*. Cambridge, UK: Cambridge University Press.

Hirsch, Fred. 1977. *Social Limits to Growth*. Cambridge: Harvard University Press.

Hobbes, Thomas. 1996 [1651]. *Leviathan; or the Matter, Forme & Power of a Common-Wealth Ecclesiastical and Civil*, edited with an introduction by J. C. A. Gaskin. Oxford, NY: Oxford University Press.

Hobsbawn, Eric. 1992. *Nations and Nationalism since 1780: Programme, Myth, Reality*, 2nd edn. Cambridge: Cambridge University Press.

Hogan, Jenny. 2005. "Editorial" *New Scientist*, Print Edition, March 12: 1.

Hopkins, Raymond and Donald Puchala. 1978. *The Global Political Economy of Food*. Madison, WI: University of Wisconsin Press. *http://www.columbia.edu/~xs23/papers/GlobalIncomeInequality.htm*

Huntington, Samuel. 1968. *Political Order in Changing Societies*. New Haven, CT: Yale University Press.

_____. 1993. "The Clash of Civilizations?" *Foreign Affairs*, 72(3): 22–49.

_____. Michel Crozier and Joji Watanuki. 1975. *The Crisis of Democracy: Report on the Governability of Democracies to the Trilateral Commission*. New York: New York University Press.

Husbands, C. 1992. "The Other Face of 1992: The Extreme Right Explosion in Western Europe." *Parliamentary Affairs*, 49(9): 267–283.

International Development Research Centre (IDRC). 1992. *The Global Cash Crunch: An Examination of Debt and Development*, Ottawa: IDRC.

International Telecommunications Union (ITU). 2006. "World's Poorest Countries Increasingly Wired, UN Agency Reports." 14th September, 3:16:42 PM (W. Europe Daylight Time, UTC+02:00). *http://www.un.org/apps/news/story.asp?NewsID=19830&Cr=information&Cr1=technology*

Jaguaribe, Helio. 1968. *Economic & Political Development; a Theoretical Approach & a Brazilian Case Study*. Cambridge, MA: Harvard University Press.

Jimenez, Viviana. 2005. "World Economic Growth Fastest in Nearly Three Decades." *Eco Economic Indicators*, Earth Policy Institute.

Jongman, A. J. 1993. "Trends in International and Domestic Terrorism in Western Europe," in *Western Responses to Terrorism*, A. P. Schmid and R. D. Crelinsten, ed. London, UK: Frank Cass Publishers.

Karlekar, Karin Deutsch. 2008. *Press Freedom in 2007: A Year of Global Decline*, Washington DC: Freedom House. *http://www.freedomhouse.org/template.cfm?page=362*

Keohane, Robert and Joseph Nye. 1975. *Power and Interdependence: World Politics in Transition*. Boston, MA: Little, Brown & Co.

Kirkpatrick, Jeanne. 1982. *Dictatorships and Double Standards: Rationalism and Reason in Politics*. New York: Simon and Schuster.

Klein, Naomi. 2007. *The Shock Doctrine: the Rise of Disaster Capitalism*. Toronto: Random House.

Kohn, Hans. 2005 [1944]. *The Idea of Nationalism*. Edison: Transaction Publishers.

Laclau, Ernesto and Chantal Mouffe. 1985. *Hegemony and Socialist Strategy: Towards a Radical Democratic Politics*. London/New York: Verso.

Lasswell, Harold. 1958 [1936]. *Politics: Who Gets What, When, How.* Cleveland: World Pub. Co.

Lefebvre, Edwige Liliane. 2003. "Republicanism and Universalism: Factors of Inclusion and Exclusion in the French Concept of Citizenship." *Citizenship Studies*, 7(1): 15–36.

Lincoln, Abraham. 1861. *First Inaugural Address 1861*, en Williams Jennings Bryan, ed. *The World's Famous Quotations*, IX (America II), New York: Funk and Wagnalls 1909; March 2003. *http://www.bartleby.com/100/448.10.html*

_____. 1863. *Speech at Gettysburg, Nov. 19, 1863*, en John Bartlett, *Familiar Quotations*, 10th edition, 1919. *http://www.bartleby.com/100/448.10.html*

Linz, Juan J. and Alfred Stepan. 1996. *Problems of Democratic Transition and Consolidation*. Baltimore: Johns Hopkins University Press.

Lipset, Seymour Martin. 1960. *Political Man: the Social Bases of Politics*. Garden City, NY: Doubleday.

Locke, John. 1986 [1690]. *The Second Treatise on Civil Government*. Buffalo, NY: Prometheus Books.

Machiavelli, Niccolò. 1998 [1532]. *The Prince*, translated and with an introduction by Harvey C. Mansfield. Chicago, IL: University of Chicago Press.

MacPherson, C. B. 1966. *The Real World of Democracy.* New York: Oxford University Press.

_____. 1977. *The Life and Times of Liberal Democracy.* New York: Oxford University Press.

Mainwaring, Scott. ed. 1995. *Building Democratic Institutions: Party Systems in Latin America.* Stanford, CA: Stanford University Press.

_____. ed. 1997. *Presidentialism and Democracy in Latin America.* Cambridge: Cambridge University Press.

Mainwaring, Scott, Guillermo O'Donnell and J. S. Valenzuela, eds. 1992. *Issues in Democratic Consolidation.* Notre Dame: University of Notre Dame Press.

Manin, Bernard. 1987. "On Legitimacy and Political Deliberation." *Political Theory,* 15(3): 338–368.

Maniruzzaman, T. 1992. "Arms Transfers, Military Coups and Military Rule in Developing States." *Journal of Conflict Resolution,* 36(4): 733.

Mansbridge, Jane. 1990. "Feminism and Democracy." *American Prospect,* Spring (1): 119–134.

Marshall, T. H. 1950. *Citizenship and Social Class.* Cambridge: Cambridge University Press.

Marx, Karl. 1971 [1841/42]. "Kritik der Hegelschen Staatsphilosophie," in Fruehschriften. Stuttgart: Kroener Verlag.

Maturana, Humberto and Francisco Varela. 1980. "Autopoiesis and Cognition: The Realization of the Cognitive." *Boston Studies in the Philosophy of Science,* 42. Boston, MA: D. Reidel Publisher Co.

Meier, Gerald. 1964. *Leading Issues in Development Economics.* New York: Oxford University Press.

Melchior, T. Kjetil and H. Wiig. 2000. "Globalisation and Inequality: World Income Distribution and Living Standards, 1960–1998," *in Studies on Foreign Policy Issues,* Report 6B. Oslo: Royal Norwegian Ministry of Foreign Affairs.

Melman, Seymour. 1970. *Pentagon Capitalism: The Political Economy of War.* NY: McGraw-Hill.

Michels, Robert. 1968 [1911]. *Political Parties.* New York: Macmillan Publishing Inc.; The Free Press.

_____. 1966 [1915]. *Political Parties: A Sociological Study of the Oligarchical Tendencies of Modern Democracy,* translated by Eden Paul and Cedar Paul. New York: The Free Press.

Milanovic, Branko. 1999. "The Ricardian Vice: Why Sala-i-Marti's Calculations are Wrong," World Bank, Development Economics Research Group, paper. *www.ssrn.com*

_____. 2003. "Can We Discern the Effect of Globalization on Income Inequalities?" World Bank, Development Economics Research Group, paper. 22 September.

_____. 2005. "Global Income Inequality: What It Is and Why It Matters?" *paper:* The Carnegie Endowment for International Peace, December.

Milgram, Stanley. (1963). "Behavioral Study of Obedience." *Journal of Abnormal and Social Psychology, 67: 371–378.*

Milgram, Stanley. 1974. *Obedience to Authority; an Experimental View.* New York: Harper & Row.

Mills, C. Wrights. 1958. *The Power Elite.* London: Oxford University Press.

Montesquieu, Charles de Secondat, Baron de. 1752, in French 1748. *The Spirit of Laws,* translated by Thomas Nugent. London: J. Nurse and P. Vaillant in the Strand, electronic version: *http://www.constitution.org/cm/sol.htm*

Moore, Barrington. 1967. *Social Origins of Dictatorship and Democracy: Lord and Peasant in the Making of the Modern World.* London: Penguin Press.

Moreno, Francisco José. 1969. *Legitimacy and Stability in Latin America; a Study of Chilean Political Culture.* New York: New York University Press.

Mouffe, Chantal. 1996. *The Laws of Hostility: Politics, Violence, and the Enlightenment,* translated by Jennifer Curtiss Gage. Minneapolis, MN: University of Minnesota Press.

Nagorski, A. and T. Waldrop. 1993. "The Laws of Blood – neo Nazi Attacks Pressure Germany to Change its Citizenship Rules." *Newsweek,* 14 June, p. 39.

Nef, Jorge. 1978. "Myths in the Study of Latin American Politics," in *Canada and the Latin American Challenge,* Jorge Nef, ed. Toronto-Ottawa-Guelph: Ontario Cooperative Program in Latin American and Caribbean Studies – OCPLACS, Canadian Association for the Study of Latin America and the Caribbean – CALACS.

_____. 1983. "Stalemate and Repression in the Southern Cone: An Interpretative Synopsis." *New Scholar,* 8: 371–385.

_____. 1985. "Violence and Ideology in Latin American Politics: An Overview," in *Violence et conflits en Amérique latine,* Daneau, M. ed. Centre québecois de relations internationales, Université Laval, Québec, PQ, Canada.

_____. 1992. "Governability and the Receiver State in Latin America: Analysis and Prospects," with R. Bensabat, in *Latin America and the Caribbean to the Year 2000,* A. Ritter, M. Cameron and D. Pollock, eds. New York: Praeger.

_____. 1995. "Demilitarization and the Transition to Democracy," in *Capital, Power and Inequality in Contemporary Latin America,* Sandor Halebsky and Richard Harris, eds. Boulder, CO: Westview.

_____. 1999. *Human Security and Mutual Vulnerability: The Global Political Economy of Development and Underdevelopment.* Ottawa: IDRC: 45–57.

Nef, Jorge and X. Núñez. 1994. *Las Relaciones Interamericanas Frente al Siglo XXI.* Facultad Latinoamericana de Ciencias Sociales, Quito, Ecuador.

Nef, Jorge and J. Vanderkop. 1989. *Food Security and Insecurity in Latin America and the Caribbean: Politics, Ideology and Technology,* Center for Food Security Research Series No. 1, University of Guelph.

Nelson, D. 1993. "Ancient Enmities, Modern Guns." *Bulletin of Atomic Scientists,* 49(10): 26.

Nikolenyi, Csaba. 1998. "The New Indian Party System: What Kind of a Model?" *Party Politics,* 4: 367–80.

O'Brien, Donal Cruise. 1972. "Stability, Order and the Erosion of a Democratic Ideal: American Political Science 1960–1970." *Journal of Development Studies,* July: 351–378.

O'Connor, James, R. 1973. *The Fiscal Crisis of the State.* New York, St. Martin's Press.

O'Donnell, Guillermo. 1994. "Delegative Democracy." *Journal of Democracy,* 5(1), January: 55–69.

O'Donnell, Guillermo, J. V. Cullell and O. M. Iazzetta. 2004. *The Quality of Democracy.* Indiana: University of Notre Dame Press.

O'Donnell, Guillermo, P. Schmitter and L. Whitehead. 1986. *Transitions from Authoritarian Rule. Prospects for Democracy.* Baltimore: The Johns Hopkins University Press.

Organization for Economic Cooperation and Development (OECD). 1991. *Employment Outlook.* Paris: OECD, July.

_____. 1992. *Employment Outlook.* Paris: OECD, July.

Osborne, David and Ted Gaebler. 1993. *Reinventing Government: How the Entrepreneurial Spirit Is Transforming the Public Sector* New York: Penguin Books, 1993.

Patel, Surendra. 1970. "The Economic Distance between Nations," in *Leading Issues in Economic Development: Studies in International Poverty,* 2nd edn, Gerald Meier, ed. New York: Oxford University Press: 13–20.

Poulantzas, Nicos. 1976. *The Crisis of the Dictatorships: Portugal, Greece, Spain,* translated by David Fernbach. London: NLB; Atlantic Highlands, NJ: Humanities Press.

Putnam, Robert D. 1993. *Making Democracy Work: Civic Traditions in Modern Italy.* Princeton, NJ: Princeton University Press.

_____. 2000. *Bowling Alone.* New York: Simon and Schuster.

Rapoport, Anatol. 1966. *Two-person Game Theory: the Essential Ideas.* Ann Arbor: University of Michigan Press.

_____. 1967. *Fights, Games, and Debates.* Ann Arbor, MI: The University of Michigan Press, 1967.

_____. 1974. *Game Theory as a Theory of Conflict Resolution,* in Anatol Rapoport, ed. Dordrecht; Boston, MA: D. Reidel Publisher Co.

Rawls, John. 1971. *A Theory of Justice.* Cambridge, MA: Belknap Press of Harvard University Press.

Reiter, Bernd. 2009. *Negotiating Democracy in Brazil. The Politics of Exclusion.* Boulder, CO: First Forum Press.

Riker, William, H. 1982. *Liberalism against Populism: A Confrontation between the Theory of Democracy and the Theory of Social Choice.* Illinois: Waveland Press.

Robinson, William. 1994. "Central America: Which Way after the Cold War?" *Notisur,* 4(8), February 25: 1–9.

Rostow, W. W. 1959. "The Stages of Economic Growth," in *The Economic History Review,* New Series, 12(1): 1–16. Published by: Blackwell Publishing on behalf of the Economic History Society.

Rousseau, Jean-Jacques. 2002 [1762]. *The Social Contract; and The First and Second Discourses*; edited and with an introduction by Susan Dunn; with essays by Gita May et al. New Haven, CT: Yale University Press.

Rueschemeyer, Dietrich, Evelyne H. Stephen and John D. Stephens. 1992. *Capitalist Development and Democracy.* Chicago, IL: University of Chicago Press.

Rueschemeyer, Dietrich, Marylin Rueschmeyer, and Bjorn Wittrock. 1998. *Participation and Democracy.* New York: Armonk.

Sala-i-Martin, Xavier. 2001. "The Disturbing 'Rise' of Global Income Inequality." *http://www.columbia.edu/~xs23/papers/GlobalIncomeInequality.htm*

Samuel, Terrence. 2005. "7,783,816,546,235 in Debt." *The American Prospect,* 10 April: 1.

Sandel, Michael J. 1996. *Democracy's Discontent. America in Search of a Public Philosophy.* Cambridge: Cambridge University Press.

Sané, P. 1993. "Amnesty's report card from hell [speech delivered in London, UK, synthesized by Kevin Kreneck]." *Globe and Mail,* 10 December.

Sartori, Giovanni. 1976. *Parties and Party Systems: A Framework for Analysis.* Cambridge, UK; New York: Cambridge University Press.

Schmitt, Carl. 1996 [1932]. *The Concept of the Political,* translated with an Introduction By George Schwab. Chicago, IL: The University of Chicago Press.

Schumpeter, Joseph. 1975 [1942]. *Capitalism, Socialism and Democracy.* New York: Harper.

Seers, Dudley. 1977. "The Meaning of Development." *International Development Review,* 2: 2–7.

Sen, Amartya, K. 1992. *Inequality Reexamined.* Cambridge: Harvard University Press.

_____. 1993. "The Economics of Life and Death." *Scientific American,* May: 40–47.

_____. 1999. *Development as Freedom.* New York: Anchor Books.

_____. 2002 "How to Judge Globalism." *The American Prospect, http://www. prospect.org/print/V13/1/sen-a.html*

Sheahan, John. 1987. *Patterns of Development in Latin America: Poverty, Repression and Economic Strategy.* Princeton, NJ: Princeton University Press.

Sheppard, Mathew. 1994. "US Domestic Interests in the Latin American Debt Crisis," in *Political Economy and the Changing Global Order,* Richard Stubbs and Geoffrey Underhill, eds. Toronto: McClelland & Stewart: 302–303.

Singer, H. W. and P. Sakar. 1992. "Debt Crisis, Commodity Prices, Transfer Burden and Debt Relief." Sussex: Institute of Development Studies.

Sklar, Holly. 1981. "Trilateralism: Managing Dependency and Democracy – An Overview," in *Trilateralism: the Trilateral Commission and Elite Planning for World Management,* Sklar, Holly, ed. Montreal: Black Rose: 1–55.

Skocpol, Theda, Peter Evans and Dietrich Rueschemeyer. 1985. *Bringing the State Back In.* Cambridge: Cambridge University Press.

Stoker, Gerry. 2006. *Why Politics Matter. Making Democracy Work.* Palgrave Macmillan.

Suskind, Ron. 2004. *The Price of Loyalty: George W. Bush, the White House, and the Education of Paul O'Neill.* New York, NY: Simon & Schuster, Rockefeller Center.

Tajfel, H. and Turner, J. C. 1986: "The Social Identity Theory of Intergroup Behavior," in *Psychology of Intergroup Relations,* S. Worchel and W. G. Austin, eds. Chicago, IL: Nelson-Hall.

Todaro, Michael. 1989. *Economic Development in the Third World.* New York: Longman.

United Nations Department of Economic and Social Development (UNDESD). 1993. *Report on the World Social Situation*. New York: United Nations.

United Nations Development Program (UNDP). 1997 *Human Development Report 1997*. New York: Oxford University Press.

UNDP. 2002. *Human Development Report 2002*. New York: Oxford University Press.

UNDP. 2006. *Human Development Report 2006*. Basingstoke, UK: Palgrave Macmillan.

United Nations Educational Scientific and Cultural Organization (UNESCO). 1982. *Transnational Corporations and Endogenous Development*. United Nations: New York.

United Nations Environmental Program (UNEP). 1999. *GEO 2000. Global Environmental Outlook*. Chapter one. Nairobi, Kenya: UNEP.

Verba, Sidney, Kay Lehman Schlozman, and Henry E. Brady. 1995. *Voice and Equality. Civic Voluntarism in American Politics*. Cambridge: Cambridge University Press.

Vilas, Carlos. 2004. "Shaky Democracies and Popular Fury: From Military Coups to People's Coups?" in *Cuadernos*. ISLAC: University of South of Florida.

Wade, Robert. 2004. "Is Globalization Reducing Poverty and Inequality?" *World Development*, 32(4).

Walzer, Michael. 1980. *Radical Principles*. New York: Basic Books.

_____. 1995. "The Civil Society Argument," in *Theorizing Citizenship*, Beiner, Ronald, ed. Albany, NY: SUNY Press.

Wardlaw, Grant. 1989. *Political Terrorism*. New York: Cambridge University Press.

Warren, Mark. ed. 1999. *Democracy and Trust*. Cambridge UK: Cambridge University Press.

Weber, Max. 1972 [1922]. *Wirtschaft und Gesellschaft*. Tübingen: Mohr.

Webster, Daniel. 1830. *Second Speech on Foot's Resolution, Jan. 26, 1830*. In Bartlett, John. 1919. *Familiar Quotations. A Collection of Passages, Phrases, and Proverbs Traced to their Sources in Ancient and Modern Literature*, Boston, MA: Little, Brown & Co.

Weller, Christian and Adam Hersh. 2002. "Free Markets and Poverty." in *The American Prospect*, 13(1): 1–5.

West, Cornel. 2004. *Democracy Matters: Winning the Fight against Imperialism*. New York: Penguin Press.

Whitehead, Laurence, ed. 1997. *The New Politics of Inequality in Latin America: Rethinking Participation and Representation*. Oxford: Oxford University Press.

Wilder, Gary. 2005. *The French Imperial Nation-State: Negritude & Colonial Humanism between the Two World Wars*. Chicago, IL: University of Chicago Press.

Winant, Howard. 2003. *The Soul of Latin America*. New Haven, CT: Yale University Press.

Wood, Ellen Meiksins. 1999. *Democracy against Capitalism*. Cambridge, UK: Cambridge University Press.

World Bank. 2005. *World Development Report 2006: Equity and Develop-ment*. Washington: The World Bank & Oxford University Press.

Worsley, Peter. 1970. *The Third World*. Chicago, IL: University of Chicago Press.

Young, Iris. 1996. *Justice and the Politics of Difference*. Princeton, NJ: Princeton University Press.

_____. 2000. *Inclusion and Democracy*. Oxford: Oxford University Press.

Zakaria, Fareed. 2003. *The Future of Freedom*. New York: W.W. Norton.

Index